Crowd Design

Florian Alexander Schmidt

Crowd Design

From Tools for Empowerment to Platform Capitalism

Birkhäuser
Basel

CONTENTS

FOREWORD BIRD

Computer and Internet have been symbols and tools of personal liberation. Stewart Brand called the computer revolution 'the real legacy of the sixties', an outgrowth of the 'counterculture's scorn for centralised authority'. The ideology was codified by Steven Levy in his 1984 book *Hackers*, summarising hacker ethics as: 'Unlimited and total access to computers; all information is free; mistrust authority – promote decentralisation; you can create art and beauty on a computer; and computers can change your life for the better.'

Current social media provides the means for unlimited conversation. *WIRED*, a magazine with its roots in the counterculture of the 1960s, which transformed into an affirmative mainstream publication, recently published the article 'How Silicon Valley Utopianism Brought You the Dystopian Trump Presidency'. They write that socioeconomic despair was profitably chanelled to elect a president who represents a threat to most of the values that the technocracy holds dear: transparency, multiculturalism, expertise, and social progress. In the greatest of ironies, the tools and the language of personal liberation have been colonised and subverted by the very forces that they were intended to topple.

Mark Zuckerberg's text 'Building Global Community' (2017), some euphemistically call a 'humanitarian manifesto', addresses these issues and asks the big question: 'Are we building the world we all want?' It continues: 'In times like these, the most important thing we at Facebook can do is develop the social infrastructure to give people the power to build a global community that works for all of us.' After having focused on connecting friends and families, 'our next focus will be developing the social infrastructure for community – for supporting us, for keeping us safe, for informing us, for civic engagement, and for inclusion of all.' This is a naïve understanding of human individuality and stubbornness and of the autopoietic nature of social dynamics, if not a frightening vision.

Florian Alexander Schmidt examines such power relations on the issue of crowdworking, depicting how a fascination for amateur design culture and open creation processes evolved into a journey into the heart of darkness of the digital labour landscape. In times of new industries, new working structures, new dependencies, and new illusions, he carefully disillusions us, exposing the process of capitalisation behind a seemingly de-capitalising occurrence, and the hierarchical grasp of power behind the seeming decentralisation of it. Tools for empowerment are meticulously disclosed as platform capitalism, as is the capitalist use of anti-capitalist rhetoric that is currently being uttered at an unprecedented global scale. The ethics of these human-made social systems are put in question and, at the nexus of potential and despair, the possibility of a novel path towards a more ethically defendable and socially advantageous model of crowdworking is put forward.

Michelle Christensen and Wolfgang Jonas
Board of International Research in Design (BIRD), April 2017

In memory of my dear friend Dr. Danny Pannicke,
whose big heart and great mind I miss very much.

ABOUT THE BOOK

The research for this book began with a fascination for amateur design culture and open creation processes online and has become a journey into the heart of darkness of the digital labour landscape. Along the way it passes the idealistic vistas of early online collaboration and maps the jungle of competing systems for the division of labour via the internet. Towards the end, it sketches out some paths that could lead to a more agreeable work environment for crowdworkers.

Having a professional background in communication design, I didn't start my research from an impartial, detached position but as someone in the thick of it – on the one hand fascinated by the implications the open-source movement and the Web 2.0-hype would have for the design world, on the other hand worried about the emergence of the first commercial platforms for creative crowdwork. I have been thinking and writing about the power shifts related to digital tools and platforms since 2006 and about creative crowdwork since 2009. As many others at the time, I used to believe that the dissemination or 'democratisation' of digital creative tools – the means of production, so to speak – would lead to a redistribution of power towards a more egalitarian, less capitalist structure of the media landscape. It took me a while to understand that this was not necessarily the case; that evidence instead showed that in the emerging platform economy, power didn't reside with those owning the tools but with those owning the platforms.

From 2012 to 2015, I worked on my PhD in the department for Critical Writing in Art and Design at the Royal College of Art in London. In the beginning of my research, I spent a lot of time participating as a designer on platforms for creative crowdwork. I started with an ethnographic approach, trying to describe the working conditions from within, from the perspective of an individual in the crowd. This phase of participant observation has deepened my understanding of the platforms. And yet, I abandoned this approach eventually, because in contrast to what I originally believed, putting myself in the shoes of the exploited crowdworkers was increasingly counterproductive for an objective analysis. I realised that I needed a more distanced, analytical view of the platforms, understanding them in their historic trajectory as well as in their contemporary variety. I wanted to understand at what point in time the widening gap between the lofty rhetoric of online collaboration and the actual practice of exploitative crowdwork had first occurred. I wondered if there was a moment in time, when the development had taken 'the wrong turn' to evolve from a spirit of online community to a winner-takes-it-all individualism.

With my shift from hands-on action research in the thick of the platforms to a historical perspective on the development of the phenomenon, my method changed into a form of discourse analysis, with the goal of exposing the interests and mind-sets of the various stakeholders by analysing how key terms were coined and narratives were spun.[1] I have developed a particular interest in those moments in the long history of the internet when the dominant explanations of technological change still celebrated the emancipatory qualities of a technology whilst the usage of the tools and platforms had already taken a different turn. In other words, I am concerned with the process by which an engaging vision of the future and the accompanying rhetoric is hollowed out over time and comes to be used to justify a technology that, in its application, is at odds with the original vision. This form of intellectual archaeology has required the excavation of both overlooked and well known primary sources which have strong explanatory power for the current state of creative crowdwork as part of the wider platform economy. As I will show, the texts that I have worked with can be reread as 'usable pasts'; narratives that can help to critique and potentially redesign our contemporary platforms in a way that is more fair and sustainable for all stakeholders.[2]

The research has sent me back through time, peeling back layer-by-layer of systems for online collaboration and the discourse on crowds, to understand their origins. The book, however, is structured in the chronological order in which the phenomena that I analyse have evolved. My original ethnographic approach dissolved into the background of the book but it has not disappeared. It has deeply informed my understanding of the platforms. Many particularities of creative crowdwork would have never come to my attention had I not participated in this type of work myself. The book has gained in depth through this methodological detour, but the decision to abandon it in favour of a more detached approach – which combines different research methods, led to a richer understanding of the historic and ideological dimension of the crowdsourcing phenomenon. It turned out to be necessary to go back in time to truly understand this very contemporary and fast-changing subject.

In addition to historical texts and current academic papers from different scholarly fields, I analysed a rich and eclectic combination of textual sources to deal with the messy reality that is happening in real time on the internet. I looked at advertising and press releases by the platforms, their on-site rules and regulations, online chat room discussions, user complaints, business reports, usage data, and economic statistics, either published by the platforms themselves, by third parties, or deduced through my own calculations. I have also conducted a number of long formal interviews with different stakeholders – crowdworkers and platform providers in particular. I deliberately searched for a broad spectrum of sources in order to reflect the different kinds of rhetoric and narratives at play in the crowdsourcing discourse, from hyperbole sales pitch, via matter-of-factual legal text, to snarky

---

1   Fairclough, *Critical Discourse Analysis: The Critical Study of Language* (2010). Wodak/Meyer, eds., *Methods of Critical Discourse Analysis* (2009). Schiffrin et al., *The Handbook of Discourse Analysis* (2003).
2   On the concept of 'usable pasts' see: Kelty, *Two Bits: The Cultural Significance of Free Software* (2008): p. 65.

sarcasm. Some of these sources are very controlled, but revealing by what they don't say, such as a lot of the data that the platforms provide; others, like some of my interviewees, are unguarded and candid about their motives.

My dissertation at the RCA forms the core of this book, but I have substantially revised and updated the text with subsequent research. In 2014 and 2015 I worked with the German labour union IG Metall as co-editor of a book on crowdwork and as researcher for a website called FairCrowdWork.org. Some of the recommendations that I make at the very end of the book have been informed by this interaction with the union.

Nevertheless, I fought against the design impulse to start producing solutions right away, thus the book is mainly analytical in character. It should be understood as a contribution to the advancement of a deeper understanding of the problem of manipulation and exploitation in crowdsourcing, the necessary foundation for working on possible solutions. The book offers precise descriptions of the present state of affairs as well as an analysis of the evolution of systems and concepts that has lead to this point: it also provides descriptions of the underlying general principles and mechanisms of contest-based creative crowdwork, some of which I could not have discovered had I not participated in the contests myself. But it was equally important not to reduce my perspective and discuss as many (often contradictory) views on crowdsourcing as possible. As the design theoretician Prasad Boradkar writes in *Designing Things* in a call for disciplinary diversity:

Each disciplinary lens sets its focus on things from a perspective that is shaped by the unique purpose of its inquiry. The questions asked, methodologies chosen and results sought are determined by disciplinary know-how, and therefore the critical knowledge generated is determined by the *situation* within which the analysis is conducted. However, it is important to note that while the disciplines bring to the study of object their unique theoretical underpinnings and specific methods of inquiry, they also share some ideological biases. In fact, interdisciplinary research is founded on the notion that there are productive areas of convergence [...] among disciplines where new scholarship can emerge.[3]

I regard my research on creative crowdwork as being located at such an area of convergence, at the intersection of management studies, human-computer-interaction research, design studies, and digital labour discourse. To my knowledge, it is the only study that analyses crowdsourcing from the perspective of design, within the context of digital labour, and with a focus on the ethics of designing these systems. It is also the only study that I know of that offers a detailed comparison of the mechanics of *microtasking crowdwork* with that of *contest-based creative crowdwork*. I use the former as a basis to bring to the fore the specifics of the latter. Many of my

---

3   Boradkar, *Designing Things: A Critical Introduction to the Culture of Objects* (2010): p. 17–18.

insights have been informed by empirical, qualitative research; namely, by my participation in the systems that I analyse. Rooted in my background as a practitioner as well as in my conviction that this is a political subject that is in dire need of a wider public discourse, it is my intention to produce knowledge in a way that is accessible and also of use outside the ivory tower of academia. Thus my work is neither theory-driven nor method-driven: instead it is probably best described with what Ian Shapiro calls a problem-based approach.[4] I agree with Shapiro in his view (and this adds to the quote from Boradkar above) that over-specialisation produces 'esoteric discourses' that lose sight of their subject of study because they revolve primarily around methodology and around commenting on each other, and thus create 'high entry costs to the uninitiated'.[5] With this book, I strive to achieve the exact opposite and write for both the expert and the wider audience alike, without sacrificing academic rigour.

Introduction and conclusion aside, the book consists of four main chapters. The first two chapters deal with the historic dimension of the crowd and of digital platforms respectively. The latter two deal with the present day division of labour in the platform economy and the particularities of creative crowdwork:

Chapter one is concerned with the historic meaning and the current connotation of the term 'crowd' and the political context in which it occurs; it is about what a physical crowd once was and what this reveals about what a digital crowd is today. The chapter analyses the historic crowd discourse and shows the power structures reflected by the original use of the term, its reinvention under the paradigm of digital platforms, and the present day echoes of its original connotation.

Chapter two deals with historic visions of tools for online collaboration that have transformed our understanding of virtual communities and crowds and that have prepared the ground for today's crowdwork platforms. The guiding question here: How can historic concepts of tools and platforms for online collaboration teach us to better understand, evaluate, and potentially revise contemporary crowdsourcing platforms? And at what point in web history did the gap between an emancipatory rhetoric on the one hand and exploitative practices on the other start to emerge? When did the proclaimed tools for empowerment turn into platform capitalism?

Chapter three is about the design of crowdsourcing. It maps the current digital labour landscape and locates creative crowdwork within a typology of the larger platform economy and its mechanisms. This chapter is about the general features and functions of platform-based business models, about the design of crowdwork platforms in general, and about those for microtasking crowdwork in particular.

Finally, chapter four focuses on the crowdsourcing of design. It investigates what differentiates the design of creative crowdwork from other methods used to

4   Shapiro, *The Flight from Reality in the Human Sciences* (2005).
5   *Ibid.* p. 178.

organise digital labour and what this teaches us about design. What are the specific challenges of contest-based creative crowdwork in contrast to microtasking crowdwork?

The conclusion provides a number of recommendations for and a discussion of potential solutions to the problem of exploitation in creative crowdwork and the platform economy, based on my analysis and my arguments from the previous four chapters.

INTRODUCTION:
COMING TO TERMS WITH CROWDSOURCING

What we are seeing with crowdsourcing is the phenomenon of creative destruction happening in near real time.
Jeff Howe, 2008[1]

Seeds grow ... the crowd will have its way, eventually.
Ai Weiwei, 2010[2]

Of Flowers Facing to the Sun and Sheep Facing to the Left

In October 2010, Tate Modern's Turbine Hall opened its doors to the art crowd for its annual exhibition of expansive sculptural installations sponsored by Unilever, a multi-national consumer goods company. Visitors encountered 1,000-square-metres of the hall's vast space covered with a thick layer of sunflower seeds, a 'social sculpture' by Chinese artist Ai Weiwei. What looked like a rich harvest of edible kernels were actually 100 million painstakingly hand-painted porcelain pebbles. The artist had paid 1,600 artisan porcelain painters for two and a half years to create the 150 tons of kernels that together made the artwork *Sunflower Seeds*. The production took place in Jingdezhen, a Chinese town that had made imperial porcelain for an entire millennium but was running out of work at the beginning of the twenty-first century. Through Ai Weiwei's project, the people of the town were able to continue to work in their traditional manner, painting porcelain either in small groups in the artisan workshop or at home with their families in a cottage industry. On average, each worker finished 68 seeds per day. According to Ai Weiwei, the workers were paid a 'slightly more than customary' living wage.[3] At the time, the minimum wage in Jingdezhen was 0.58 USD per hour.

Five years earlier, in November 2005, the young American media artist Aaron Koblin heard of a new service online retailer Amazon had just launched (with hardly anyone taking notice). Amazon Mechanical Turk, as it was called, started to offer its customers access to what the company dubbed '*artificial* artificial intelligence' – that is: the seemingly computational processing of repetitive tasks that require human intelligence. Amazon had quietly set up an invisible, distributed workforce – an online crowd – to process cognitive tasks that computers were not yet capable of solving. For only a few cents per HIT (Human Intelligence Task), the workers in this

---

1   Howe, *Crowdsourcing* (2008).
2   Weiwei, Faurschou Foundation, aiweiweiseeds.com (2010).
3   Hancox,'Art, Activism and the Geopolitical Imagination' (2012).

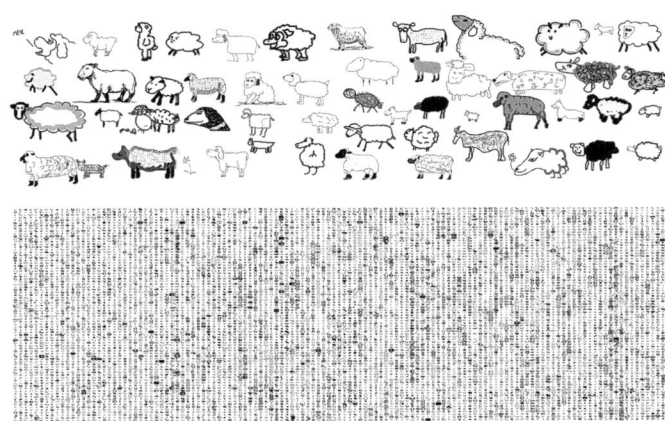

1 Aaron Koblin, *The Sheep Market*, 2006.

newly established crowd could now be addressed like processors in distributed computing. This could be done not only by Amazon but also by its clients, because the company had transformed its internal tool into an open, multi-stakeholder platform for digital labour. In theory, everybody could now instantly become a 'requester' or a 'provider' of microtasking crowdwork – in other words an employer or a worker.[4]

Koblin was intrigued by what he saw as 'an irresistible medium for experimentation' and he later wrote that he was 'immediately curious about the ramifications of exploiting the human qualities of workers in contrast to the tasks commonly automated through centuries of labor management systems.'[5] After a few preliminary tests, he developed *The Sheep Market,* an artwork consisting of 10,000 hand-drawn sheep, created by workers on Mechanical Turk and later exhibited online and in a gallery space. Koblin provided the workers with a simple digital drawing tool and paid them two cents for drawing 'a sheep facing to the left'. The tool recorded the workers' every brush stroke and made it possible to replay the drawing process as an animation. The creation of the 10,000 sheep took 40 days at a total labour cost of 200 USD; the average time to draw a sheep was 115 seconds and the workers earned on average 0.69 USD per hour.[6] The total number of 7,599 unique IP addresses from which sheep were contributed indicates the approximate number of workers involved. However, as typical for Mechanical Turk, the process was completely anonymous and therefore opaque with regard to who the workers actually were and

4   Legally, it is a highly contested question in crowdwork whether the people in the crowd of a specific platform are employees or independent contractors. I will come back to this in chapter three.

5   Koblin, *The Sheep Market,* Masters' Thesis (2006).

6   On Amazon Mechanical Turk the labour costs for a project the size of Sunflower Seeds would have been around 200,000 USD, but Ai Weiwei of course also had to pay for materials, transport, storage, etc.

where they came from (opaque for Koblin, not for Amazon).[7] Ai Weiwei was still able to travel to the place of production and meet the workers he had hired personally – Koblin only saw a string of letters and numbers that represented the workers in Amazon's interface.

Ai Weiwei and Aaron Koblin paid similar, and by global standards, very low wages to their workers, but both artists mention that the workers were happy about the job-opportunity and asked for more work, even though in both cases, the workers didn't quite understand what they were working on. The workers could not see the full picture they contributed to, an aspect typical for crowdsourcing. Both artists orchestrated and aggregated the labour of the crowd to create something that is more than the sum of its parts, with regard to its meaning as well as to its economic value. Both artists were able to sell parts of the work with a substantial profit.[8]

By doing so, Ai Weiwei and Aaron Koblin ask crucial questions about the cultural values and the monetary value of outsourced work on a globalised labour market, about the relationship between the individual initiator and the masses of workers complying with the request, and about contemporary forms of repetitive, alienating and exploitative labour. At a time when more and more work is becoming completely automated, the two artists turn to mass *manu*facturing in its most literal sense as handicraft mass production. Both artists point at the asymmetry of knowledge and power in these systems of mass outsourcing or *crowd*sourcing, and even though they perpetuate this power structure, they also encourage us to contemplate the role of the individual in the crowd, by showing individual brush strokes and lines drawn by hand – traces that, in the case of *The Sheep Market*, couldn't have been achieved by a machine and, in the case of *Sunflower Seeds*, would have been rendered meaningless if created mechanically.

By choosing sunflower seeds and sheep respectively, both artists employ age-old and highly charged crowd-metaphors to explore the contemporary relationship between the individual and the masses. While each sheep and seed is unique, this individuality becomes meaningless in relation to the total number of individuals involved in the work. With the symbolic choice of sheep as a motif, Koblin uses the old association of the crowd with a gullible herd. The individual is reduced to an animal, exchangeable and subordinated to the guidance and control of a shepherd, and with no understanding of the larger economic parameters of its existence: namely that it will either constantly have to produce wool – that it will be fleeced again and again – or eventually eaten.

Koblin's choice of symbol therefore can be read as a critique of the workers' naivety or of the dehumanising aspects of Amazon's marketplace for digital labour,

7   Theoretically, the same worker could have logged in from different IP addresses.
8   Koblin sold the sheep in groups of twenty, for twenty USD per printout (under the protest of some of the crowdworkers, as he describes in his thesis); Ai Weiwei sold a large amount of seeds for an undisclosed price to Tate Modern, smaller amounts were auctioned at Sotheby's for £3.50 a seed. See: Kennedy, 'Tate Buys Eight Million Ai Weiwei Sunflower Seeds', *The Guardian* (2012).

now often described as a 'digital sweatshop'. Ai Weiwei's critique cuts both ways, too, and refers to Western consumerism's reliance on cheap outsourcing, as well as to Eastern communist and post-communist power structures in his home country. In China, sunflower seeds are not only a ubiquitous snack but have been used as metaphor for the crowds in communist propaganda, where chairman Mao was depicted as the sun and his people as sunflowers, orientating their heads and seeds towards his shining light. In a similar way, the seeds in the Turbine Hall all point to Ai Weiwei as the source of power, the commander of the giant invisible workforce that has created the seeds.

The total number of 100 million individual seeds in the Turbine Hall is already hard to grasp, but China now has thirteen times that many people. Often referred to as 'the world's factory' the country quintessentially stands for the outsourcing of manufacturing jobs. 'Designed in California, assembled in China' can be read on every Apple product, and the firm is just one of many technology companies that have completely outsourced their production to China. For the West, this division of labour still seems to be the key to success in a globalised, digitised world – that is until China catches up and also provides the design part of the job.

As I will show in the first chapter of this book, our notion of 'the crowds' or 'the masses' was informed in the late nineteenth century as a reaction to what was then an explosion in population growth. But this development with all its grave consequences is being dwarfed by the current population growth in China. Ai Weiwei's *Sunflower Seeds* make this palpable, at least to some extent.[9]

While the book at hand is centred on Europe and the English-speaking parts of the world, it is important to keep in mind that the future of the crowd and of crowdwork is likely to take place in Asia. After the outsourcing of manufacturing jobs to China, we can now observe the outsourcing of service and design jobs to countries such as Indonesia, the Philippines, and India. While the last wave of outsourcing occured at the level of companies, crowdsourcing is now having the same effect at the level of individuals.

The juxtaposition of *The Sheep Market* and *Sunflower Seeds* shows the differences between traditional, location-based forms of material production and the orchestration of seemingly placeless, distributed, 'digital labour' via dedicated platforms. Aaron Koblin and Ai Weiwei achieved what only artists can do. They condensed the many conflicting aspects and ambiguities of outsourced creative labour into a single and formally reduced piece of work that still contains all the complexities of the issue. Their work and their personal standpoint remain deliberately ambiguous and open for interpretation by the individual spectator and the collective judgement of the art crowd.

---

9   Ai Weiwei wanted the visitors to be able to touch the seeds and walk around on them like on a beach of
     pebbles, but British Health & Safety regulations ruled otherwise.

2 'Respectfully wish Chairman Mao eternal life', Chinese Poster, artist unknown, 1968.

敬祝毛主席万寿无疆

The goal of this book, however, is to take a more analytical approach, to trace the history of the phenomenon and to map the present day complexities of crowdsourcing in general and creative crowdwork in particular and thus to contribute to an analytical understanding of its social, ethical, economical, and political implications. The overarching questions are: How have these systems evolved historically? How are they currently designed? And can they be designed in a way that is fair and sustainable for all stakeholders?

Coming to Terms with Crowdsourcing

The challenge of writing about a contemporary, technology-driven topic like crowdsourcing in the form of a slower-paced academic study is that the subject is such a fast moving target. The problem is not only the short half-life of the technology itself. It is the terminology that is evolving at an even quicker rate. Nothing is older than yesterday's buzzwords. Unfortunately, we can't quite do without the neologisms because often there is not a neutral alternative to contrived, sometimes deceptive, but already widely adopted terms such as 'cloud computing'.[10] It is difficult to decide which neologism to adopt because they all come with their own biases and hover somewhere between still being over-hyped, already hackneyed, or too specialised and technocratic. What complicates things further is that different academic

10   The 'cloud' was once more appropriately called a 'server farm' and is best described with 'someone else's computer'.

disciplines adopt varying terms for very similar phenomena – or use identical names for different phenomena. The language in this field is dominated by a Silicon Valley-centric group of start-up entrepreneurs, venture capitalist, technology evangelists, and business-consultants – all competing to give the next big thing a catchy title.

The publisher Tim O'Reilly is a prime example of such spin-doctory. He popularised the term 'Web 2.0', played a crucial role in rebranding 'free software' into 'open source software' (see chapter three) and the DIY scene into the 'Maker Movement'. Silicon Valley critic Evgeny Morozov attacked O'Reilly for being a 'Meme-Hustler' with 'buzzwordophilia' and showed how he framed the public dialogue about technology in a dumbed-down, superficially optimistic, business-friendly way.[11] Even O'Reilly himself speaks of his practice as 'meme-engineering'. Those earning an arbitrage from being one step ahead in the 'hype-cycle' have an incentive to sustain a constant atmosphere of urgency through inflated neologisms sold to those in fear of being left behind.

The concept of the 'hype cycle' itself is already part of this game. It was introduced by Gartner Inc., a firm that describes itself as 'the world's leading information technology research and advisory company.'[12] Every year, the company maps the current position of emerging technologies, all on the identical curve. According to Gartner, every new technology has to undergo five distinct phases: the 'Innovation Trigger', the 'Peak of Inflated Expectations', the 'Trough of Disillusionment', the 'Slope of Enlightenment', and finally the 'Plateau of Productivity'.

It is obviously very simplistic to plot everything new under the (Californian) sun onto that same curve, with the promise of reaching 'enlightenment' later along the way. Yet the 'hype cycle' is intuitively appealing and has a strong 'sense of truth' to it. Its steep rise and fall in the first half of the curve fits, in retrospect, many of the technology buzzwords. Yet, the number of words and concepts that eventually dissolve into nothingness is much higher than Gartner's optimistic curve suggests. And yet, in July 2013, Gartner estimated that 'crowdsourcing' just made it over the Peak of Inflated Expectations, heading for Disillusionment. Crowdsourcing was scheduled to reach the Plateau of Productivity between 2015 and 2018.[13] As of 2017, it can be stated that crowdsourcing is far from becoming obsolete and has instead evolved into an industry in its own right, but it is also true that the hype has moved on to new buzzwords; all the more reason for a sobering look at the persisting structures that have been designed for 'the crowds' as users.

Out of a long array of overlapping, often conflated, but not necessarily interchangeable terms and concepts – such as *collective intelligence, cognitive surplus, human*

---

11 Morozov, 'The Meme Hustler: Tim O'Reilly's Crazy Talk', *The Baffler* (2013).

12 Gartner.com, about section (2017).

13 The curve is accessible for free online, but the 87 page report itself costs $1,995 US dollar, a sum that prevents me from finding out how exactly the positioning of the different technologies is done.

computation, co-creation, prosuming, produsing, distributed thinking, democratising in-
novation, open innovation, social product development, user-innovation, user-generated
content, mass collaboration, mass creativity, we-think, and wikinomics – it is crowdsourcing that has survived and made it into the dictionaries. So what exactly is it?

In 2010, the *Oxford Dictionary* still defined 'crowdsourcing' as: 'the practice
whereby an organisation enlists a variety of freelancers, paid or unpaid, to work on
a specific task or problem.'[14] The weakness of this definition was, that it also holds
true for a conventional design agency that selects a handful of paid freelancers or
unpaid interns. In this definition, the crucial novelty and driving force behind the
concept of crowdsourcing was lost: Which is that through the method of conducting an *open call over the internet* it has become possible to tap into an external workforce of hundreds of thousands of people with extremely low transaction costs.

In 2013, the *OED* updated its definition and now even commented on the fact,
that the dictionary itself was originally the result of a crowdsourcing endeavour.[15]
Its new definition of crowdsourcing: 'The practice of obtaining information or input into a task or project by enlisting the services of a large number of people, either
paid or unpaid, typically via the Internet.'[16] It was the journalist Jeff Howe who
coined the term in June 2006 in an article for *Wired*. Under the title 'The Rise of
Crowdsourcing' the lead read: 'Remember outsourcing? Sending jobs to India and
China is so 2003. The new pool of cheap labor: everyday people using their spare
cycles to create content, solve problems, even do corporate R&D.'[17] Howe had
realised that a new source of value creation was emerging that included labour of
hitherto seemingly passive internet into the value chain of companies – not just as
a side effect but as the core of a new type of business model.[18] Even though Howe
didn't invent the phenomenon, he gave it the name that stuck.[19] As it turned out,
many people online were willing to work practically for free if the tasks were small
enough or fun to do. In their aggregate form as crowds, these people even self-assigned to their preferred tasks. Companies engaged in crowdsourcing can thus not
only save money in wages they would otherwise have to pay regular employees, they
also save expenses in 'human resource' management.

---

14 *Oxford Dictionary of English* (2010).
15 The OED originally built on the work of hundreds of unpaid readers contributing thousands of support-
    ing quotations. See: Matthew/Harrison, eds., *The Oxford Dictionary of National Biography* (2004). 'Tweet,
    geekery and epic crowdsourcing: an Oxford English Dictionary update', OED blog post (2013).
16 Oxford English Dictionary, definition of crowdsourcing (2017).
17 Howe, 'The Rise of Crowdsourcing', *Wired* (2006).
18 Tim Berners-Lee, inventor of the world wide web, reject the notion that users where passive before the
    advent of Web 2.0. For Berners-Lee, user-participation was always the core of the www. Also Olia Lialina
    shows in her research that users were very inventive in the 1990s, when they designed their homepages
    from scratch. See: Lialina et al. *Digital Folklore* 2009.
19 As Howe wrote later, he had developed the term already in 2005 with his colleague Mark Robinson in
    preparation for the article in *Wired*. The term 'Web 2.0', usually attributed to Tim O'Reilly, was actual.y
    also coined by a colleague of his, Dale Dougherty.

There is a close connection but also a notable shift in emphasis from Tim O'Reilly's description of web trends in 2004 – which led to the introduction of the term 'Web 2.0' – to Howe's observations in 2006 – which led to the term 'crowdsourcing'. 'Web 2.0' was a marketing term that emphasised the empowerment of the individual user, who supposedly now acquired a voice,[20] became an active contributor and was provided with various tools for media production, publication, and public self-expression – for example through citizen journalism on blogs, or by creating videos for YouTube. The term crowdsourcing, however, shifted the perspective from the *individual user* towards *masses of users* and especially towards methods that allowed the aggregation of their myriad contributions. The coinage of the term crowdsourcing made visible, and at the same time amplified, the endeavour to take commercial advantage of the surplus cognitive and creative capacities of the masses online. Both concepts went through a media-hype, but while the term Web 2.0 withered away over time, the term crowdsourcing stayed. Its meaning, however, oscillated already at its inception. Jeff Howe himself provided two definitions for crowdsourcing, the 'white paper version', concise and apt, and the 'sound bite version', catchy but misguiding:

The White Paper Version: Crowdsourcing is the act of taking a job traditionally performed by a designated agent (usually an employee) and outsourcing it to an undefined, generally large group of people in the form of an open call.

The Sound Bite Version: The application of Open Source principles to fields outside of software.[21]

At the root of the original definition, we thus find the source of an enduring conflict, caused by the entanglement of two seemingly similar concepts, which however must not be used interchangeably. The sound bite version is misguiding because there are several fundamental differences between the principles of crowdsourcing and the principles of 'Free/Libre and Open Source Software' (FLOSS).[22] Variations of the sound bite version even suggested that crowdsourcing is 'like Wikipedia, but with everything' – an interpretation also at the core of Don Tapscott's management book *Wikinomics*.[23] The problem with the sound bite version is that it conflates crowdsourcing with what Yochai Benkler has defined as *commons-based peer production*, already in 2002.[24] I will come back to this important point in chapter three.

---

20 An attitude not unlike that represented in the 'Cluetrain Manifesto' by Levine/Weinberger et al. (1999).
21 Howe, 'Crowdsourcing: A Definition' (2006).
22 'Free Software' is the older concept, developed by Richard Stallman, 'Open Source Software' has a different emphasis and there is an on-going dispute between the two camps. 'FLOSS' is the all-encompassing term. See p. 101.
23 Tapscott/Williams, *Wikinomics* (2008).
24 Benkler, 'Coase's Penguin, or Linux and the Nature of the Firm'. *The Yale Law Journal*, 112 (2002).

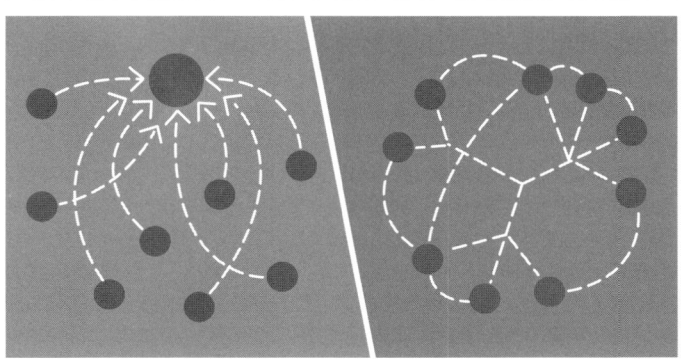

3 Principle of Crowd-sourcing (on the left) versus that of Open Source and Commons-based Peer Production.[25]

For now it should suffice to say that the results of crowdsourcing are typically neither open, nor do they become part of the commons at the end of the creation process. The contributors in crowdsourcing – *the crowdsourcees* or *crowdworkers* – do not produce something primarily for themselves, their peers, or the greater public, but for *the crowdsourcer*, a private entity, typically a company, which is not part of the crowd and recruits the workers from an outside position. The crowd is encouraged to produce something according to someone else's *brief* and in the predefined *time frame* of that person or entity. In *commons-based peer production*, self-organised individuals solve problems and produce things for themselves and their community of peers, the fruits of the labour become part of the commons. This difference can thus be distilled as: crowd-to-company versus peer-to-peer – or – many to few versus many-to-many.

Even though hybrid forms exist and many people understand crowdsourcing in the sense of the sound bite version as an overarching concept, it is crucial to maintain and emphasise the distinction. I will therefore build on the 'white paper version' of the definition, also because it makes clear that crowdsourcing is about work that once had the form of a regular job and is now being outsourced to a *large*, *undefined* and *open* group. While Howe's double definition caused some confusion, his original article in *Wired* made unmistakably clear that it was not commons-based peer production that he had in mind. With one half of its etymological roots in 'outsourcing' the term crowdsourcing has a lineage of cheap labour written directly into its DNA:

Welcome to the age of the crowd, (where) [...] distributed labor networks are using the Internet to exploit the spare processing power of millions of human brains. [...] The labor

25 Fittingly, this visualisation from 2010 is itself part of the commons: (opensource.com/business/10/4/ why-open-source-way-trumps-crowdsourcing-way – accessed January 2017). I will include URLs only in exceptions like this were the source has no searchable title. Most of my sources are available online, but the locations and URLs often change over time. It is therefore much more efficient to just enter the titles into a search engine than to copy an URL manually from a printed book.

isn't always free, but it costs a lot less than paying traditional employees. It's not outsourcing; it's crowdsourcing.[26]

As a consequence of understanding crowdsourcing in this narrow sense of outsourcing labour to an online crowd for commercial purposes, I will exclude several similar phenomena, such as 'crowdfunding' and 'user-generated content' from the detailed discussion in this book. In the beginning of chapter three, I will briefly map these adjacent fields in the larger platform economy and provide clear distinctions between them. They are important fields of research in their own right, but this book is concerned primarily with the crowd as a source of labour (chapter three), and creative labour in particular (chapter four). To avoid confusion with related concepts, I will use the term *crowdwork* to refer to crowdsourcing in what I regard as its original narrow sense. The term has been used by other researchers before and is often used interchangeably with 'crowd work', 'crowd labour', or 'crowd-labor'.[27] The following definition is my own:

Crowdwork is labour previously performed by a designated employee or freelancer, that is outsourced via an open call on an intermediary online platform, to a large and undefined group of people (crowdworkers), who have to follow a specific brief and time frame to finish the task. The crowdsourcer offers payment and other incentives for participation and in turn owns the results of the process.

The best way to distinguish *crowdwork* from *user-generated content* or *commons-based peer production* is to look for a brief, i.e. a description of how a job has to be done; a narrow *time frame* in which the job has to be finished; and a *change of ownership* of the results after the job has been done. In *user-generated content* and *commons-based peer-production*, the product of the work typically has an immediate use-value for the crowdsourcees and even the general public. In crowdwork proper this is not the case. The results are *primarily useful for* the external party who initiated the process.

---

26 Howe, 'The Rise of Crowdsourcing' (2006).

27 The first use of the term 'crowdwork' I could find, written in one word in an academic paper is: Silberman/Irani/Ross, 'Ethics and Tactics of Professional Crowdwork' (2010). An early example of the separate spelling is: Kittur et al., 'The Future of Crowd Work' (2013); one of the authors of the previous paper, Michael S. Bernstein, also used the term 'crowd labor' before: Bernstein et al. 'Soylent: A Word Processor with a Crowd inside' (2010). The term 'crowd labor' was used already two years earlier by Brabham, 'Crowdsourcing as a Model for Problem Solving' (2008). I am aware that in Marxist Theory, a distinction is made between 'work' and 'labour', but in the general discourse, this difference is usually ignored. I chose 'crowdwork' over 'crowd labour' because it is more general, less politically charged, and in sync with the term 'crowdworker'. For a detailed theoretical distinction see: Fuchs/Sevignani, 'What Is Digital Labour? What Is Digital Work? What's Their Difference?' (2013). These authors write: 'Labour is a necessarily alienated form of work, in which humans do not control and own the means and results of production. It is a historic form of the organisation of work in class societies. Work in contrast is a much more general concept common to all societies. It is a process in which humans in social relations make use of technologies in order to transform nature, culture and society in such a way that goods and services are created that satisfy human needs.'

The Future of Work: Between a Rock and a Hard Place

Over the last ten years since its inception as a commercial practice, crowdwork has evolved from a niche web phenomenon into a global industry that now affects millions of workers. In order to understand the rise of crowdwork, it is necessary to keep the bigger picture in mind – not only globalisation and outsourcing briefly mentioned above, but also the economic melt-down of 2008 and the two macro-trends of automation and platform capitalism as the new forms of value creation.

In their much discussed study from 2013, 'The Future of Employment', Carl Benedikt Frey and Michael Osborne from the Engineering Science department at Oxford University asked: 'How susceptible are jobs to computerisation?'[28] They showed that after the crash of the financial industry in late 2008, the global economy, and especially that of the US, experienced a 'jobless recovery'. Productivity and profits had recovered quickly and are now higher than before the crisis, but unemployment rates remained high in many countries. Frey and Osborne argue that this was made possible by an unprecedented degree of automation through advanced computerisation and they see this development continually gaining momentum. In their analysis, the two researchers look at the entire spectrum of sectors with regard to the probability of the jobs becoming automated in the next two decades.

They build on the task categorisation of David H. Autor, professor for economics at MIT, who 'distinguishes between workplace tasks using a two-by-two matrix, with routine versus non-routine tasks on one axis and manual versus cognitive tasks on the other.'[29] Previously, it had predominantly been the manual, routine tasks that were suited for automation, but through substantial advances in – and the combination of – big data, sensor-technology, robotics, and algorithms, non-routine and cognitive tasks are also more likely to become automated.

Google's new fleet of self-driving cars is just one apt example of this trend, and also Uber announced that it is working towards getting rid of human drivers eventually.[30] Likewise, Foxconn, the infamous Apple-manufacturer, has revealed its plans to replace parts of its suicidal workforce in China with ten thousand 'Fox-bots'.[31] As Terry Gou of Foxconn told reporters in July 2014, 'Cheap labor no longer exists. Wages are the same everywhere due to the free flow of information through the Internet [...] We hope to use robots to make robots in 5 to 10 years.'[32]

---

28 Frey/Osborne, 'The Future of Employment' (2013).
29 Autor et al., 'The Skill Content of Recent Technological Change', *The Quarterly Journal of Economics* (2003).
30 Biggs, 'Uber Opening Robotics Research Facility In Pittsburgh To Build Self-Driving Cars', *TechCrunch* (2015).
31 In 2010, more than a dozen Foxconn workers at the company's largest plant in Shenzhen committed suicide by jumping from the factory rooftops – arguably because of the harsh working conditions. Foxconn reacted with the installation of safety nets around its buildings and by making the workers sign an agreement not to kill or harm themselves. See: Johnson, '1 Million Workers. 90 Million iPhones. 17 Suicides. Who's to Blame?', *Wired* (2011).
32 Luk, 'Foxconn Plans to Make its Own Industrial Robots', *Wall Street Journal* (2014).

Frey and Osborne emphasise that they are not predicting anything (a point frequently lost in popular reports about the study), but are merely evaluating systematically which jobs could *potentially* become totally automated. The number they come up with is 47% in the next twenty years. The remaining 53% 'are occupations that involve complex perception and manipulation tasks, creative intelligence tasks, and social intelligence tasks, which are unlikely to be substituted by computer capital over the next decade or two.'[33] Frey and Osborne describe these three areas as 'engineering bottlenecks for computerisation' and from the perspective of the design profession, these findings are good news.[34] Arguably, good designers are by training situated right at the intersection of the three 'engineering bottlenecks' that prevent automation. In the words of the two researchers from Oxford:

Because creativity, by definition, involves not only novelty but value, and because values are highly variable, it follows that many arguments about creativity are rooted in disagreements about value. Thus, even if we could identify and encode our creative values, to enable the computer to inform and monitor its own activities accordingly, there would still be disagreement about whether the computer appeared to be creative. In the absence of engineering solutions to overcome this problem, it seems unlikely that occupations requiring a high degree of creative intelligence will be automated in the next decades.[35]

And yet automation is only one of the macro-trends transforming the labour landscape at the moment. Tasks that can't be automated can often be outsourced, not only to companies but also to the masses of freelancing crowdworkers online; globalisation, recession, and jobless growth make it likely that somewhere around the world there is always a crowd willing to work for pennies. So, cheap labour continues to exist after all. Crowdsourcing and automation go hand in hand, with the former often preparing the way for the latter (see chapter three); and while creative labour is not well suited for automation, it is all the more susceptible for crowdsourcing (see chapter four).

---

33 Frey/Osborne (2013): p. 27.
34 With design profession I mean the sum of all people who make a living by designing things, products and services, i.e. for whom these activities are a vocation with common standards. I would also include professional associations such as AIGA in the US and AGD in Germany, as well as the schools teaching design and the trade journals writing about design. But I also count in people without formal training in design – autodidacts, disconnected from the established institutions, who nevertheless generate their main source of income through designing things. In contrast, when I use the term 'amateur' in the context of design, I mean those who design things as a hobby, out of passion, but without serious intention to make a living from it. I use the phrases 'professional designer' and 'amateur designer' without value judgement – both groups can produce design of high or low quality.
35 Frey/Osborne (2013): pp. 25–26.

Sharing as a Euphemism for Renting

As of 2017, the most deceptive and endemic term peddled by tech entrepreneurs for at least the last two to three years is the so-called 'sharing economy'.[36] In the rhetoric of this latest spirit of capitalism *sharing is the new buying!* In a period marked by high rates of unemployment, precarious labour, rampant debt, foreclosures and evictions in the US, and harsh austerity programs in many parts of Europe, Silicon Valley has taken on the seemingly anti-capitalistic mantras 'buy less', 'sharing is caring', and 'love thy neighbour'. Yet, behind this lofty language a global rent-extraction scheme is operating on an unprecedented scale. In 2013, the Silicon Valley business strategist Jeremiah Owyang founded a consulting firm called Crowd Companies which states as its mission: 'to bring Empowered People & Resilient Brands together to collaborate for Shared Value.'[37]

The Collaborative Economy is an economic model where people are creating and sharing goods, services, space and money with each other in what is also known as the Sharing Economy. Some people are also building their own products, known as the Maker Movement. Combined, this movement means the crowd is getting what they need from each other. The bold question we'll ask and answer is 'What role do companies play if people get what they need from each other?'[38]

This is obviously marketing jargon, Owyang is trying to combine as many buzzwords as possible into one paragraph. Yet it tellingly reveals a gap in the narrative that people like Jeremiah Owyang and Tim O'Reilly have been spinning over the last decade. The narrative is that the individual has been increasingly empowered through digital tools and a culture of self-sufficient sharing among peers. But this doesn't tally with the emergence of commercial monopolies of incredible wealth and power, especially in the so-called 'sharing economy'. So, what exactly is the role that companies play if the crowds get what they need from each other?

    The answer is simple: the role merely successful companies now play is that of the platform provider. What at first sounds like the neutral provision of infrastructure, a humble technical service to support and connect individuals in the crowd is the core architectural principle across the new digital economy – reaching far beyond what is occurring online, also capitalising the physical assets of users participating in these systems. The story of the empowered user is increasingly a myth distracting from the fact that the true power resides with those building the platforms and coordinating the users in their aggregate form as crowds. The flow of

36   The term that is used interchangeably with the equally misguiding 'collaborative economy' and 'collaborative consumption'.
37   crowdcompanies.com/about.
38   *Ibid*.

venture capital and the astronomic valuations of companies that supposedly revolve around non-commercial sharing leave no doubt about that.

The 'sharing economy's' greatest success stories so far are the two Silicon Valley based platforms Uber, founded in 2009 and Airbnb, founded in 2008. These companies frame the rental of private cars and homes as a social, decentralised, peer-to-peer exchange, based on sharing and collaboration, while in fact they introduce a fierce neoliberal logic and conditions of precarious labour into areas of life which had hitherto not been part of the market. Every citizen is regarded as a potential 'micro-entrepreneur' by theses schemes and even one's own bed becomes an 'under-utilised asset' that can and should be capitalised. All the risks are outsourced to private individuals – the users – and regulations that society had once installed to protect the individual, such as fire safety regulations in the case of hotel rooms, insurances for drivers, and passengers in the case of public transport and generally all kinds of workers' protections are 'routed around' by these new platforms.

Most importantly, the platforms that are performing well in the 'sharing economy' are quickly evolving into monopolies in their respective domains. As with Microsoft, Facebook, Google, Amazon, Apple, and eBay before, we are once again confronted with a winner-takes-it-all situation in which platform companies use network effects to become the de-facto global standard for an entire industry. Huge profits nowadays are made when one of these 'lean' start-ups manages to 'disrupt' a large industry in the physical world, with the help of little more than a highly scalable smartphone app, without having to own assets, by externalising all the risk to the crowd, and by taking a cut from every transaction made via the platform across the globe. A common example is Instagram (now owned by Facebook), a platform that with 15 employees achieved what Kodak Eastman once needed 140,000 employees for – billions of dollars are still being made but they remain with the founders and venture capitalists and are not redistributed through wages.[39] Technology critics like the virtual reality pioneer Jaron Lanier argue that the pattern of disruption is leading to an erosion of the middleclass in the USA and in Europe.[40] Indicative of just how much profit is expected to be made at the top of the pyramid are the latest venture capital rounds by Airbnb, which in total raised 3.2 billion USD at a 30 billion USD valuation of the company (as of 2016); and Uber, which by 2016 had raised almost $9 billion dollars and had a 62.5 billion USD valuation.[41] No wonder venture capitalists can't get enough of the 'sharing economy'.

The deceptive term should therefore be avoided and is replaced in the following with the much more appropriate term 'platform capitalism', which also includes

39 Timberg, 'Jaron Lanier: The Internet Destroyed the Middle Class', *Salon* (2013); Leslie, 'Kodak vs Instagram', *New Statesman* (2014).

40 Lanier, *Who Owns the Future* (2013).

41 Rosoff, 'Airbnb is now worth $30 billion', *Business Insider*, (2016). Carson, 'Uber is raising another $2 billion at a $62.5 billion valuation', *Business Insider* (2015).

platforms for crowdwork and gigwork (see chapter three).[42] Martin Kenney, Professor of Human and Community Development at the University of California Davis, was the first person who spoke of platform capitalism in a presentation addressing the consequences of digital labour in 2014:

The assembly line gives you the corporate capitalist (and industrial union). The Cloud gives you the platform capitalist (and contingent labor).[43]

The term platform capitalism points to the underlying structure as well as to the commercial intent. Analysing the digital economy through the lens of platform capitalism shifts the focus of the debate to this new form of centralised power. In chapter three I will discuss in greater detail the mechanics of the platform business model and how the older, location-independent crowdwork relates to the newer, location-based gigwork. Essentially, the two are the most important branches of digital labour within platform capitalism. Often, these platforms are also described as digital tools, but it is crucial to acknowledge that they are tools of a higher order, that serve multiple users with different roles and usage rights. A tool can be in full control of just one user, no strings attached. Platforms, however, always have multiple stakeholders with potentially conflicting interests. Platforms are therefore inherently political. Groups of users can exert control over each other by means of the platform, but it is the platform owner who has the structural advantage in such a system architecture.

Designing Tools for Conviviality

The term 'design' is even more overused and ambiguous in meaning than many of the words and concepts I have discussed in this introduction so far. It ranges from: everything done with a purpose or intent, such as the planning or plotting of a scheme; the development and definition of the shape and functionality of a new physical, mass-produced object through drawings, prototypes, and blueprints; the styling or perceived beautification of goods then sold as *design*-editions supposed to fashionably stand out from the seemingly un-designed regular products and boost sales; and it ends with things like 'nail-design', where fancy ornaments and

---

42 Kessler, 'Pixel and Dimed: On (Not) Getting by in the Gig Economy', *Fast Company* (2014).
43 Kenny, 'Rethinking Labor (and Capital) in the Era of the Cloud' (2014). The term was then picked up by the German journalist, internet expert and business consultant Sascha Lobo in a column for *Spiegel Online*, partly building on a blog-post by the German journalist Julius Endert, Lobo, 'Auf dem Weg in die Dumpinghölle – Sharing Economy wie bei Uber ist Plattform-Kapitalismus', *Spiegel Online* (2014). Endert, 'Von Der Sharing-Lüge und anderen Internet-Märchen', *JBlog*, 2014. See also: Olma, 'Never Mind the Sharing Economy: Here's Platform Capitalism', *Institute of Network Cultures* (2014).

visual effects are applied to fingernails and other surfaces without structurally changing anything about the thing itself. The most general yet elegant definition of design is probably that of Herbert Simon: 'Everyone designs who devises courses of action aimed at changing existing situations into preferred ones.'[44]

In order to address the challenging design problems that we are faced with by the rise of digital platforms, it is illuminating to turn to two authors who were not designers themselves but who provided us with an understanding of design concerned not with discrete objects but with social systems and institutions: In 1973 the Austrian philosopher, catholic priest, and social critic Ivan Illich published the book *Tools for Conviviality*,[45] which in turn was a strong influence on the Swiss sociologist and design theoretician Lucius Burckhardt, especially on his famous essay 'Design is Invisible' from 1980.[46]

Both texts emphasise that institutions are man-made and can thus be re-designed in order to be truly of service to the people, instead of being geared exclusively towards growth and profit. They offer a framework for analysing design from an ethical and social perspective. I am going to build on their work in this book.

In 'Design is Invisible' Burckhardt criticises the common misconception of seeing design merely as an array of objects and is critical of the designers' impulse to solve every encountered problem with the creation of a new thing. Instead of dividing the world into isolated objects, it should be analysed as a succession of interlocking and nested systems (or institutions) that also include invisible yet human made components. One of his examples is a street corner which 'encompasses, above and beyond the visible dimension, elements of an organisational system comprised of bus routes, timetables, magazine sales, traffic light sequences and so on.'[47] An intervention to improve the design of such a system should not stop with a redesign of its visible, physical components such as a bus stop or a newsstand but must also expand to invisible things like the pricing structure of magazines, so that people who have to catch a bus can buy them quickly and conveniently. It is not necessarily the best solution to replace it with a fancy vending machine, because the newsstand also serves a communicative function. Burckhardt shows that these design decision have social implications for the system of the street corner that stretch far beyond the potential shape of the vending machine.[48] He criticises that within the restrictions of a typical design brief, designers often lack the freedom to question the systemic dimension of the social institutions into which they

---

44 Simon, *The Sciences of the Artificial* (1996): p. 11, originally published 1969.
45 Illich, *Tools for Conviviality* (1973).
46 Burckhardt, 'Design ist unsichtbar' (1980). Translation in: Fezer/Schmitz ed., *Lucius Burckhardt Writings* (2012).
47 Burckhardt, 'Design is Invisible' (1980).
48 Burckhardt's systemic perspective on the interplay of humans, objects, institutions, rules and conventions is at times reminiscent of Bruno Latour's Actor-Network-Theory (ANT), in the sense that also here things, even immaterial things, can have a strong agency and form interconnected social systems when used by humans.

intervene. They are instead reduced to devising a new and seemingly better designed object within very narrow parameters – even when yet another object no matter how well designed, does not improve the system as a whole.

Thus Burckhardt calls for a 'socio-design' that transcends the fixation on objects and emancipates designers to intervene on the level of institutions or systems of interpersonal relationships.

When Burckhardt wrote his text in the early 1980s, it was still incomparably harder for designers to intervene in relationships on this systemic level. And one can also argue that it is a bit self-aggrandising of the designers to think they are qualified to solve problems on these abstract and immaterial levels. But now that networked digital technology reaches into every nook and cranny of society, the design of social systems and platforms, often by small groups of designers and engineers has become much easier. In today's nested platform economy a single app can potentially have a huge economic and interpersonal impact on a global scale. Industrial design students at the Rhode Island School of Design, for example, developed Airbnb.

New digital tools and platforms obviously have interfaces of a specific aesthetic, but more relevant than their shape, colour, and style are the invisible power structures that the interface is an expression of, and the social relations that it allows or prevents. The affordance of such system, its implicit assumptions about the user, what it allows the user to do, what it reports about the usage and to whom, and how openly it communicates what it does to the user – together make up the politics of the interface. In my understanding of design, these are all design issues – decisions about functionality, usability, and responsibility with huge social implications. The question inevitably arises as to whether the designers serve the users, as they like to regard themselves, or the financiers of the system who might not always have the users' best interest in mind.

Burckhardt is right when he argues that the responsibility and potential of design must not stop at the shape and surface of things. I think his approach is even more relevant today than it was in the 1980s, because the complexity and social impact of immaterial and invisible social and political features applied to the field of design has increased substantially through digital technology. There has been a power shift from autonomous tools for individual use, to platforms that orchestrate a gamut of possible social roles and interactions via their respective interfaces.

Largely in accordance with the concerns of this book Burckhardt points out: 'Jobs are also designed; not only in the traditional sense of design but in terms of the way the production process is broken down into various types of task, which actively demand or render redundant the laborers' skillsrange, and foster or hinder cooperation.'[49] This type of design decision in the context of digital platforms is

49 Burckhardt, 'Design is Invisible' (1980).

what this book is mainly about. Building on Illich, Burckhardt asserts that designed objects are not neutral but can potentially be *evil*:

Is there such a thing as evil objects? Goods are harmful when they foster our dependence on systems that ultimately pillage our resources, or desert us. Without doubt we are all attached to such systems, and this makes us liable to blackmail. However we can still influence the extent of our dependency. We should avoid those objects that compel us to buy more accessories. We should distrust media that provide a one-way flow of information, even though we can no longer do without them. We should exercise restraint in buying and using any goods that isolate us.[50]

Here, Burckhardt looks at the problem through the eyes of the *consumer*; a figure that later was transformed into a *user*, a *'prosumer'*, and eventually the new subcategory of the *crowdworker*. But the essential ethical problems of *centralisation, dependency*, *isolation*, *asymmetric flows of information*, and *exploitation* are even more prevalent within digital systems today than they had been for the consumer of physical goods in the past. De-centralisation and refraining from trying to solve every problem with the design of new objects or tools are two of the remedies he suggests. Burckhardt encourages designers to understand 'invisible design' as 'design that consciously takes into account the invisible overall system comprised of objects and interpersonal relationships.' This is also the perspective that I take for my critique of crowdsourcing platforms as designed systems with a wide-ranging social impact.

As mentioned above, Burckhardt was influenced by Illich's book *Tools for Conviviality*, which incorporates the design of institutions, the social impact of technical innovation, the limits to industrial growth in a capitalist society, and the fair distribution of wealth and power in a globalised and industrialised world. Illich was from Vienna originally, but for years he travelled through South America and eventually settled in Cuernavaca in Mexico in 1961, were he founded a research centre and language school. His philosophy was formed by studying how Western industrial nations imposed their value system on the so-called third world countries of South- and Central America through export of industrial tools and institutions.[51] Through his first-hand experience of this cultural and technological imperialism, Illich developed an ethics of tool use that evaluates their social impact from the perspective of individuals and local communities in the global South. Illich's philosophy is pertinent for the subject of this book because it forms an important opposition to the world view of utopian technological determinism that has evolved from the counterculture scene around the *Whole Earth Catalog* into an ideology that is

---

50 *Ibid.*
51 Gajardo, 'Ivan Illich', *Prospects: The Quarterly Review of Comparative Education* (1993).

common in the current rhetoric coming from Silicon Valley through publishing outlets such as *Wired* magazine and O'Reilly Media.

I will discuss this in detail in chapter two. Here it suffices to say that the Californian techno-utopian worldview is trying to solve all social, political, and ecological problems with continuously more advanced digital tools and platforms, designed in a global one-size-fits-all manner. This worldview is characterised by a strong belief in technological progress and a lack in reflexivity regarding long-term unwanted social side effects of rolling out certain technologies globally and in total ignorance of the local legal situation. Most importantly this 'Californian Ideology' is an explicitly libertarian worldview that sees all forms of government intervention as a problem generally hindering entrepreneurial ventures and innovation. Libertarian hardliners like venture capitalist Peter Thiel (investor in Facebook, PayPal, Seasteading, Palantir, Trump) have openly declared that they want technology to overcome politics. In Thiel's worldview, the (deeply undemocratic) technology-corporations are an ideal model with which to replace representative government and get things done more efficiently.[52]

It is insightful for our understanding of digital tools and platforms to compare Illich's concept of convivial tools with that of the countercultural hippies and hackers in the twentieth century and with that of today's crowdsourcing advocates. I use Illich and Burckhardt's tool ethic as a framework to develop an ethic of crowdsourced creative work. Since crowdsourcing today is a truly global phenomenon that thrives on the inequalities of income and influence between developing and developed countries, it is instructive to see these tools not just from the perspective of the Global North but from that of the disenfranchised people in the 'emerging markets' of the Global South. Their perspective is crucial for the evaluation of crowdsourcing. It would be a fallacy to only see the phenomenon through the eyes of highly educated and well-connected Western professionals. Crowdsourcing might be perceived as a threat to established professions but could well offer an opportunity for all those previously excluded by high entry barriers such as academic degrees.[53]

New technological tools can be both constructive and destructive for society. They can be constructive at first, but then turn out to become increasingly destructive over time. Illich sees a connection between the potential destructiveness of a tool and the scale of its application. In his view, tools that are rolled out globally at an industrial scale tend towards being destructive on the local level and in the long

---

52 Meerman, 'Cybertopia: Dreams of Silicon Valley', TV documentary, Backlight (2015).
53 Probably, Illich would have been in favour of the erosion of professions and the devaluation of academic degrees that crowdsourcing can cause, as he advocated a 'deschooling' of society, in the sense that expensive degrees should not be used as entry barriers to keep the poor out of certain professions, but he would have certainly opposed the centralisation of power that is another consequence of commercial crowdsourcing platforms. See: Illich, *Deschooling Society* (1999).

run also with regard to the sustainability of the whole system. The question we must therefore ask is whether a new technology solves more problems than it creates.

According to Illich, it is not uncommon for new technologies to go through what he calls 'two watersheds' – a first turning point at which the productivity and usefulness of a tool is substantially increased through industrial methods so that it can be beneficial to most people, and a second turning point, later in the development, when the focus on growth, efficiency, and quantification of outputs is scaled up to such an extent that the balance between positive and negative social consequences is reversed again. Two of the fields in which Illich has identified such turning points are healthcare and mobility.

In the first example, Western medicine reached its first watershed when cures against age-old diseases and primary health care became accessible to a large proportion of the population and its second watershed when hospitals became extremely expensive institutions focusing their financial resources primarily on the prolonging of life through high-tech machines for the richest people in society. In the second example, transportation became cheap, accessible, and useful for the broad population through the railroad system and reached a second watershed with private cars that demanded expansive highway systems, with detrimental effects on the environment and the quality of life on various levels.

Such turning points can also be identified in the history of online collaboration. The dissemination of networked personal computing, with its focus on the empowerment of the individual user and widespread access to decentralised digital tools can be regarded as a first watershed moment. The shift of perspective from the individual user to crowds of users in their aggregate form, characterised by the rise of centralised online platforms 'for the crowd', can be regarded as the second watershed moment. With regard to the mind-set of those designing the new tools, the shift from thinking about how to best create productive tools for the individual user, to creating platforms to harness the creativity and productivity of crowds of users can hardly be overestimated.

The second watershed is the point at which an infrastructural change in scale and quality on a global level leads to an increase in negative consequences on the individual as well as on the social level. To be clear here: of course these shifts are always multifaceted in their consequences and never just good or bad. I agree with Illich though, that as a society we need to have a keen eye on the long-term balance between negative and positive consequences of our technological tools and keep in mind their social costs, not just the private revenues. Constructive social tools, which solve more problems than they create, are what Ivan Illich calls Tools for Conviviality.

Chapter One: The Reinvention of the Crowd

THE MORE THE WISER

On whatever lines the societies of the future are organised, they will have to count with a new power, with the last surviving sovereign force of modern times, the power of the crowds.
Gustave Le Bon, 1895[1]

This chapter is concerned with historic notions of the crowd in comparison with those defining the discourse today. Certain aspects of what a crowd was have remained remarkably stable over time, while others have changed substantially.

In the classic literature on crowds there is some disagreement regarding the differentiation between 'the crowd', 'the masses', and 'the mob'.[2] In some of the key texts the wording changed between the three terms when they were translated. The most influential historic text on the subject, Gustave Le Bon's *Psychologie des Foules* from 1895, was published in English under the title *The Crowd: A Study of the Popular Mind*, and in German under *Psychologie der Massen*.[3] Depending on the context, the French 'la foul' is translated as 'mob', 'masses', or 'crowd' in both English and German.[4]

The British historian and psychoanalyst Daniel Pick writes that 'since at least the late 19th century [...] psychologists, criminologists and sociologists [...] substituted 'crowd' for 'mob', not to insist on the 'neutrality' of the object they scrutinised, but to signify the cool, clinical detachment of their investigations.'[5] And John Carey, literary critic and Professor of English at Oxford, argues that 'the difference between the nineteenth-century mob and the twentieth-century mass is literacy.'[6]

I will come back to the complex relationship between 'the crowd' and 'the masses' in the next section. What is uncontroversial and can therefore be stated here very briefly, is that 'the masses' is the most neutral, abstract, and all-encompassing term, 'the crowd' is the one that changed and diversified its meaning the most over time, and the 'the mob' is the one that remained most stable in its negative connotation – an unequivocally derogative way to refer to group behaviour at its lowest.

The research tool Google Books Ngram Viewer (fig. 5) shows us how frequently 'the crowd' was used in English publications between 1800 and 2008 – also in comparison with 'the masses' and 'the mob'. *The masses* dominated the larger part of the

---

1   Le Bon, *The Crowd: A Study of the Popular Mind* (1895).
2   To a lesser extent also 'the public' and 'the multitude'.
3   Le Bon, *The Crowd: A Study of the Popular Mind* (1895) page numbers from the 2005 edition.
4   In German exists a differentiation between 'Menschenmenge' (crowd) and 'Menschenmasse' (masses), though it's a blurry one, too.
5   Pick, 'Thousands of Little White Blobs', London Review of Books (1989): pp. 20–22.
6   Carey, *The Intellectuals and the Masses* (1992): p. 5.

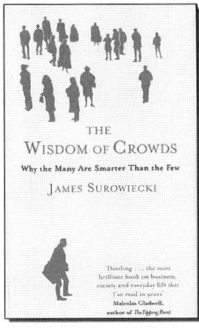

4 Covers of six influential contemporary books on crowdsourcing: Surowiecki (2004), Howe (2008), Shirky (2009), McGonigal (2011), Tapscott (2008), Rheingold (2002). All covers take a birds-eye perspective, looking down at the crowd. The individual seems unimportant from this vantage point.

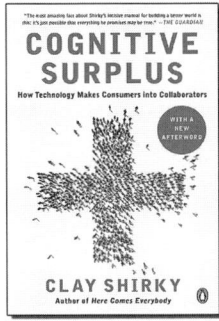

twentieth century, with a small peak in 1918 and two remarkable peaks in 1941 and 1968, followed by a steep and steady decline until the year 2000. The frequency of *the crowd* rose throughout the nineteenth-century, sharply peaked at the turn of the century only to then, with the exception of small bumps in 1932 and 1968, slowly fall out of use until the late 1970s. Since then, *the crowd* has been on the rise again and it is clearly the most common of the three terms in literature today – almost on the level of its old heights again. Without reading too much into the graph, it can be observed that the popularity of the terms used to describe mass phenomena correlates with historic events such as World War II and the counterculture movement of the late 1960s.

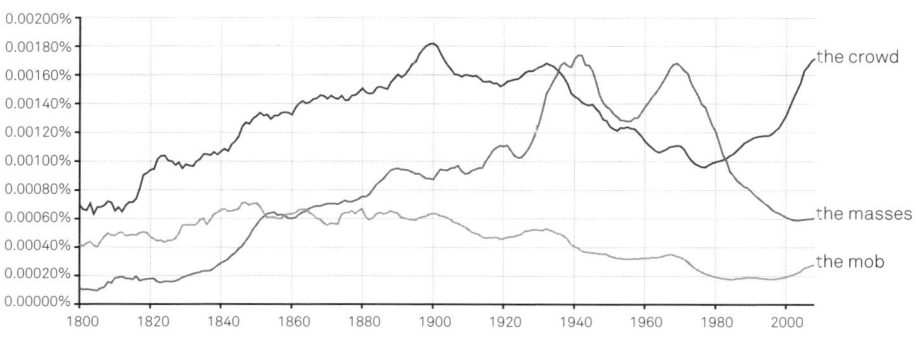

5 Usage of 'the crowd', 'the masses', and 'the mob' in English-language publications between 1800 and 2008.[7]

The steep rise in the use of *the crowd* at the end of the nineteenth century and at the beginning of the twenty-first century is remarkable and suggests that it is a diagnostic of social change. But in contrast to the two peaks in the usage of *the masses,* it is not immediately obvious what influenced or connects the two phases. If one looks at the content of the most influential publications on crowds in these two historic phases, however, it becomes clear – as I will show in the following – that in both periods, the authors were concerned with the arrival of the masses.

At the first peak of crowd literature, the authors were worried about the crowds physically appearing in the cities – from a criminological as well as political angle, thinking about how to best keep the crowds at bay and prevent them from causing destruction through riots or gaining political power through strikes and other forms of public protest. At the second peak, the most read authors were writing about the crowds arriving on the internet – and they were looking at them often from an economic point of view, thinking about the productivity of the crowds, about their uploading user-generated content to digital platforms, and how to best make a profit from that; some were also concerned about a lack of cultural gate-keepers and feared a decline in the quality of media production. And yet in both periods, briefly before 1900 and briefly after 2000, the crowd was typically looked down on from the higher vantage point of the incumbents and the elites. As it turns out, a crowd is always *them* – its other people in their aggregate.

The classic image of the crowd was that of a disorganised gathering of people with a dynamic that could quickly turn a group of cheering spectators into a raging mob. An unruly force, despised and feared by those in power, and frequently ascribed the qualities of a wild animal – aggressive, destructive, impulsive, emotional, hard to control, and not susceptible to reason. This image gained particular relevance during the Industrial Revolution in Europe, when a steep rise in population combined with

---

7   Google Books Ngram Viewer.

massive urbanisation led to overcrowded tenements, people densely packed living under grim conditions, never far away from taking to the streets, potentially picking up dangerous ideas about political revolution. In the late nineteenth and early twentieth century, many authors tried to understand what drives *the mob*, *the crowd,* or *the masses* psychologically and how these people, gathering outside on the street, could be kept at bay; how they could be manipulated in favour of the ruling classes, turned into consumers, or be educated to live up to the democratic power that now 'unfortunately' lay in their hands. The crowd discourse back then took place in front of a general shift towards political democratisation and early consumerism.

The most seminal text on the subject at the time was published by the French social psychologist Gustave Le Bon in 1895. His influence extends via Sigmund Freud and Edward Bernays and far into twentieth century practices of crowd control, crowd manipulation, propaganda, and public relations. With *The Crowd: A Study of the Popular Mind* Le Bon established Crowd Psychology as a new academic field. He argued that 'crowds can never accomplish acts demanding a high degree of intelligence' and argued that a decision by a group would in any case be worse than that of an intelligent individual. A century later, the American author James Surowiecki would write: 'Gustave Le Bon had things exactly backward. If you put together a big enough and diverse enough group of people [...], that groups decision will, over time, be 'intellectually (superior) to the isolated individual,' no matter how smart or well-informed he is'.[8] What informed these two radically opposed positions?

After having studied the French Revolution of 1789 and the aftermath of the Paris Commune of 1870, Le Bon was convinced that by joining a crowd every human would degenerate and succumb his or her will to the brutish and animal-like hive mind that seemed to act as an independent being with a psychology of its own. In this new 'group mind' the particular character of each individual would dissolve into an average character, but the new collective mind would in turn also display new characteristics such as a 'sentiment of invincible power', which the individuals had not previously possessed.[9] The individual would sacrifice his personal interest to the collective interest and the collective would in turn loose any form of fear, conscience, or responsibility that might have restricted the individual.

This analysis had a great influence on Sigmund Freud who developed it further in his book, *Group Psychology and the Analysis of the Ego*. 'The apparently new characteristics which [the individual in the crowd] then displays', Freud wrote, 'are in fact the manifestations of this unconscious, in which all that is evil in the human mind is contained as a predisposition.'[10] Although Freud also had some minor criticism to offer, he marvelled about 'Le Bon's deservedly famous work' and quoted the 'brilliantly executed picture of the group mind' over many pages.[11] Freud saw in

8   Surowiecki, *The Wisdom of Crowds* (2005): from the introduction.
9   Le Bon *The Crowd*, p. 22.
10   Freud, *Group Psychology* (1922): p. 10.
11   *Ibid.* p. 5 and 22.

Le Bon's description of the relation between the crowd and state an equivalent to his own observations on the unconscious mind:

> For our mind, that precious instrument by whose means we maintain ourselves in life, is no peacefully self-contained unity. It is rather to be compared with a modern State in which a mob, eager for enjoyment and destruction, has to be held down forcibly by a prudent superior class.[12]

What Freud is doing here, is an inversion and internalisation of the crowd. The term does not refer to actual people outside on the street any longer, instead it becomes a metaphor for negative forces inside the individual – either way, they had to be supressed!

Astonishingly, in the early years of the twenty-first century, we see an almost total inversion of the negative connotations the term crowd previously had. The crowd suddenly started to appear as a source of knowledge, creativity, and productivity, not only in a metaphorical sense but also as a core element in the business plans and value chains of countless companies. In the image that was now painted of the crowd, it was even seen fit to solve complex problems in research and development. However, at the same time it lost in political and destructive power. Those in charge did not see it as a threat any longer. As it turned out, a virtual crowd could be organised through digital platforms into a docile mass and it didn't expect to gain real democratic control over these structures.

How did this reinvention of the crowd come about? As I have already mentioned in the introduction, it was Jeff Howe who introduced the term 'crowdsourcing' in an article for *Wired* in 2006. He was the first to explicitly write about the crowd as a source for cheap labour. What Howe failed to acknowledge at the time, however, was that his usage of the term 'crowd' was clearly influenced by the journalist James Surowiecki, who's book *The Wisdom of Crowds: Why the Many are Smarter Than the Few,* had been published already in 2004.[13] It was Surowiecki who deliberately and successfully triggered a paradigm shift in the prevailing notion of the crowd.

Surowiecki's choice of title as well as the main message of his book mirrored and inverted that of an early classic of crowd literature: Charles Mackay's *Extraordinary Popular Delusions and the Madness of Crowds*, published in 1841.[14] Mackay's book consits of detailed description of historic hypes and speculative bubbles – cases in which groupthink and information cascades had caused entire populations to collectively run wild. The most vivid example in *Madness of Crowds* is the 'Tulipomania',

---

12 Freud, 'My Contact with Josef Popper-Lynkeus' (1932): p. 219.
13 Surowiecki, *The Wisdom of Crowds* (2005).
14 Mackay, *Extraordinary Popular Delusions and the Madness of Crowds* (1841): page numbers from the 1995 edition.

which occured in the Netherlands in the early seventeenth century. Over the course of about thirty years, tulips had grown from an obscure Turkish flower into an almost mandatory status symbol, and 'it was deemed a proof of bad taste in any man of fortune to be without a collection of them.'[15] Tulips rose so quickly in value that they became an object of speculation and a tremendous financial bubble grew out of the trade with the bulbs (ending in an inevitable crash). 'In 1634, the rage among the Dutch to possess them was so great that the ordinary industry of the country was neglected.'[16]

Surowiecki didn't argue against such obvious examples for the madness of crowds. His point was simply that it is a question of controlling the circumstances for collective decision-making. He was able to show, with an array of empirical evidence from various fields of research that under certain conditions, a crowd was indeed able to deliver better results than any expert. In a sense, Surowiecki's book was an amplified echo of a revelation that had already been made a hundred years earlier by the British polymath, eugenicist, and statistician Francis Galton, a cousin of Charles Darwin. In 1907 Galton had published a short article in *Nature* titled 'Vox Populi'.[17] It was based on data from a weight-judging competition at a livestock fair in Plymouth, where 800 visitors had estimated the weight of a particular ox after slaughtering. The crowd consisted of expert butchers and farmers as well as random spectators. Galton assumed that 'the average competitor was probably as well fitted for making a just estimate of the dressed weight of the ox, as an average voter is of judging the merits of political issues on which he votes [...]'. 'In these democratic days', he wrote, 'any investigation into the trustworthiness and peculiarities of popular judgments is of interest.' Galton originally set out to prove the inferiority of crowd judgement, only to discover quite the opposite. To his surprise, the 'Vox Populi', the voice of the people, was correct within an aberration of just one per cent. Their median estimate was 1,207 lb., the actual weight was 1,198 lb. 'This result is, I think, more creditable to the trustworthiness of a democratic judgement than might have been expected', Galton concluded.

James Surowiecki updated and greatly extended this historic insight with many case studies from the late twentieth century and derived rules from these observations on how to best organise so-called 'prediction markets' with the power of crowds.[18] One of his examples was the TV show 'Who Wants to Be a Millionaire?',

---

15 *Ibid*. p. 75.
16 *Ibid*. p. 76. Mackay reports that: At the height of the hysteria, one singular bulb of the particularly rare type 'Viceroy' was exchanged for 'two lasts of wheat, four lasts of rye, four fat oxen, eight fat swine, twelve fat sheep, two hogsheads of wine, four tuns of beer, two tons of butter, one thousand lbs. of cheese, a complete bed, a suit of clothes and a silver drinking cup.'
17 Galton, 'Vox Populi', *Nature*, 75 (1907): p. 450–451. All of Galton's quotes here are from these two pages.
18 Surowiecki, *Wisdom of Crowds*, p. 96 ff.. See also: Surowiecki, 'The Science of Success', *The New Yorker* (2007). In prediction markets people can bet on things like 'election outcomes, current events, and product sales. Rather than relying on the gut instincts of a single decision-maker, prediction markets tap the collective intelligence of everyone playing the market.'

in which a competitor had to answer an array of questions of increasing difficulty. When the competitor didn't know the answer, he or she could ask the audience or call a preselected assumed expert. The show ran for a long time and the results are well recorded; according to Surowiecki, the 'experts' on the phone were right in about sixty-five per cent of the cases, while the audience chose the correct answer with an average of ninety-one per cent.[19]

A popular experiment similar to that of Galton is to let a group guess the number of beans in a jar. If the number of participants is large enough, there will be a great variety of answers but the average estimate will be very close to the actual amount. The reason for this is that everybody in the crowd uses different strategies, or heuristics, to 'guesstimate' the number – and people tend to be equally far off in both directions, so that the wrong answers cancel each other out on average. The resulting number is almost always more precise than the guess of the best individual. According to Surowiecki, this is only true, however, when the participants are not allowed to discuss their estimations beforehand. If they do, 'groupthink' emerges and people make their decision dependent on others.[20] A so-called 'information cascade' then causes the individuals not to use their own heuristics but let someone else take the lead – the average drifts off significantly from the actual number in the jar.[21] Surowiecki hence argues that aiming for consensus is not a good strategy for decision making in groups.[22] According to him, there are four preconditions that have to be fulfilled in order to get the best possible results from a crowd.[23] Its members have to be *diverse*, *independent*, and *decentralised* and there has to be an *overarching mechanism to aggregate* the variety of ideas and opinions. These aspects (especially the last one) are the foundation of the crowdsourcing platforms that started to emerge since around 2005 – they are, first and foremost, a mechanism for aggregation, for harvesting the input of diverse, independent, and decentralised individuals, freelancers and hobbyists, from all over the world, on a massive, industrial scale.

Surowiecki didn't look at crowds as a source for labour and profit, and he wasn't interested in online platforms. He saw them as a source of information or knowledge and was keen to understand the parameters that allowed crowds to outperform experts. His book was highly influential, but it could only unfold its full potential in combination with another counter-intuitive revelation – that on the

---

19 Surowiecki, *The Wisdom of Crowds*, p. 4.
20 *Ibid*. p. 45.
21 *Ibid*. p. 66.
22 This questions the public voting mechanisms on platforms for creative crowdwork and also the practice of brainstorming in groups, so popular in design and in 'design thinking'. See also Jonah Lehrer on brainstorming as a myth 'Groupthink', *The New Yorker* (2012).
23 The question remains for whom the results will be best and according to what standards. There are big differences between factual results that are either right or wrong, functional results such as code, that either work or don't, and qualitative results – as in many areas of design – that are on a spectrum between better or worse, but can not be measured objectively or automatically. In these letter cases the crowd is often used to evaluate the quality of results.

internet, people were willing and capable to do complex tasks almost for free. Digital technology, so it seemed, substantially changed the behaviour (and the meaning) of the crowd.

In 2003, Howard Rheingold published his book *Smart Mobs*, in which he wrote about how widespread dissemination of mobile phones would change group behaviour and allowed for intelligent, coordinated behaviour.[24] This idea still lives on in the term 'flashmob'. Yet, Rheingold failed to achieve what Surowiecki did for the crowd. Smart or not, the connotation of *the mob* remained negative – as in 'mobbing' and of course the 'lynch mob'.

24 Rheingold, *Smart Mobs: The Next Social Revolution* (2003).

THE PHYSICAL AND THE VIRTUAL CROWD

Most classical authors on crowds agree that the concept has its roots in the bodily experience of being in a physical crowd in the streets. The key question here is, which of its features continue to exist when the crowd becomes virtual?

It was the German writer and Nobel Laureate Elias Canetti who in 1962 provided the most emphatic and insightful contribution to the crowd discourse. For thirty years he worked on his book *Crowds and Power* and the text is exceptional because it is not written from the elitist perspective otherwise so typical in the field of crowd literature. Canetti doesn't start his discussion of crowds as an armchair observer but from his own emotional experience of being submerged and carried away in a crowd. The book begins with the assertion that 'There is nothing that man fears more than the touch of the unknown [...] It is only in a crowd that man can become free of this fear of being touched. That is the only situation in which the fear changes into its opposite. [...] Ideally, all are equal there; no distinctions count, not even that of sex.'[25] By becoming part of a dense crowd of people, this 'Urangst' (fundamental fear) is overcome and inverted – which results in a feeling of boundlessness and empowerment. For Canetti, the experience of the overcrowded physical space, where bodies are pressed against each other, is at the root of what constitutes a crowd.

According to Canetti, those in the physical crowd long for the brief moment of what he calls 'discharge', in which all distinctions between them collapse into a feeling of equality. 'It is for the sake of this blessed moment, when no-one is greater or better than another, that people become a crowd. But the moment of discharge, so desired and so happy, contains its own danger. It is based on an illusion; the people who suddenly feel equal have not really become equal; nor will they feel equal for ever.'[26] Elias Canetti strongly emphasises a second core feature of crowds, and this one is particularly pertinent to online crowds: openness.

The urge to grow is the first and supreme attribute of the crowd. It wants to seize everyone within reach; anything shaped like a human being can join it. The natural crowd is the open crowd; there are no limits whatever to its growth; [...] 'Open' is to be understood here in the fullest sense of the word; it means open everywhere and in any direction. The open crowd exists so long as it grows; it disintegrates as soon as it stops growing. [...] The openness which enables it to grow is, at the same time, its danger.[27]

Against the backdrop of Canetti's description of what a crowd originally was, we can see more clearly what constitutes a virtual crowd today. Online crowds lack the

---

25 Canetti, *Crowds and Power* (1981): p. 15.
26 *Ibid*. p. 17–18.
27 *Ibid*. p. 16.

core feature of earlier crowds: the physical confirmation through touch and a shared space, and thus the physical feedback of possessing strength in numbers. The overwhelming, empowering, and liberating moment of becoming one with others is hard to achieve if everybody sits alone in front of the computer. In an online crowd, only those who actively engage in communication with others are visible. Those who stay passive disappear in the eyes of the others – they become invisible 'lurkers' who might still be watching what is going on, but have become indistinguishable from those who have left the crowd for good. An online crowd demands far less commitment, or none at all, and one can argue that it is only perceived as a crowd from the outside. On the inside, everybody stays alone. The members of a virtual crowd have no sensual feedback about the presence of the others and the size and strength of the crowd they are in. Participation in a march, for example, might be brief, but while it lasts it demands and communicates total bodily presence and this intensity contributes to the reciprocal increase in strength. In short, when it comes to a feeling of empowerment, the virtual crowd is inferior to the physical crowd.

But when it comes to the question of openness in connection with growth and stability, the online crowd is superior to that on the street. Its potential for growth is truly unlimited by space and time, especially if a crowd does not emerge spontaneously around a certain cause, but is organised in a persistent online platform with long-term goals. Today's crowdsourcing platforms have millions of registered users and exist for many years. 'Anything shaped like a human being' can join here, too, but in addition the platforms provide an outer structure that allows the virtual crowd to persist continuously over time (even though its members might constantly change). However, this feature also makes it difficult to estimate the true power and size of online crowds.

Anyone who has ever enlisted to join an online crowd platform (and registration with a user name and an email address is almost always the mandatory prerequisite), typically continues to be counted indefinitely. Often only the platform providers themselves really know what percentage of a crowd is actually still active. MySpace and Second Life are good examples for online platforms that still exist, but have been abandoned by the crowds. Joining an online platform demands far less commitment than, say, joining a rally on the street. People can slip in and out of their role of being part of the crowd within seconds, disappear for months with ease, or be very active in many online crowds at the same time. But even those who are active on an online platform are not as visible to others in the crowd as they would be in a shared space like a street because the activities between the members of the crowd are often compartmentalised into small groups.

Canetti not only differentiates between *open* and *closed* crowds, with regard to how they grow; but also between *quick* and *slow* crowds, with regard to how immediate the crowd's goals are and between very different emotional driving forces of crowds. His examples here include the *fleeting crowd,* which is in a state of panic and disintegration, *the baiting crowd*, which tries to take down a public figure like a hunting pack or a mob, and the *prohibitive crowd*, which can be observed in a strike.

I will come back to the question of closed crowds in chapter four and the conclusion, because there is an important connection between unlimited openness and low pay in commercial crowdwork. If funds are limited (and they always are) but the crowd can grow indefinitely, fair pay is not possible.

The fleeting crowd is a category that is not relevant online – people don't have to run for their life on a virtual platform, they simply log off and don't come back. The baiting crowd, however, occurs in many forms on the internet today – in spontaneous but very destructive mobbing and trolling behaviour on platforms like Twitter and in the comments section of practically every online article that touches on a political subject. It also occurs in an organised form in the public exposure of academic plagiarism committed by prominent political figures. The most famous example of this is the German crowdsourcing project GuttenPlag and its spin-offs attacking other politicians who have copied and pasted their dissertations.[28]

Finally, the prohibitive crowd could potentially be a concept worth reviving in the context of crowdwork as a form of protest and self-organisation to counter exploitative working conditions.

The French sociologist and criminologist Gabriel Tarde, a friend of Gustave Le Bon, also saw the physical gathering of people as the essence of the phenomenon. In 1898 he published 'The Public and the Crowd'. In this paper, he differentiated between *crowds* as one of the oldest forms of human association, whose members are co-present, who share the same space at the same time, and thus are limited in size, and *publics*, which are only made possible through modern media (at his time the printing press, newspapers, railroads, telegraph). Media had created a sense of collective awareness and belonging across the physically dispersed members of a *public*.[29] It made the public potentially unlimited in size, but also influenced the behaviour of its members. For Tarde, a public was defined by critical discussion and thus tended toward heterogeneity while a crowd became homogenous over time.[30] (Seen from this perspective, one could argue that in today's polarised political climate of filter bubbles, echo chambers, fake news, and 'alternative facts', the public discourse has degenerated to separated homogenous crowds shouting at each other instead of engaging in a critical discussion with the goal to draw closer to the truth through better arguments ...)

Today's online crowds share some of the features of Tarde's publics, and yet it would be wrong to speak of the working crowds online as publics, because they do not typically come together to engage in critical discourse but to separately produce

28 PlagDoc/Kotynek, 'Reflections on a Swarm', guttenplag.wikia.com (2012).
29 Paraphrased after: McPhail, *The Myth of the Madding Crowd* (1991): p. 7.
30 *Ibid*. See also: Trotter *Herd Instinct* (1924), discussed on p. 053 ff.

something for someone else.[31] It is tempting to simplify the discourse on crowds by reducing the term to people physically gathered in one place and find a new one for abstract, virtual, or digital crowds. Literary critic John Carey insists on a distinction between the *actual crowd* – which for him is a throng on the street, and the *abstract mass* – which for him is merely a linguistic device contrived by the elites to 'eliminate the human status of the majority of people – or, at any rate, to deprive them of those distinctive features that make users of the term, in their own esteem, superior.'[32]

[...] masses do not exist. [...] Crowds can be seen; but the mass is a crowd in its metaphysical aspect – the sum of all possible crowds. [...] It turns people into a conglomerate. It denies them the individuality which we ascribe to ourselves and to people we know.[33]

Even though this distinction between the 'abstract mass' and the 'concrete crowd' sounds plausible and useful, it has never been as clear-cut as John Carey would like it to be. As we saw with the example of Charles Mackay and the tulip-craze, 'the crowd' was understood in an abstract sense already in 1841 (by this British author, so it is not a matter of imprecise translation) to describe dispersed groups of people that shared a common interest or obsession, but not necessarily the same space. This type of crowd could form or loose its ascribed collective mind in a more *distributed* and *asynchronous* fashion than during a sudden panic in the streets – criteria also essential of the modern day productive crowd online, which is invisible, too, but typically still not referred to as the masses. This makes sense if one wants to maintain a distinction between the totality of all people and *particular* crowds. In that sense, the following distinction by American sociologist Herbert Blumer from the 1940s is helpful: 'Crowds are defined by their shared emotional experiences, but masses are defined by their interpersonal isolation.'[34]

Even though crowds online don't necessarily have a shared emotional experienced, it is true that they are gathered around a certain cause. In crowdfunding, where the crowd pools its resources to finance a shared goal, they also gain strength in number, just as the physical crowd in the street does. There are also examples where the crowd collaborates, where it pools its labour to achieve a shared goal, as in the case of GuttenPlag or in citizen science. However, in crowdwork, individuals are typically in competition with each other, fighting for a very limited pool of resources (payment, reputation, and attention). Here, the fact that they are eventually alone in the crowd becomes particularly clear.

---

31 On page 098 ff., I briefly outline Christopher Kelty's concept of 'recursive publics' as a particular form of online community of programmers that not only constantly discusses but also alters the infrastructure in which it is conversing and working.
32 Carey, *The Intellectuals and the Masses* (1992): from the introduction.
33 *Ibid.* p. 21.
34 Cited after: Glynn et al., *Public Opinion* (2016): p. 12.

Crowds can be seen as a sub-unit of the masses, they have an inside and an outside, a direction and a time frame. They are certainly distinct from a community, in which the members know each other, build bonds, share a history and responsibilities, and are far less exchangeable than they are in a crowd. It is possible and common to be involved in several online crowds and still be alone, without reliable social bonds that make a community. Becoming a member of a crowd is not tied to any obligations.

To some extent, the members of an online crowd (in contrast to a crowd in a shared physical space) resemble what German media philosopher Günther Anders has called 'Masseneremiten' – or 'mass hermits' – in his early criticism of television in 1956.[35] Similar to Marshall McLuhan, Anders argued that the technical format of the media is much more relevant in the formation of its audience than its content. In a similar manner to Jean Baudrillard, Anders argued that the mediated image would become more real than the actual world, which in turn would be reduced to a *matrix*, a raw blueprint – mere material for the constant stream of images derived from it.[36] Instead of participating in the world with other people, the masses in front of the TV would be actively transformed into passive, isolated consumers of images and indirectly of mass-produced goods. Anders wrote that 'modern mass consumption takes place as a sum of solo performances: each consumer is an unpaid domestic worker employed in the production of the mass man.'[37]

Anders was ahead of his time when he pointed out the increasingly blurry distinction between work and leisure, which caused consumers to become unpaid domestic workers for – and the product of – media corporations. 'It is true, of course,' Anders wrote about the recipient, 'that he is a domestic worker of a very unusual type, because of the nature of his work: his self-transformation into a mass-man through his consumption of mass-produced commodities, that is, through his leisure.'[38] The members of online crowds are physically isolated, similar to the people Anders described, but not as passive as he feared. Anders was 'right on the money' when he explained:

The process is completely paradoxical insofar as the domestic worker, instead of being paid for this collaboration, must even pay for it himself; especially for the means of production (the radio or television and, in many countries, even for the broadcasts), by the use of which he allows himself to be transformed into the mass-man.

35 Anders, *Die Antiquiertheit des Menschen / The Obsolescence of Man* (1956).
36 The respective chapter in Anders' book is called: 'The World as Phantom and Matrix', it also appeared as a separate article in the magazine *Dissent* (1956), here with the very contemporary sounding subtitle *'On Work and Play in the Industrial Society'*.
37 Anders, *The Obsolescence of Man* (1956): §2 p. 108. 'Massenkonsum findet heute solistisch statt – Jeder Konsument ist ein unbezahlter Heimarbeiter für die Herstellung des Massenmenschen.'
38 *Ibid.* p. 5 in the English translation from 2014.

This is also the case in crowdsourcing: people pay for the means of production but are not paid for their work. *The masses* refers the totality of a people, the group to which mass media and mass manufacturing was catering in the twentieth century – basically everybody.

For the Spanish philosopher José Ortega y Gasset, the problem of 'mass-man' emerged because in the relatively short period between 1800 and 1914, the population of Europe had risen from 180 millions to 460 millions in just three generations and had produced a gigantic 'mass of humanity'. Due to the development of democracy, the loathed mass-man was now politically in charge, but according to Ortega y Gasset, neither intellectually nor morally fit for the task.[39] Similar arguments were made when the masses arrived online, about a hundred years later.

Society is always a dynamic unity of [...] minorities and masses. The minorities are individuals or groups of individuals which are especially qualified. The mass is the assemblage of persons not specially qualified. By masses, then, is not to be understood, solely or mainly, 'the working masses'. The mass is the average man. In this way what were mere quantity – the multitude – is converted into a qualitative determination: it becomes the common social quality, man as undifferentiated from other man, but as repeating himself a generic type.[40]

The aspect of lacking qualifications is interesting with regard to crowdsourcing today, because there it is not seen as a bug but rather a feature. The fact that there are no gatekeepers, nobody asks for qualifications, and anybody who thinks he or she is fit for the task can join, is often triumphantly framed as a blow against elitism.

For Ortega y Gasset, the mass-man is an abstract category – it is anybody who lacks ambition and reflectiveness and is not willing to subjugate himself to reason, reflection, and ambition. Ortega y Gasset's worldview is a mixture of elitism and meritocracy. He does not defend an elite based on the right of birth but one that is based on intellectual rigour, and the willingness to take responsibility for the future course of civilisation. 'Nobility is defined by the demands it makes on us – by obligations, not by right. *Noblesse oblige.*'[41] He strongly argues in favour of education, but also points out that even academics frequently regress into the lower ranks of mass-man – as soon as they become complacent, accept intellectual commonplaces, and stop aiming for distinction through critical thinking. Ortega y Gasset's problem with the masses is that they *feel* empowered through mass produced goods and mass media and that they actually *are* politically empowered through the right to vote, but that they supposedly don't realise that this level of civilisation can only be maintained and further elevated by not taking it for granted. 'We live in a time,' he

39   Ortega y Gasset, *The Revolt of the Masses* (1929), page numbers from the 1993 edition.
40   *Ibid.* p. 13.
41   *Ibid.* p. 63.

wrote in 1929, 'when man believes himself fabulously capable of creation, but he does not know what to create. Lord of the things, he is not lord of himself.'[42] He ascribes two fundamental traits to the mass-man: 'the free expansion of his vital desires, and therefore, of his personality; and his radical ingratitude towards all that has made possible the ease of his existence. These traits together make up the well-known psychology of the spoilt child.'[43] While he unmistakably despised the masses, he didn't want to oppress or manipulate them, but to transform them into worthy heirs of a humanist civilisation.

Ortega y Gasset often writes in an alarmist tone, predicting that 'the mass crushes beneath it everything that is different, everything that is excellent, individual, qualified and select.'[44] The masses are, in his view, about to destroy the foundations of civilisation: 'Civilisation is before all, the will to live in common. A man is uncivilised, barbarian in the degree in which he does not take others into account.'[45] The book is an urgent and passionate pledge for liberalism and the overcoming of nationalism. The rise of fascism and the outbreak of World War II that followed only a few years after the publication of *The Revolt of the Masses* gave Ortega y Gasset's concerns, in hindsight, a prophetic quality. Sadly, with the rise of populism that has become visible and successful during the wake of the Brexit and the Trump election and in many right-wing parties across Europe in 2016, Ortega y Gasset has become very relevant again today.

---

42 *Ibid*. p. 44.
43 *Ibid*. p. 58.
44 *Ibid*. p. 18.
45 *Ibid*. p. 76. – In antiquity, the barbarians were those who *still* lived outside of civilisation. In Silicon Valley a new generation of libertarian 'barbarians' like Peter Thiel invest in 'Seasteading' – platforms floating in the high-see or near the coasts of 'host nations', on which new micro-nations are supposed to be founded. Seasteaders want to leave civilisation to not be hindered by any government in their entrepreneurial endeavours. Now that neither California nor even the internet is a frontier anymore, new territories have to be created off the coast. The goal is to create private island states without any government regulations. Seasteading is platform capitalism put to the extreme.

FEAR AND LOATHING IN THE IVORY TOWER

In *The Intellectuals and the Masses* Oxford professor of English John Carry has meticulously compiled and studied a vast collection of citations showing the *Pride and Prejudice among the Literary Intelligentsia* between 1880–1939.[46] It is an impressive documentation of the widespread hatred among well respected British poets and writers such as Virginia Woolf, Aldous Huxley, and H. G. Wells towards emerging mass culture and mass-man. Carey shows that what infuriated the intellectual elites more than anything was mass education, which they argued was at the same time futile and dangerous. It seems that old elites felt threatened in their intellectual hegemony. At the very least, they wanted to draw a line between their own professional practice and the emerging multitude of amateurs in the world of art and literature. Carey quotes T. S. Eliot from a 1938 essay:

There is no doubt that in our headlong rush to educate everybody, we are lowering our standards [...] destroying our ancient edifices to make ready the ground upon which the barbarian nomads of the future will encamp in their mechanized caravans. [...] Students should return to the cloister, where they would be 'uncontaminated by the deluge of barbarism outside.[47]

The evocation of a defensive battle that the formerly small and privileged 'creative class' would have to fight in order to hold the edifice of high culture is typical for this kind of sentiment. The call for a defence against the cultural barbarism of the masses has its historic precursors as well as its as recurring echoes in the debates around amateurism and dilettantism.

Already in 1799, the German national treasures Johann Wolfgang von Goethe and Friedrich Schiller were preparing a manifesto against dilettantism. Even though Goethe himself was a dilettante in many artistic fields, he saw himself as a natural born artist and fantasised about 'flushing away legions of dilettantes' in a deluge of criticism 'like ants in a rainstorm'.[48]

That same lamentation about the erosion of high culture we saw at the end of the eighteenth and nineteenth century reached another peak at the beginning of the twenty-first century with the advent of the masses online. A prime example here is the work of British-American author Andrew Keen. In *The Cult of the Amateur:*

---

46 Carey, *The Intellectuals and the Masses* (1992).
47 Carey, p. 15.
48 '(...) denn wir überschwemmen geradezu das ganze liebe Tal, worin sich die Pfuscherei so glücklich angesiedelt hat. [...] so werden sie schreien, daß man ihnen ihre Anlagen verdirbt, und wenn das Wasser vorüber ist, wie Ameisen nach dem Platzregen alles wieder in den alten Stand setzen. Doch das kanr nichts helfen, das Gericht muß über sie ergehen. [...] Es soll eine gewaltige Sündflut werden.' Goethe, *Briefwechsel zwischen Schiller und Goethe: 1794–1805, Band 3*. English: Goethe, *The Collected Works 3* (1994).

How Today's Internet is Killing Our Culture from 2007, he warns: 'The monkeys take over. Say good-bye to today's experts and cultural gatekeepers.'[49] Keen refers to a metaphor from mathematics, the so called 'infinite monkey theorem', which states that even a group of monkeys, given that it is infinitely large and has an unlimited amount of time for hacking randomly into a typewriter would eventually write a masterpiece of Shakespearean quality. In the words of Andrew Keen:

Today's technology hooks all those monkeys up with all those typewriters. Except in our Web 2.0 world, the typewriters aren't quite typewriters, but rather networked computers, and the monkeys aren't quite monkeys, but rather Internet users. And instead of creating masterpieces, these millions and millions of exuberant monkeys – many with no more talent in the creative arts than our primate cousins – are creating an endless digital forest of mediocrity.[50]

There is no question for Keen what to do about this situation: 'Instead of developing technology, I believe that our real moral responsibility is to protect mainstream media against the cult of the amateur.'[51] His argument is not unlike that of Ortega y Gasset: because the masses are uneducated and not susceptible to reason, they destroy the infrastructure created by their noble ancestors, unwittingly tearing down what empowered them in the first place.

The use of animal metaphors, like ants or monkeys is a common trope in the discourse on the crowds and the masses. Neither are they always used in a derogative way, especially when they refer to social animals forming herds, packs, flocks, swarms, hives, and colonies. Strength in numbers is especially helpful for the favourable alteration of the environment, as exemplified by beehives, anthills, and termite mounds.

In his book about herd instinct published in 1924, the British surgeon Wilfred Trotter discusses the extraordinary increase in strength, intelligence, sensitivity, alertness, and resilience that animals gain in groups.[52] In these formations, animals act as one being; a behaviour that can be very advantageous for flight and attack, as exemplified in herds of sheep and packs of wolves. Trotter wrote about animals, but with a political agenda and with human crowds in mind.

According to Trotter, the key features, which allow this behaviour to emerge, are 'gregariousness' and 'herd instinct'. However, the increase in strength through collective action comes at a price, Trotter explains. The trick to 'act as one', can only be accomplished by a high degree of suggestibility towards the other members of the group. Individuals have to take all impulses that they receive from their immediate neighbours as *a priori truths* and must act accordingly, without thinking about

---

49 Keen, *The Cult of the Amateur* (2007): p. 9.
50 *Ibid.* p. 2 ff.
51 *Ibid.* p. 204.
52 Trotter, *Instincts of the Herd in Peace and War* (1924).

whether they are valid. 'It is of especial importance', writes Trotter, 'to note that this suggestibility is not general, and that it is only herd suggestions which are rendered acceptable by the action of instinct. Man is, for example, notoriously insensitive to the suggestions of experience.'[53] Interesting in the context of today's creative crowdwork is the idea that the herd instinct Trotter describes is hostile to innovation:

Anything which tends to emphasize difference from the herd is unpleasant. In the individual mind there will be an unanalysable dislike of the novel in action or thought. It will be 'wrong', 'wicked', 'foolish', 'undesirable', or as we say 'bad form', according to varying circumstances which we can already to some extent define.[54]

In chapter four, I will return to the question of how the crowd is able not only to accept but also to create innovations. Trotter's theories haven't aged well, partly because as he was writing in the wake of World War I, he pushed the use of animal metaphors too far, and slipped from biology into propaganda. In later parts of the book he connected the perceived character of whole nations to certain animals, namely, the Germans to wolves and the British to bees.[55] According to historian Marlise Rijks, this 'introduction of national prejudice into scientific theory' has 'discredited his work for later generations.'[56] But his shift in perspective towards strength in numbers as a biological principle, as well as the question how far animal metaphors can appropriately be stretched, are still relevant for today's discussion of crowd phenomena.

Among all the animal metaphors for crowds, it is the worker bee that has the most positive connotations. The Freelancers Union in the US uses the beehive as its logo and has also built the visual identity of its social networking platform 'Hives' on this metaphor.[57] Bees not only display complex, emergent behaviour and collaboratively build intricate structures, they also industriously create a product that can be harvested by others.[58] Already in Bernard Mandeville's poem *Fable of the Bees* from 1705, the hive served as a parable to illustrate economic principles such as the division of labour and the creation of wealth. 'Harvesting the hive' (or 'harnessing the hive' – a weird mix of metaphors) are frequently used expressions to refer to crowdsourcing; and the German word for crowdsourcing even is 'Schwarmauslagerung' – meaning, the outsourcing to the hive.[59] Bees are a vivid image to illustrate structure, emergent complex behaviour, and collective intelligence, and I frequently use the beehive metaphor myself to draw attention to the question of who

53 *Ibid*, p. 32.
54 *Ibid*. p. 32.
55 *Ibid*. p. 179.
56 Rijks, *Conceptualizing the Masses* (2011).
57 Horowitz, 'Hives: A Community for the New Workforce', *Freelancers Union* (2014).
58 Ramírez, *The Beehive Metaphor: from Gaudi to Le Corbusier* (2000).
59 Early examples in the context of collective intelligence digital labour: Kelly, *Out of Control* (1995). Herz, 'Harnessing the Hive' (2002).

is providing the infrastructure (or platform) for the hive and who is harvesting the honey.

It is important to keep in mind, however that the social animal metaphor does not work on the level of the individual human being. It can easily aggravate the tendency to let the individual in the 'swarm' appear meaningless and dispensable – a worker drone born into a rigid system that cannot be changed. Such metaphors can even be misused to justify totalitarian notions of society. Much more problematic even than referring to social insects, and quite common as well, is the evocation of bacteria and microbes as metaphors for the crowd. Gustave Le Bon wrote in 1895:

Civilisations as yet have only been created and directed by a small intellectual aristocracy, never by crowds. Crowds are only powerful for destruction. [...] In consequence of the purely destructive nature of their power crowds act like those microbes which hasten the dissolution of enfeebled or dead bodies.[60]

It is a recurring theme that also John Carey found in his research for *The Intellectuals and the Masses*, and he pointed out that what originally might have been just harmless rants in the private letters of esteemed thinkers, over time developed into outspoken demands for cruel and drastic measures. Faced with the quickly growing numbers of common people crowding the cities, rage and disgust reached new heights and 'dreaming of the extermination or sterilization of the mass or denying that the mass were real people [became] an imaginative refuge for early twentieth-century intellectuals.'[61] While these authors looked backwards in admiration to Nietzsche, and indulged themselves in rhetorical crowd hate, they eventually lay the ideological groundwork for the actual terror and annihilation of millions through fascism.[62] Stephen Reicher, professor of social psychology at the University of St Andrews and one of today's leading experts on crowd dynamics, writes that the equalisation of the crowds with bacteria, as in this example above by Le Bon was eventually picked up by fascists as a rhetorical device to justify the Holocaust:

Certainly, Le Bon influenced a plethora of dictators and demagogues, most notoriously, Goebbels, Hitler and Mussolini. This influence was not in spite of but rather an expression of Le Bon's intentions. He repeatedly urged contemporary establishment figures to employ his principles in order to use the power of crowd for, rather than against, the state. His perspective matched the concerns of the age in their entirety: fear and fascination in equal measure; denigration of the collective intellect, harnessing of collective

---

60 Le Bon p. 10.
61 Carey, p. 15.
62 Friedrich Nietzsche famously wrote in *Twilight of the Idols* (1889): 'What? You seek something? You wish to multiply yourself tenfold, a hundredfold? You seek followers? – Seek zeros!'

energy. [...] The majority of his crowd text is, in fact, essentially a primer on how to take advantage of the crowd mentality, how to manipulate crowds and how to recruit their enthusiasms to ones own ends.[63]

Le Bon himself argued that through crowd manipulation, all wars are fought. If the crowds have been 'suitably influenced [they] are ready to sacrifice themselves for the ideal with which they have been inspired.'[64] Part of his study therefore resembles Niccolò Machiavelli's *The Prince* from 1532 (who used the term 'multitude' when he meant the crowd).

---

63 Reicher, 'The Psychology of Crowd Dynamics', *Blackwell Handbook of Social Psychology* (2001): pp. 182–208.
64 *Ibid*. p. 65.

THE BUSINESS OF CROWD MANIPULATION

Even though it is likely that Hitler was influenced by Le Bon's *Study of the Popular Mind* and used it to his own ends, it must also be said that Le Bon was not a fascist. Obviously, an elitist tone runs throughout Le Bon's book and his sentiments are anti-democratic, but this is not the case for his political reasoning:

In spite of all the difficulties attending their working, parliamentary assemblies are the best form of government mankind has discovered as yet, and more especially the best means it has found to escape the yoke of personal tyrannies. They constitute assuredly the ideal government at any rate for philosophers, thinkers, writers, artists, and learned men – in a word, for all those who form the cream of a civilisation.[65]

Le Bon acknowledges the democratic axiom that the only true and legitimate power comes from the people, only then to develop a set of tools and mechanisms that those in power should use to manipulate public opinion at their will. He writes that 'a knowledge of the psychology of crowds is to-day the last resource of the statesman';[66] and goes on to show that for true change, strong iconic images have to be implanted in the collective mind to control their behaviour – the simpler the better – since the crowd is not susceptible to reason.

[W]hen crowds have come, as a result of political upheavals or changes of belief, to acquire a profound antipathy for the images evoked by certain words, the first duty of the true statesman is to change the words without, of course laying hands on the things themselves [...] that is to say, in replacing words evoking disagreeable images in the imagination of the crowd by other words of which the novelty prevents such evocations.[67]

Although Le Bon's influence on dictators had arguably the graver consequences, the most interesting aspect in the context of this book is Le Bon's legacy with regard to the manipulation of crowds for commercial purposes. In the early twentieth century, the crowd was manipulated through propaganda and public relations into seemingly boundless consumption. At the beginning of the twenty-first century, with the advent of crowdsourcing, people figured out how to harness the enthusiasm of the crowds to perform free labour.

The most influential figure for the application of crowd psychology in the service of capitalism is Edward Bernays. A nephew of Sigmund Freud, he was a consultant for the US government during World War I, where he successfully

---

65 *Ibid*. p. 199.
66 *Ibid*. p. 11.
67 *Ibid*. p. 102.

orchestrated the propaganda efforts of the country. When the war was over, he privatised his techniques of mass manipulation and started to offer his services to big corporations with remarkable success. His famous book *Propaganda* published in 1930 opens with the following sentence:

The conscious and intelligent manipulation of the organized habits and opinions of the masses is an important element in democratic society. Those who manipulate this unseen mechanism of society constitute an invisible government which is the true ruling power of our country.[68] [...]
   The minority has discovered a powerful help in influencing majorities. It has been found possible so to mold the mind of the masses that they will throw their newly gained strength in the desired direction.[69]

Like Le Bon, Bernays explicitly acknowledges that, in the wake of democracy, power technically resides with the majority. But in spite of this, he is committed to help the minority stay in charge. Because it cannot overrule and dominate the masses openly anymore, the minority has to become invisible and rule with the special tools that Bernays is happy to provide. He offers his service to those in power and at the same time assumes himself already to be part of that secret elite. At least he tries hard to impose that image on his readership through conspiratorially writing about 'our will':

If we understand the mechanism and motives of the group mind, is it not possible to control and regiment the masses according to our will without their knowing it? The recent practice of propaganda has proved that it is possible, at least up to a certain point and within certain limits.[70]

In the book, Bernays still tried to rid the term propaganda of its negative connotation, but he already seemed to sense that this would be futile; after all, the term itself was part of the US propaganda effort during World War I to make the people believe that propaganda was a bad thing, exclusively practiced by the enemy. So, Bernays did what Le Bon and his uncle had also recommended – he changed the words without laying hands on the thing itself and thus made himself known as the father of 'public relations'. According to the contemporary public relations expert Tim Burt, who has taken on the job description 'reputation manager' and wrote the book *Dark Art: The Changing Face of Public Relations,* the insights of *Propaganda* are still valid for his industry.[71]

68 Bernays/Miller, *Propaganda* (2005), p. 37, first published 1930.
69 *Ibid*. p. 47–48.
70 *Ibid*. p. 71.
71 Burt, *Dark Art: The Changing Face of Public Relations* (2012).

Bernays's career went from strength to strength and in one of his most success-ful propaganda campaigns he established a method that leads directly to the core of this book: a design contest on a massive scale. In the early 1920s, Procter & Gam-ble, the multinational consumer goods company, today engaged in creative crowd-work on the *open innovation* platform InnoCentive.com, hired Bernays to improve the image and the sales of the soap brand Ivory. The 'public relations coucil' came up with the idea of a soap 'sculpture competition for children because they were, as Bernays explained, the 'natural enemies of soap'.[72] Bernays's solution was to invent an affordable and egalitarian hobby from scratch and he managed to charge plain white soap with values such as creativity, individuality, and self-expression. Not un-like today's Maker Movement after the financial crash of 2008,[73] the contest was sold to the public as a nostalgic return to manual skills in times of mechanised and alienating work – even though it primarily served to sell more mass-produced soap. The first *National Soap Sculpture Competition in White Soap* was conducted in 1924 and had 500 participants; in 1931, the annual contest had already 5,000 submissions and it continued thereafter for several decades. In *Propaganda*, Bernays reveals how he put his theory of crowd manipulation into practice:

A number of familiar psychological motives were set in motion in the carrying out of this campaign. The aesthetic, the competitive, the gregarious (much of the sculpturing was done in school groups), the snobbish (the impulse to follow the example of a recognized leader), the exhibitionist, and – last but by no means least – the maternal. All these mo-tives and group habits were put in concerted motion by the simple machinery of group leadership and authority. As if actuated by the pressure of a button, people began work-ing for the client for the sake of the gratification obtained in the sculpture work itself.[74]

The similarity, especially of that very last sentence, to today's crowdsourcing contests for design, is striking. Through clever manipulation, the natural creative impulses that people have are redirected and orchestrated to serve corporate interests without the participants taking much notice or at least without them being bothered by it.

Bernays was convinced that in order to influence the crowd, one should not speak directly to its lower rank members – instead, one had to win over the people the crowd looked up to, influence them and speak with their voice. Bernays was fa-miliar with Trotter's theory of herd instinct and, unsurprisingly, he was especially interested in its principles of suggestibility.[75] Having learned also from Freud, Ber-

72 Museum of Public Relations, 'Edward Bernays speaks about his work for Ivory Soap', video available on YouTube.
73 Schmidt, 'The Feeling of Control – Die Revolution Wird Nicht 3D gedruckt' (2013). The essay deals with the politics of the so-called Maker Movement and shows a direct connection between the financial crash of 2008 and a return to private handicraft work as a means to regain a feeling of control in times of economic depression.
74 *Ibid*. p. 81.
75 Bernays, p. 44.

nays furthermore knew that the message could not simply be 'buy more soap' but had to appeal to subconscious desires and be aligned with the pursuit of higher values and the perceived greater good, like in today's volunteer crowdwork (see chapter three).

The reasons for participating in these crowd creativity projects back then and today are very similar. People either have an alienating and unfulfilling job which they try to counterbalance with a creatively fulfilling and productive hobby, or they have a lot of free time on their hands because they have been made redundant and try to put that downtime to good use in order to stay skilled, motivated, and focused.[76]

Edward Bernays didn't invent crowd creativity contests, but he refined the concept at a comparatively early point in history. Not only did he change the image of the product; customers also had to consume vast amounts of the product in order to take part in the competition. That is to say, Procter and Gamble only made profit from the crowd at the very end of the value chain. In modern crowdsourcing, however, the crowd provides labour at almost all stages of the value chain: from ideation, through research and development to production, marketing, and market research.

It wasn't until the twenty-first century that Bernays's ingenuity to commercially harness the crowds urge to be creative was surpassed. In today's iteration of these methods, the crowd is 'nudged' into producing goods that feed back into the value chain at an early stage and that can be resold or form the basis of innovative new products. As I will show in chapter four, today's contest-based creative crowdwork can take the form of marketing, market research, product design, and production – all wrapped into one.

76 See: Marshall, 'Clean Cuts' (2008); and also: Gelber, *Hobbies: Leisure and the Culture of Work in America* (1999).

FROM GLOBAL BRAIN TO COLLECTIVE INTELLIGENCE

As long as the masses were imagined as the rabble in the streets, most authors in classic crowd literature treated them with a mixture of fear and disgust – either openly or thinly veiled. This worldview transformed however into more lofty notions through a change of perspective with regard to the timescale and through a systemic, global viewpoint directed towards a more distant future. When the writers on mass phenomena widened their perspective to think about connected humanity in an abstract sense, large groups of people started to appear to have the potential for a glorious next phase in evolution.

In the organicist version of this, society is seen as a biological superorganism consisting of many specialised organs that are in constant synergetic interaction. In 1897, Herbert Spencer based his *Principles of Sociology* (1897) on the assumption that society is an evolving 'social organism' defined by ever growing complexity and internal processes of integration and differentiation – a division of labour so to speak – following a universal law of evolution.[77]

It was the worldview of cybernetics, which in the middle of the twentieth century popularised the view of society and even the whole planet as one integrated system with many interlinking subsystems. It allowed an analysis of living and non-living actors as one interconnected system of mathematically describable feedback loops. In these modern imaginings, the internet becomes the central nervous system of humanity and the individual becomes a node in an all-encompassing information processing organism – a global brain.

The Belgian cyberneticist Francis Heylighen traces the idea of society as one single organism back to antiquity, but it is only with the advent of network technology and cybernetics that the metaphor transforms into a political and technological agenda. Heylighen distinguishes between three different but often interwoven strands of the concept: the organicist, the encyclopedist, and the emergentist vision, depending on whether the global brain is seen as a social organism, a universal knowledge system, or a spiritual planetary consciousness that will eventually emerge.[78] It is beyond the scope of this book to go into the intricacies of these concepts, but I would like to briefly mention why this seemingly progressive vision is problematic.

It was the British physicist Peter Russell who coined the term and published the book *The Global Brain* in 1982.[79] He saw society and nature as one conscious

---

77 Spencer also coined the famous phrase 'survival of the fittest.'
78 Heylighen, 'Conceptions of a Global Brain: A Historical Review' in: *From Big Bang to Global Civilization* (2012). The emergentist vision has its contemporary version in people believing in the Singularity.
79 Lovelock, 'Gaia as Seen through the Atmosphere', *Atmospheric Environment* (1967); and: Russell, *The Awakening Earth: The Global Brain* (1984); and the animated short film version 'The Global Brain – Peter Russell' (1983) available on YouTube.

system, building on the 'Gaia Hypothesis' by the British maverick polymath James Lovelock, Russell emphasised the New Age spiritual aspect of the idea. Believers in the Gaia Hypothesis, paradoxically see humanity with its infrastructure and network technology as the intelligent nervous system of the planet and, at the same time, as the cancer of the earth. On the one hand, the 'natural' equilibrium of a system that stabilises itself through feedback loops is praised, on the other hand, the system is supposed to be regulated through coordinated interventions.

As Heylighen points out: 'The organicist view is not just rejected on the left by Marxists, but on the right by advocates of 'laissez-faire' economics, who abhor the idea of individuals as merely little 'cells' subordinated to a collective, which they see as a justification for totalitarian systems such as those created by Mao, Hitler or Stalin.'[80]

The encyclopedist version of the global brain is usually referred to as the 'World Brain'. It was introduced and popularised by the science-fiction writer H. G. Wells, who was in turn influenced by the encyclopaedic endeavours of the enlightenment thinkers Denis Diderot and Jean le Rond d'Alembert.[81] Wells was obsessed with a vision of the World Brain in form of an encyclopaedia that was supposed to be much more than just a knowledge retrieval system. The reorganisation of the world's knowledge would be the first step. He imagined a global government – unifying humanity and preventing all future wars. Wells envisioned a future utopia in which humanity would be free from toil, thanks to mechanisation and automation. New intellectual occupations, such as the constant editing of a shared global encyclopaedia (very similar to today's Wikipedia) would keep the global network of intellectual workers busy:

You see how such an Encyclopaedic organization could spread like a nervous network, a system of mental control about the globe, knitting all the intellectual workers of the world through a common interest and a common medium of expression into a more and more conscious co-operating unity and a growing sense of their own dignity, informing without pressure or propaganda, directing without tyranny.[82]

Indeed a crowdsourcing utopia! But this very cybernetic sounding 'directing without tyranny' is the great contradiction in Wells's vision, because he frequently also writes about an 'Open Conspiracy' by a class of technocrat 'Samurai', that will control the New World Order – much like Edward Bernays's idea of the 'invisible government'.

---

80 Heylighen, p. 3.
81 Wells, *World Brain* (1938). Citations here from online version without pagination: (gutenberg.net.au/ebooks13/1303731h.html).
82 *Ibid.*

As the Australian information scientist W. Boyd Rayward shows in great detail, Wells's belief in a centralised version of the world brain, in which a superior class of man undemocratically directs the world with the best intentions and for the better, leads him to visions of total control and a justification of eugenics.[83] The various global brain fantasies sound promising at first: with the help of technology, humanity will be able to merge the totality of its cognitive capacities into a super brain that will then steer the planet into a better future. They are the opposite of the derogative notions of the primitive crowds, but they disrespect the individual human in a different way, because the single being, larger groups, and even politics eventually become meaningless. As soon as all brains are connected, according to these visions, a supreme being will emerge, be it biological, technological, hybrid, or virtual. The only option that remains for lesser humans is to have faith and give in to a totalitarian, technological, or biological determinism. Yet, as a species, we can't make collective decisions without politics and it would be fatal to hand over control to a quasi-religious belief in self-organising networks, monitored by an invisible technocratic or cybernetic government.

With the advent of the world wide web in the 1990s, the old vision of connecting all human brains to form a single superorganism suddenly seemed within reach. In 1994, the French sociologist and philosopher Pierre Lévy coined the term 'collective intelligence' to describe 'mankind's emerging world in cyberspace'.[84] Lévy wrote a book that is particularly characteristic of the moment in time when it was published – the internet had arrived, its power had become evident, but was not yet fully realised and its direction still left room for speculation and deliberation. Lévy's worldview and ambitions are deeply humanist throughout the text. His ideas build on those of social computing pioneers such as Douglas Engelbart (who I will introduce in the next chapter) and set out to strengthen and integrate the individuals on the fringes of society. He wants their potential contributions to be taken seriously, treated with respect, and integrated in a meaningful way. For him, collective intelligence is:

[...] a form of universally distributed intelligence, constantly enhanced, coordinated in real time, and resulting in the effective mobilisation of skills. [...] The basis and goal of collective intelligence is the mutual recognition and enrichment of individuals rather than the cult of fetishised or hypostatized communities.[85]

For Lévy, it is important to distinguish this vision from any totalitarian tendencies that diminish the role of the individual human. According to the French sociologist, the failure to recognise the other as an intelligent being is to deny him his social

---

83 Rayward, 'H.G. Wells's Idea of a World Brain: A Critical Reassessment' (1999).

84 Lévy, *Collective Intelligence* (1997); first published in French: *L'intelligence collective: Pour une anthropologie du cyberspace* (1994).

85 *Ibid.* p. 13.

identity. Collective intelligence 'is a global project whose ethical and aesthetic dimensions are as important as its technological and organisational aspects.'[86] True collective intelligence, as understood by Lévy, would be a 'real time democracy' and the antithesis of any totalitarian system; it would be based on slow, distributed collective deliberation by the many, without any power in the hands of the few. It is marked by a 'laborious but continuous construction of a collective and interactive debate in which everyone can contribute to formulating questions, establishing positions, proposing and weighing arguments, making and evaluating decisions.'[87] It does not mean simple online voting (or 'clicktivism', as it is today called) but hard work. The question is how many people would be willing to constantly engage in such an ongoing discourse without representatives. For Lévy, collective intelligence offers a third way; neither the 'stupidity of crowd behaviour' nor the oppression through hierarchy and authority. 'Intelligent communities are the direct antithesis of the incoherence and brutal immediacy of crowd behaviour and yet do not channel the community into a rigid structure.'[88] However I would argue that there are limits to the size a community can be before becoming either a crowd, with no internal structures or some form of state, with rigid structures.

Throughout the book, Lévy argues decidedly against central control of the 'global brain' and against the manipulation of the masses through demagoguery and propaganda. In a talk that Lévy gave in Sao Paulo in 2014, he reemphasised his position to 'augment the human intellect' (a goal set out by Douglas Engelbart), pointed out that collective intelligence in animals is not to be confused with that among humans, strongly dismissing the cultish belief in artificial intelligence as represented by institutions such as the Silicon Valley based Singularity University and its hope for Transhumanism. 'My perspective is humanist – not post-humanist. It is a continuation of the traditional humanism, centred on the development of the person and the development of the community – the idea is human development.'[89]

Over the last century, this vision appeared in different guises, but the core idea remained the same and is closely connected to the rhetoric that was used after 2006 to advertise crowdsourcing as the next big thing: The networked collaboration of the entirety of humanity was propagated as a means to prevent a global catastrophe. The fight against climate change in particular was used as the ultimate justification for commercial crowdsourcing. It was prominently used by people like Thomas Malone, director of the MIT Center for Collective Intelligence, and by management consultant Don Tapscott, author of the books *Wikinomics* and *Macrowikinomics*.[90] The subtitle of Macrowikinomics is *Rebooting Business and the World,* leaving no doubt about the order of Tapscott's priorities. The book is built around the claim

86 *Ibid*. p. 10.
87 *Ibid*. p. 80.
88 *Ibid*. p. 81.
89 'Pierre Lévy Talks about Collective Intelligence at Senac' (2014), talk available on YouTube.
90 Tapscott/Williams, *Wikinomics* (2008). Tapscott, *Macrowikinomics* (2010).

that the world is broken, but our new digital tools and platforms will lead to 'the birth of a new civilisation' based on mass collaboration, openness, sharing, integrity, interdependence, and of course, crowdsourcing.[91]

Now that our 'world in cyberspace' has fully emerged and turns out not to be averse to or resilient to the agglomeration of power and the reduction of humans to mere parts in the machine, it is important to recall that Lévy's core idea behind collective intelligence was more ambitious. Through people like Thomas Malone, who is also Professor of Management at the MIT Sloan School of Management, the concept has evolved (or has been downgraded) to a business model or the basis for a manipulation technique. Asked in an interview by *The Economist* about the future of work and the opportunity for management to take advantage of collective intelligence, Malone answered that 'one advantage is that you can sometimes get work for less money if you are enticing people to work for free. The deeper question is, how do you motivate people to do the things you want them to do?'[92]

Malone went on to explain that marketing has been traditionally aimed at getting people to buy things – now, these instruments would be better used to keep people motivated to work as volunteers. According to Malone, people can be motivated by money, love, and glory and he wants to emphasise the latter two to enhance the effectives and the collective intelligence of businesses. Malone's ideas approach Bernays's here and diverge from Lèvy's.

The metaphor of the global brain, woolly as it may be, still has currency for the MIT, as becomes clear in a paper from 2013 by the Center for Collective Intelligence titled 'Programming the Global Brain'.[93] The authors describe their paper as a 'call to arms' for research with the goal to 'fully exploit the enormous potential of the global brain.' They speculate about how a 'social operating system' could be designed in order to get the best output and the most reliable results. Unsurprisingly it is written from the perspective of those doing the programming of the human machine. The authors see the global brain as an 'idea ecology' able to 'host a constant ferment of idea generation, mutation, recombination, and selection, analogous to biological evolution.' It is supposed to take the form of an intellectual supply chain, and 'fortunately, the global brain also provides access, at least currently, to a huge human "cognitive surplus", so that, for instance, quality mechanisms based on previously-unthinkable levels of redundancy have become practical.'[94] They point out that the programmers of the 'social operating system' will have to become 'societal architects', who are to 'master the art of programming our planet's emerging global brain' in order to address not only the huge opportunities of scientific and social

---

91 Tapscott Group, 'From Crowdsourcing to Kony 2012: Macrowikinomics: New Solutions for a Connected Planet' (2012), promotional video, available on YouTube.
92 Malone, 'The Future of Work with MIT's Thomas Malone', interview with *The Economist* (2013), available on YouTube.
93 Bernstein/Klein/Malone, 'Programming the Global Brain' *MIT Center for Collective Intelligence* (2012).
94 *Ibid*. p. 3.

progress but also global 'existential threats of unprecedented seriousness, such as the environment.'[95]

The architecture of such a 'social operating system' is also at the heart of this book, but my perspective is a humanist one, not primarily concerned with an efficient design of the system but with its ethics and the implications for the individuals working within it. Charlie Chaplin wonderfully illustrated in Modern Times (1936) how the individual industrial worker was always in danger of being reduced to a cog in the machine. In post-industrial times the danger is to be a mere processor, a neuron in the distributed computing operation of the global brain.

95 *Ibid.* p. 5.

Chapter Two: Early Concepts of Online Collaboration

AUGMENTING HUMAN INTELLECT

The first detailed anticipation of networked personal computing and online collaboration emerged from (and was a reaction to) the large-scale interdisciplinary research for nuclear warfare. Vannevar Bush, born in 1890, had been at the Department of Electrical Engineering at the Massachusetts Institute of Technology (MIT) since 1919. There he worked on early analogue computers and code breaking devices before he became dean of the MIT School of Engineering in 1932. Much of his research was defence-related and in 1941 he was among the initiators and eventually became the major scientific coordinator of the Manhattan Project, which led to the development and ultimately the detonation of the atomic bomb. Bush coordinated the activities of about six thousand leading American scientists in the application of science to warfare.[1] However, towards the end of the war, he made an intellectual leap and developed an *a priori* description of decidedly civil personal computing and online collaboration. In July 1945, Bush published the article 'As We May Think' in *The Atlantic*.[2] In his text, he outlined his vision of the so-called 'Memex' – a design fiction of a *personal computer* meant to support *individual* knowledge workers and foster their collaborative exchange of information *among peers*. At this remarkable moment in history, only two months after the surrender of Germany and a month before the bombings of Nagasaki and Hiroshima, the director of Pentagon's Research Office tried to redirect the efforts of his colleagues towards non-military efforts. As Bush wrote in *The Atlantic*: 'It is the physicists who have been thrown most violently off stride, who have left academic pursuits for the making of strange destructive gadgets. [...] Now, as peace approaches, one asks where they will find objectives worthy of their best.' Bush saw this new and worthy challenge in a computer aided personal information management system. He was worried that the rapidly growing amount of human knowledge would make itself unmanageable, that important scientific findings might therefore remain unnoticed, leading to a wasteful doubling of effort due to a lack of access and navigation of existing knowledge.

As H.G. Wells with his ideas for the World Brain, Bush too, had observed the great advances in the miniaturisation of technology and was intrigued by the possibilities of microfilm as a storage medium. He was convinced that soon the '*Encyclopaedia Britannica* could be reduced to the volume of a matchbox', its material production 'would cost a nickel, and it could be mailed anywhere for a cent.' He did not foresee the advent of the microchip but still projected a whole system of information management for the individual user. The objective that he outlined was to free

---

1   Bush, 'As We May Think', *The Atlantic* (1945), all quotes by Vannevar Bush in this section are from this article.
2   *Ibid.*

the brain of the user from repetitive tasks (in stark contrast to today's crowdsourcing services such as Amazon Mechanical Turk that, as will be described later, just outsource the repetitive and burdensome tasks to the brains of other people, to the crowd online), in order to allow full concentration on the creative tasks at hand: 'For mature thought there is no mechanical substitute', Bush wrote, but for everything else there will be 'powerful mechanical aids. [...] We may some day click off arguments on a machine with the same assurance that we now enter sales on a cash register.'

Bush not only prophesied modern input devices, automated processing of information and logical operations to click through on a high symbolic level (like natural language, in contrast to code); he also envisioned advanced tools for data retrieval that would allow users to visually browse through libraries of books and academic papers stored in the Memex and to control the 'selection device' by spoken language. He furthermore criticised the shortcomings of the way information is traditionally indexed in libraries, where it has to be traced down from subclass to subclass and can only be in one place at a time.[3] 'The human mind does not work that way', Bush wrote, 'it operates by association. With one item in its grasp, it snaps instantly to the next that is suggested by the association of thoughts, in accordance with some intricate web of trails carried by the cells of the brain.'[4] The user of the Memex would be able to index and link all kinds of information associatively – meaningfully joining the content in his private database with a keystroke.

Thus he builds a trail of his interest through the maze of materials available to him [...] he sets a reproducer in action, photographs the whole trail out, and passes it to his friend for insertion in his own memex, there to be linked into the more general trail. [...] Wholly new forms of encyclopedias will appear, ready made with a mesh of associative trails running through them, ready to be dropped into the memex and there amplified.[5]

At a time when the oldest computer had just been running for four years and microchips were not yet invented, Bush was already thinking about search engines, hyperlinks and, most importantly, collaborative open knowledge production – almost like Wikipedia.

It was not a coincidence that this vision, if only indirectly, came out of the development of the nuclear bomb. Bush's job was to coordinate a research endeavour of unprecedented scale with many separate teams of scientists working in parallel – similar conditions to those that led Tim Berners-Lee to develop the 'world wide web' standard at CERN, much later between 1989 and 1991. With the important difference that at the Manhattan Project information was deliberately distributed

3 The argument for dynamic filing order was picked up again much later by: Weinberger, *Everything Is Miscellaneous* (2007).
4 Bush, 'As We May Think' (1945).
5 *Ibid.*

for security reasons, so that nobody who worked there (except a few people like Bush and Oppenheimer) would have the full picture.[6]

This splitting up of one large task into many separate smaller tasks to be solved in isolation and later aggregated and reassembled is also the method applied today in microtasking crowdwork although not in the service of innovation (see chapter three). In large-scale innovation projects such as the one Bush was orchestrating, classic top-down bureaucratic control alone would not have been successful: out of necessity the military-industrial-academic complex therefore pioneered a post-industrial mode of collaboration, based on interconnected flexible teams of experts.

Most remarkable is that when Bush was finished with the bomb, he went on to design a computer and a concept of networked collaboration that was not intended to serve government and its large research facilities, let alone commerce. He imagined his Memex as a tool for the empowerment of the individual knowledge worker, as a medium to freely share ideas with peers. This is also the crucial point that differentiates Bush's encyclopedist imaginary future from that of H. G. Wells. From someone who had successfully managed the division of labour of 6,000 people one might have expected to develop a computing system to better coordinate large groups of intellectual workers and outsource tasks to them in a top-down manner. Instead, Bush designed a system that he wanted to work with himself, a tool for the empowerment of the individual user, not a centralised platform to coordinate and control the work of others.

It took two decades until the first steps were taken towards the realisation of the Memex. But already in 1945, Bush's ideas left a lasting impression on the person that would undertake these steps. When Douglas Engelbart stumbled upon Bush's article in *The Atlantic*, he was a twenty-year-old navy radar technician stationed on a small island in the Philippines.[7] After he returned from the war, he studied electrical engineering and then started working for an aeronautics research centre in Mountain View, California, at the heart of what would later become known as the Silicon Valley. In 1950 he realised that he wanted to contribute something meaningful to the world, 'something that would enable people to collectively understand the scope and nature of the world's problems and the potentials for their solution.'[8] He decided to devote his life to the task of empowering the individual, with the help of the computer, to *augment the user's intellect* and make Vannevar Bush's vision of the Memex real.

---

6   Else, *The Day After Trinity*, documentary film, USA (1980).
7   Engelbart' biographical information here is partly paraphrased after: Markoff, *What the Dormouse Said* (2006), and a talk Engelbart gave on 22 August 2007 at the Google Headquarters in Mountain View, available on YouTube.
8   *Ibid.*

However, Engelbart was ridiculed when he told colleagues at the University of California, Berkeley about his ambitious plans.[9] His ideas where not regarded as an appropriate research topic. At the time, computers were massive mainframe machines doing arithmetic calculations, primarily for military purposes. The long-term goal, following the work of Alan Turing and John von Neumann, was *artificial intelligence* – nobody was interested in 'augmenting the intellect of the user'. Indeed, there wasn't even such thing as an individual user at that time. The huge machines had to be shared by many scientists, most of whom only had indirect access. His colleagues warned Engelbart to keep quiet about his visions if he wanted to establish a career and not stay an assistant forever. Yet, he stuck to his and Vannevar Bush's vision and in 1962, at the Stanford Research Institute, he published an extensive report for the Air Force titled 'Augmenting Human Intellect: A Conceptual Framework'.[10]

Engelbart argued that 'after all, we spend great sums for disciplines aimed at understanding and harnessing nuclear power. Why not consider developing a discipline aimed at understanding and harnessing "neural power?" In the long run, the power of the human intellect is really much the more important of the two.'[11] This at first almost sounds like today's crowdsourcing concept of 'harnessing the cognitive surplus' through 'human computation', but Engelbart was not aiming for repetitive and simple microtasks – quite the opposite. He wanted to significantly increase the complexity of tasks that individuals could deal with. He described a holistic system of human computer interaction that did not focus on technical specifications but rather on the workings of the human intellect, the creation of knowledge, and the manipulation of symbols:

By 'augmenting human intellect' we mean increasing the capability of a man to approach a complex problem situation, to gain comprehension to suit his particular needs, and to derive solutions to problems. [...] By 'complex situations' we include the professional problems of diplomats, executives, social scientists, life scientists, physical scientists, attorneys, designers [...]. We do not speak of isolated clever tricks that help in particular situations. We refer to a way of life in an integrated domain where hunches, cut-and-try, intangibles, and the human 'feel for a situation' usefully co-exist with powerful concepts, streamlined terminology and notation, sophisticated methods, and high-powered electronic aids. (1a1)[12]

9   *Ibid.*
10   Engelbart, 'Augmenting Human Intellect' (1962).
11   Paragraph 6e – the specific numbers for each paragraph are a structural element of Engelbart's Augmentation System. He tried to overcome the page metaphor in the digital realm and I will stick to his system here whenever I quote from the 1962 paper.
12   *Ibid.*

Engelbart outlined what we take for granted today; real-time digital text editing programs that allow easy copying and pasting of text fragments and that include dictionaries and auto-complete features. He also aimed to make semantic text editing tools that would make visible how an argument is structured and link back and forth inside its logical structure. But his system would not be limited to text editing. Right from the beginning he thought about the way designers could benefit from working with the computer. His very first example in *Augmenting Human Intellect* is that of an architect creating and collaborating with the help of the machine, yet to be designed by Engelbart:

Let us consider an augmented architect at work. He sits at a working station that has a visual display screen some three feet on a side; this is his working surface, and is controlled by a computer (his 'clerk') with which he can communicate by means of a small keyboard and various other devices. (1a11)

A structure is taking shape. He examines it, adjusts it, pauses long enough to ask for handbook or catalog information from the clerk at various points, and readjusts accordingly. He often recalls from the 'clerk' his working lists of specifications and considerations to refer to them, modify them, or add to them. These lists grow into an ever-more-detailed, interlinked structure, which represents the maturing thought behind the actual design. (1a14)

All of this information (the building design and its associated 'thought structure') can be stored on a tape to represent the design manual for the building. Loading this tape into his own clerk, another architect, a builder, or the client can maneuver within this design manual to pursue whatever details or insights are of interest to him – and can append special notes that are integrated into the design manual for his own or someone else's later benefit. (1a18)

Remarkably, about half of this academic research report written for the US Air Force takes the form of a design fiction. Engelbart places the reader in a conversation with Joe, the imagined future user of the speculative augmentation system, who explains patiently all the functions of the tool and how he uses the system to get his work done. Engelbart also included thoughts about ergonomics: how the future user would sit comfortably in front of multiple screens; how he would best switch from one device to another, depending on what types of symbols he would want to manipulate; and where an input device such as a stylus pen would have to be positioned.[13] Speaking with the voice of Joe from the future, Engelbart outlined his long-term goal, the use of the augmentation system for group collaboration:

---

13   In 1963 Ivan Sutherland's 'Robot Draftsman' Sketchpad pioneered the manipulation of graphics directly on the screen with a stylus pen as a tool. See: Sutherland, 'Sketch Pad' in *Proceedings of the SHARE Design Automation Workshop* (1964).

We have experimented with having several people work together from working stations that can provide inter-communication via their computer or computers. That is, each person is equipped as I am here, with free access to the common working structures. There proves to be a really phenomenal boost in group effectiveness over any prev ous form of cooperation we have experienced. They can all work on the same symbol structure, wherever they might wish. If any two want to work simultaneously on the same material, they simply duplicate and each starts reshaping his version – and later it is easy to merge their contributions. The whole team can join forces at a moment's notice 'pull together' on some stubborn little problem, or to make a group decision. [...] (3b9a)

We feel that the effect of these augmentation developments upon group methods and group capability is actually going to be more pronounced than the effect upon individuals methods and capabilities, and we are very eager to increase our research effort in that direction. (3b10)

In the context of this book, the most important aspect of Engelbart's work is that he was the first person who actually started to build a system for elaborate online group collaboration – not just for knowledge workers in general but also for designers in particular. He always imagined the group collaboration to be taking place among peers: he never mentions hierarchies, the outsourcing of tasks to others, or the control of subordinates and their performance through the machine. Already in 1961, for example, he and his colleagues had created a voting-device for instant feedback in group discussions. A speaker could continue talking as long as the real-time ratings submitted by the group through special devices didn't fall below fifty per cent.[14]

Engelbart's paper is marked by a decidedly humanist view of technology and a strong belief in the capabilities of the individual user, if only he or she was provided with the proper tools. Not unlike his contemporaries Richard Buckminster-Fuller and Stewart Brand, Engelbart is deeply concerned with the growing challenges for humanity on a global scale. He sees the responsibility and the possibility of tackling theses problems in the hands of the individual (which would be the 'Comprehensive Designer', in Buckminster-Fuller's parlance). And while Brand, as I will show in the next section, demanded – and provided – 'access to tools' with his *Whole Earth Catalog*, Engelbart worked hard to design such tools. It is a worldview that is typical for the 1960s in the US and that has been perpetuated into the present through the success of the Californian tech-industry. Fuller, Brand, and Engelbart didn't expect the solution for society's big problems to come from some top-down state institutions, from Big Government, so to speak. Instead they were firm believers in bottom-up distributed technological empowerment of the individuals,

14   Markoff, *What the Dormouse Said,* p. 45. An analogue contemporary version of this was the hand signals developed by the Occupy Movement to communicate during public speeches and to make decisions based on consensus.

who could then self-organise into groups of collaborators. This became almost like a mantra in the early history of online collaboration: Provide *individuals* with proper hardware and software *tools*, encourage all these users to connect over a *network*, and thus enable them to solve the world's problems through *bottom-up, decentralised collaboration*.

Engelbart's approach to tackle research, development, and design problems was very advanced at the time and it remains relevant for designers today. His method, which he called 'bootstrapping' was a combination of planning and intuition, calculation, and tinkering. He applied scientific quantitative methods but also emphasised the importance of a 'feel for a situation' and a hands on approach. He didn't aim at design products in the sense of finished artefacts: instead he was interested in fostering a system of iterative development processes that revolved around tools for designers and other creative users, who in turn, would be augmented or empowered to solve cognitive tasks and designerly problems.

For Engelbart, such a holistic approach was necessary in order to tackle the hard and complex problems (or 'wicked problems' as design theorist Horst Rittel would later call it) that society was facing.[15] With this synthesis of theory, practice, planning, intuition, improvisation, prototyping, failure, and reiteration, Engelbart was very close to Buckminster Fuller's design science approach.[16] In contrast, those who around the same time tried to establish a rigorously scientific methodology for design in the wake of the Design Methods Movement (John Chris Jones and Christopher Alexander, building on the ideas of Herbert Simon)[17] veered from one extreme to the other. First they were over-scientific, only to then distance themselves from science altogether, to finally find a synthesis in *'designerly ways of thinking'* and *'knowing'* (Nigel Cross) and the *Reflective Practitioner* (Donald Schön).[18]

In Engelbart's conceptual framework from 1962, there are also insights relevant for today's open-source software endeavours and the attempts and difficulties to apply them to other fields such as product design. He pointed out that programming was particularly suited for these open approaches because it can be immediately tested and verified. He also mentioned the beneficial recursiveness in software development, in the sense that the tools that are being developed are of immediate use for those who create them. The first point has a modern equivalence in *facts* on Wikipedia, which can be checked and are *either true or false* (at least in principle; in reality, there are 'edit wars'). Collective decision-making is relatively easy in cases where there is a result that can be objectively measured. The second point made here by Engelbart is equally important: programmers often solve a problem primarily for their own purpose and then 'donate' the solution to a community of peers with similar skills, which in turn can then easily verify if the solution works and

---

15 Rittel/Webber, 'Dilemmas in a General Theory of Planning' (1973).
16 'A Design Science Primer', Buckminster Fuller Institute, online, bfi.org.
17 Jones, *Design Methods* (1980); Simon, *The Sciences of the Artificial* (1996).
18 Cross, 'Designerly Ways of Knowing' (2001); Schön, *The Reflective Practitioner* (1983).

adapt and integrate it into other projects, due to the modularity and openness of the source code.

In programming, the tools and the product are the same. All is code, and what counts is what it does, not how it looks on the surface. This allows programmers to *collectively* re-programme the digital environment in which they are working together. These arrangements constitute what anthropologist Christopher Kelty calls a 'recursive public' (as I will explain in more detail on p. 089 ff.).[19] Attempts to apply these open-source principles to fields such as product design and graphic design have proven to be difficult, because design decisions are not based on functionality alone. They are also based on aesthetics and individual values and the best solution can't be measured or decided objectively. What is more: many designers like to start from scratch and create something unique, custom-tailored, and with the signature style of the auteur designer. Modular systems are popular, but less so if they are cobbled together from other people's heterogenous modules. Collective aesthetic decisions are met with scepticism. As they say, a camel is a horse designed by a committee. These are some of the reasons why open design didn't take off to an extent comparable with the widespread application and success of open-source software (or the crowdsourcing of design, for that matter).

In 1957, five years before he published 'Augmenting the Human Intellect', Engelbart had started working on the practical implementation of his 'Augmentation Framework'. He undertook his research at the magnetics laboratory of the Stanford Research Institute (SRI) in Menlo Park, first without any special funding and against the conviction of most of his fellow engineers, who believed that the future belonged to artificial intelligence. In 1963, he did however manage to secure the crucial support from J. C. R. Licklider, a visionary and influential computer scientist who was at the time responsible for the allocation of funds of the Advanced Research Projects Agency (ARPA).[20] Licklider had published a paper concerned with similar questions and hence recognised the relevance of Engelbart's project.[21] In 'Man-Computer-Symbiosis', written in 1960, he argues that it will still take 'a fairly long time' for true artificial intelligence to emerge.[22] Until that happens, a symbiotic partnership is needed in which 'men will set the goals, formulate the hypotheses, determine the criteria, and perform the evaluations. Computing machines will do the routinizable work needed to prepare the way for insights and decisions in technical and scientific thinking.'[23] Licklider had observed his own working patterns and came to the conclusion that about eighty-five per cent of his 'thinking

---

19 Kelty, *Two Bits*, 2008.
20 Formed as ARPA in 1958, in response to the 'Sputnik Shock', to ensure US-dominance in Cold War military research; named into Defence Advanced Research Projects Agency (DARPA) in 1972; renamed back into ARPA in 1993, and back into DARPA again in 1996.
21 Licklider, 'Man-Computer Symbiosis', *IRE Transactions on Human Factors in Electronics* (1960).
22 He mentions a study by the Air Force according to which it would take at least 20 years to achieve AI of military significance; he adds that it might only take 10 years or maybe 500 years.
23 Licklider, 'Man-Computer-Symbiosis' (1960).

time' was wasted on 'activities that were essentially clerical or mechanical' and that his 'choices of what to attempt and what not to attempt were determined to an embarrassingly great extent by considerations of clerical feasibility, not intellectual capability.'[24] All this, Licklider realised, could in principle be outsourced to a computer if the machine was designed as a personal support system.

Even though it is slightly problematic that Licklider's choice of term symbiosis seems to suggest that human and machine co-exist on the same level, Licklider does not fall into the trap of technological determinism in the vein of Kevin Kelly.[25] Instead, he sustains a humanist perspective and offers valuable insights for today's crowdsourcing discourse, because he distinguishes between systems in which the machine supports the human and those in which that relationship is reversed:

'Mechanical extension' has given way to replacement of men, to automation, and the men who remain are there more to help than to be helped. In some instances, particularly in large computer-centered information and control systems, the human operators are responsible mainly for functions that it proved infeasible to automate. Such systems [...] are not symbiotic systems. They are 'semi-automatic' systems, systems that started out to be fully automatic but fell short of the goal.[26]

Today's microtasking crowdwork, the type pioneered by Amazon Mechanical Turk, can be described as failed automation in Licklider's terms – and is referred to by crowdwork expert Mary L. Gray of Microsoft Research as 'the last mile of automation' – the remaining bits that still have to be solved by humans.[27] However, with the unfortunate twist that in today's crowdwork there are two classes of humans: those who use the computer in a seemingly 'symbiotic' way by outsourcing repetitive 'clerk-like' tasks to the machine; and those at the receiving end of the machine who end up having to do nothing but these seemingly 'routinizable' tasks that the upper class is not willing to do and the machine is still not capable of. What we see in these areas today is certainly not a man-machine-*man*-symbiosis – at least not for the microtaskers at the other end of the machine. What we see unfolding after 2005 is a dystopian, semi-alive processing machine, in which superior users neither have to know nor care whether the computer is doing the work itself or is outsourcing it to users further down the hierarchy of the system.

Back in 1960, Licklider dreamed of a network of digital 'thinking centers' that would be 'connected to one another by wide-band communication lines and to individual users by leased-wire services. In such a system, the speed of the computers

24 *Ibid.* – With 'clerical' Licklider means the 'clerk-like' repetitive, technical data processing tasks that also Engelbart was writing about.
25 Kelly, *What Technology Wants* (2010).
26 *Ibid.*
27 'Mary L. Gray on Digital Labor Economies & Demands for an Ambient Workforce', talk given at the The Berkman Klein Center for Internet & Society at Harvard University, 2015, available on YouTube.

would be balanced, and the cost of the gigantic memories and the sophisticated programs would be divided by the number of users.'[28] In 1963, he made the advancement of intellectual capability through networked computing an explicit goal for the ARPA and kicked off the precursor of today's internet in the now famous 'Memorandum For Members and Affiliates of the Intergalactic Computer Network.'[29] It was a perfect match with the goals of Douglas Engelbart who, thanks to funding from Licklider, was subsequently able to establish his Augmentation Research Center (ARC) in Menlo Park.

In the same year, the mathematician John McCarthy from MIT started the Stanford Artificial Intelligence Laboratory (SAIL) in Santa Cruz, also funded by ARPA. Now there were two ARPA research hubs in the Bay Area. In the words of the Californian technology journalist John Markoff they were philosophical enemies: one offered a humanist vision for the future of computing, the other a mechanist vision.[30] Yet, to the surprise of many who had believed in the rapid progress of artificial intelligence, it was Engelbart's approach that eventually led to today's world of interconnected personal computing and online collaboration. Five decades later, despite great advances in AI, the advent of human-like artificial intelligence remains an imaginary future.

In the following five years, with only a small team of seventeen engineers and researchers, Engelbart invented the mouse (together with Bill English), the graphic user interface, the text editor, video conferencing, and hypertext. In December 1968 he presented what he now called 'oN-Line System' or NLS in the legendary 'Mother of all Demos' at the Fall Joint Computer Conference in San Francisco.[31] He gave a ninety-minute presentation in front of about a thousand experts in a format that was later widely adopted by Steve Jobs and many others in the tech industry. Engelbart impressed the audience deeply by directly augmenting his presentation with the very technologies that he was presenting. His newly developed medium became the message of his presentation. For the well choreographed show, he was connected live over an 'on-line, closed circuit television hook-up to the SRI computing system in Menlo Park', where his team was based.[32] Behind his back was a huge video projection that not only showed what Engelbart had on a screen in front of him, but also the master of ceremonies himself – in Skype-like manner he appeared in an overlay window on the larger projection. Engelbart switched back and forth to his engineers who showcased their work on parts of the system. On his screen, he live-edited text documents and nested lists by clicking on specific sections with the newly invented mouse and flipped through different representational forms using a special keyboard.

28 *Ibid*.
29 Licklider, 'Memorandum For Members and Affiliates of the Intergalactic Computer Network' (1963).
30 Markoff, p. 46.
31 Engelbart, 'Mother of all Demos' (1968), see: (sloan.stanford.edu/mousesite/1968Demo.html).
32 (*Ibid.*) Quote from the 1968 conference announcement.

Engelbart's system was designed for group collaboration via the internet and so he had already included this crucial feature – online connectivity – in his 1968 presentation. It was an outlook on the ARPANET, the first proper connection of which was only established on the 1st September 1969, five weeks after the first man had set foot on the moon. Engelbart's Augmentation Research Center was one of the first two nodes of what would grow into the internet. The 'Mother of All Demos' was a key moment in the early history of online collaboration and the pinnacle of Engelbart's career, but it was quickly followed by an unexpected demise of his institute. It had been his strong belief that in order to solve complex problems, one would need complex tools. He had imagined his final 'Augment' system to eventually have fifty thousand instructions, which the user would have to learn like a foreign language in order to then be empowered by it. The general trend in computing, however, moved decidedly towards ease of use and rendered Engelbart a quaint outsider again.

The complexity of the tools Engelbart insisted on was not the only problem for the Augmentation Research Center. According to John Markoff, the centre also fell victim to 'New Age mumbo jumbo', endemic in the California of the early 1970s.[33] It was the type of fashionable but devastating psychological group work described so vividly in Tom Wolfe's essay 'The "Me" Decade'.[34] Starting in 1971, first Bill English and, within five years, almost all of Engelbart's engineers migrated to the newly founded Xerox PARC (Palo Alto Research Center), taking all their insights and inventions with them. In 1974, J.C.R. Licklider finally terminated the ARPA funding for Engelbart's lab. The next important steps on the way to today's personal computing then happened at Xerox PARC under the leadership of Alan Kay. In 1973, the company created, but never marketed, the 'Alto' personal computer, which, after a visit the research centre 'inspired' Steve Jobs and Steve Wozniak to create the first Apple Macintosh computer in 1984.[35] Apple took a lot of credit for inventing the personal computer, the mouse, and the graphical user interface while their achievement lay in transforming the foundational work of Engelbart, Kay, and their teams into an attractive consumer product. Between the early 1970s and the early 1990s, innovation was driven by the idea of offering small personal desktop computers for the average user. The idea to connect all these private machines into a collaborative network, always a primary goal for Engelbart, was neglected for two decades.

33 Markoff, p. 209.
34 Wolfe, 'The "Me" Decade and the Third Great Awakening', New York Magazine (1976).
35 Thacker et al., 'Alto: A Personal Computer', Computer Structures: Principles and Examples, (1979).
    See also: Smith/Alexander, Fumbling the Future: How Xerox Invented, Then Ignored, the First Personal Computer (1999).

THE KOOL TOOLS OF THE ELECTRIC COMMUNARDS

Hippie communalism and libertarian politics formed the roots of the modern cyber-revolution.
Stewart Brand[36]

To change the rules, change the tools.
Lee Felsenstein[37]

From the 1960s onwards, computing technology was beginning to be applied more broadly, not just by military research projects but also as a tool for administration in large institutions such as universities. Here it took the form of large-scale, top-down bureaucratic systems. In the early 1970s, the vision of personal computing also came within reach of a fledgling bottom-up hobbyist scene. During this period computers acquired an image in public that was divided between a fear of oppression from large organisations and hopes for individual empowerment through digital tools. It was the latter image that turned out to be more influential during the decades that followed, but things still looked different in the mid 1960s.

Activists of the Free Speech Movement at the University of California, Berkley expressed the negative image that computers had most vocally in 1964. The students rallied against the introduction of computers by the university administration because they felt commodified and depersonalised by the apparatus – humans reduced to machine-readable pieces of paper. As Hal Draper, one of the activists at the time put it: 'The mass university of today is an overpowering, over-towering, impersonal alien machine in which [the student] is nothing but a cog going through pre-programmed motions – the IBM syndrome.'[38]

An illustration from a newsletter of the Free Speech Movement depicted the university as a hierarchical structure with capitalists at the top of the pyramid, pulling the strings of the puppet-like principal and teachers who in turn supervise the constant output of mass-fabricated, punch-card-like students. In their fight for dignity as human beings, the students appropriated a sentence that was printed on every punch card as a technical advice and made it their slogan: 'Please do not fold,

---

36 Brand, 'We Owe It All to the Hippies', *Time* (1995).
37 Felsenstein, born 1945 is a former American counter-culture activist and pioneer of personal computing, who was strongly influenced by Ivan Illich's book Tools for Conviviality. The quote above is his most famous motto. 'For his influence on the technical and social environment of the early personal computing era' he became Fellow of the Computer History Museum in Mountain View in 2016.
38 Berkley librarian Hal Draper, quoted after Turner, *From Counterculture to Cyberculture* (2006), citations from the 2008 edition, p. 12.

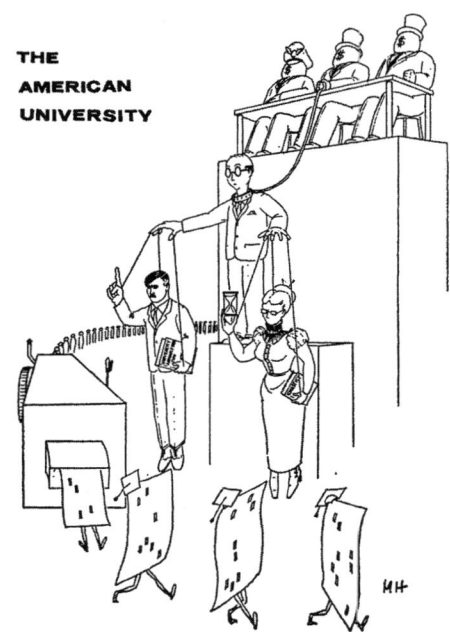

THE
AMERICAN
UNIVERSITY

6 Illustration from the W.E.B. Du Bois Club
newsletter, Berkeley 1964.[39]

spindle or mutilate me!'[40] Apparently, these students didn't yet think that they could gain any control over the digital tools they felt objectified by. Their critique of the machine was harsh, even though by today's standards, what they were confronted with – computerised student administration – appears to be quite harmless and inevitable for efficiency reasons. The most interesting question here is how the image change came about, which combined the student protest demand for 'power to the people' with the later demand for personal computing for the people?

The most in-depth academic study on this important historic shift in perspective comes from Fred Turner, Professor at the Department of Communication at Stanford University. In his book *From Counterculture to Cyberculture*,[41] Turner shows that the movements that opposed 'the establishment' in the United States in the 1960s essentially fell into two camps: the New Left and the Communards. Groups like the Free Speech Movement and the Black Panthers belonged to the New Left.

39 Illustration via Steven Lubar's 'Do Not Fold, Spindle or Mutilate' (1992); W.E.B. Du Bois was an African-American sociologist and civil rights activist; the W.E.B. Du Bois Clubs of America was a youth organisation sponsored by the Communist Party between 1964–1970. Many of its documents are archived on the website of the Free Speech Movement (fsm-a.org).

40 See: Lubar, '"Do Not Fold, Spindle or Mutilate"', *Journal of American Culture* (1992); Lubar, *InfoCulture* (1993).

41 Turner, *From Counterculture to Cyberculture* (2006).

They tried to change society by getting involved in politics through agitation, pro-test marches, and the formation of political parties. In contrast, the Communards rejected the traditional 'game' of politics. They believed that large political institutions could not be trusted; that such structures were part of the problem, not the solution. Change was instead meant to emerge through providing individual actors with *empowering tools for thought and for autarchy*. While the New Left rallied against technology, the Communards tried to figure out how to get their hands on it and use it for their own purposes.

The Communards advocated a change in perception and consciousness through experimental forms of living outside of conventional society. They followed Timothy Leary's dictum to 'turn on, tune in and drop out' – in a psychedelic as well as in a practical sense. The goal was to walk away from government and all that it stood for, the military draft for the Vietnam War, as well as the alienating workplaces of large organisations. They wanted to become spiritually enlightened and techno-logically augmented on a small scale and form networks of self-reliant, self-suffi-cient nodes – communes – scattered across the USA but in contact with each other.

A key figure for this shift of perception with regard to digital tools and for the formation of today's computing culture is Steward Brand. He had an almost un-canny omnipresence across the important events and publications that changed the image that computers had over several decades. In contrast to Bush, Engelbart, and Licklider, he was not an engineer but a publicist, designer and networker, a platform builder, business consultant, event organiser, and media producer. He didn't directly design the new tools himself, but strongly shaped the narrative that grew around them.

Brand, born in 1938, graduated from Stanford in 1960 with a degree in biology. Thereafter, he went to the army for two years before he studied design and photogra-phy in San Francisco. At Stanford, he was inspired by Gregory Bateson and Norbert Wiener, from whom he adopted a cybernetic view of ecological systems, and by Marshall McLuhan and Richard Buckminster Fuller, from whom he took on a decidedly positive, maverick, hands-on approach to the rapidly changing media and technology landscape.

Brand transcended and connected various remote avant-garde subcultures across the country, from artists experimenting with new media and technology, to scientists exploring cybernetics, biology, and programming, to groups like the Merry Pranksters, who were experimenting with psychedelic drugs. He had earned his credentials for managing multimedia presentations such as the legendary 'Mother of all Demos' from 1968, in which Douglas Engelbart presented his innova-tion to a larger public, through organising the legendary Trips Festival in 1966 – a massive psychedelic event and the first concert of the band The Grateful Dead, which, much later, played an important role on the WELL, one of the first online communities, co-founded by Brand in 1985. The WELL then became formative for the Electronic Frontier Foundation (EFF), founded 1990 by John Perry Barlow, lyricist of The Grateful Dead. The influential magazine *Wired,* founded in 1993, also has its roots in the WELL and the immediate personal network of Stewart Brand.

Brand organised the first Hackers' Conference in 1984, merged hacker ideals with hippie ideals, advocated the idea of 'personal computing', popularised the phrase 'information wants to be free', and through his various outlets propagated a worldview in which individualists empowered by tools, self-organised in decentralised, non-hierarchical ways, in order to address social and environmental issues while avoiding conventional forms of politics. He is still very active (and controversial) as an environmentalist – advocating nuclear power – and as a biologist trying to revive extinct species through synthetic biology. With his Long Now Foundation, he is trying to encourage long-term thinking.[42]

It is the seemingly paradoxical mixture of ecological and social goals with contested technological means that has been characteristic of Brand since the 1960s. Early on, he popularised leftist ideas of the 1960s counterculture as well as libertarian and techno-utopian visions for the future – a mix that was later described as the 'Californian Ideology' in a radical polemic written by Richard Barbrook and Andy Cameron in 1995, and as 'Digital Utopianism'.[43] In short, Brand functioned as a catalyst for the conversion of countercultural ideas into the self-image of the Silicon Valley-based software-industry that is dominating our digital culture today. This continuity was further explored by a recent and influential exhibition at the Haus der Kulturen der Welt in Berlin curated by Diedrich Diederichsen and Anselm Franke, entitled: 'The Whole Earth: California and the Disappearance of the Outside'.[44]

Stewart Brand's most influential contribution, among his many activities, was the *Whole Earth Catalog,* first published in the autumn of 1968.[45] In it, he catered to the rural needs of the Communards but combined with ideas from cybernetics and the advent of early computing. Many years later, Steve Jobs described the *Catalog* as a 'Bible of his generation'.[46]

For Stewart Brand and the communities that he connected, computers were not at all seen as a threat that would turn people into cogs, instead, machines were regarded as a welcomed addition to the wide spectrum of tools, compiled in the *Catalog* that promised the empowerment of the individual. The first line of the *Catalog*

---

42 Brand, 'Reviving Extinct Species', *The Long Now Foundation* (2013).
43 Barbrook/Cameron, 'The Californian Ideology', *Mute* (1995); and: Turner, *From Counterculture to Cyberculture* (2006).
44 Diedrich Diederichsen and Anselm Franke curated the exhibition 'The Whole Earth: California and the Disappearance of the Outside' at Haus der Kulturen der Welt in Berlin (2013). The catalogue was published under the same title at Sternberg-Press (2013). I build my recapitulation of Stewart Brand's influence on early ideas of online collaboration partly on these secondary sources. Yet more important are the primary sources, the many articles and interviews that Brand himself and his immediate network published since the 1960s up until now, and the documentations of the many events that he organised.
45 *Whole Earth Catalog*, Volume 1, 1968.
46 Steve Jobs in his commencement speech at Stanford University (2005).

ambitiously announced: 'We are as gods and might as well get good at it.'[47] The project had started with a campaign that Brand ran in February 1966. At the time he distributed buttons asking the question: 'Why haven't we seen a photograph of the whole earth yet?' Inspired by Buckminster Fuller, NASA, and LSD, he had come to the conclusion that such a photograph would intuitively bring 'Bucky's' message across 'that people act as if the earth is flat, when in reality it is spherical and extremely finite, and until we learn to treat it as a finite thing, we will never get civilization right.'[48] The iconic picture, shot by a NASA satellite in 1967 became the cover of the first *Whole Earth Catalog*. The overarching idea was to inspire a global consciousness and encourage taking responsibility for mankind's new power unleashed by technology – 'think global, act local'. The *Catalog* tried to achieve this by providing, as the subtitle announced, *'access to tools'*, and this was meant literally as well as metaphorically. The self-proclaimed function of the publication was to serve its *'users'* (not readers!) as an 'evaluation and access device'.[49] And indeed, Brand offered his *users* an extraordinarily heterogeneous mix of *tools*, reaching from advice on goat husbandry to construction plans for geodesic domes; from cutting edge theoretical texts on cybernetics and evolutionary biology to advertisements for gadgets such as walkie-talkies, radio transmitters, and pocket calculators – exactly the type of objects described in 1965 by the English architectural critic Reyner Banham in 'The Great Gizmo':

A characteristic class of US products – perhaps the most characteristic – is a small self-contained unit of high performance in relation to its size and cost, whose function is to transform some undifferentiated set of circumstances to a condition nearer human desires. The minimum of skills is required in its installation and use, and it is independent of any physical or social infrastructure beyond that by which it may be ordered from catalogue and delivered to its prospective user. A class of servants to human needs, these clip-on devices, these portable gadgets, have coloured American thought and action far more deeply – I suspect – than is commonly understood.[50]

This particular class of objects stood in a paradoxical relationship with the history of the American Frontier, libertarianism, and eventually the counterculture. The gizmos

47 Brand later admitted that he had 'stolen' the line from the 1968 book *A Runaway World*? by British anthropologist Edmund Leach, which begins with: 'Men have become like gods. Isn't it about time that we understood our divinity? Science offers us total mastery over our environment and over our destiny, yet instead of rejoicing we feel deeply afraid. Why should this be? [...]' ('We are as gods', wholeearth. com). The line can also be read as a response to Robert Oppenheimer, chief creator of the atomic bomb, 'the gadget', as they called it, who, in a 1965 TV interview cited from a Hindu scripture: 'Now I am become Death, the destroyer of worlds.'
48 Brand, 'Photography Changes Our Relationship to Our Planet', Smithsonian Photography Initiative (archive.org).
49 *Ibid.*, p. 3.
50 Banham. 'The Great Gizmo.' *Design Quarterly* 12 (1965). Quoted after: Banham/Sparke, *Design by Choice: Ideas in Architecture*, 1981.

and gadgets allowed a heightened self-dependence and promised to enable a Walden-like 'life in the woods', but they were also mass produced consumer goods, bought through mail-order shopping catalogues such as the one published by Sears Roebuck. Shopping catalogues like these were important inspirations for Brand, but he added a political agenda, while trying to stay out of conventional politics. The eclectic mix of physical gadgets and tools for thought was meant to change society in a bottom-up, decentralised, non-authoritative way.

However, the back-to-the-land movement of the late 1960s, which was the original audience of the *Whole Earth Catalog,* was short lived. Within only a few years, starting around 1965, thousands of communes emerged, but most of them had already disappeared again in the early 1970s. It was around the time of this anti-climax, in June 1971, that Brand published *The Last Whole Earth Catalog.*[51] And yet, he continued to propagate his worldview of systems theory, participation, collaboration, individual empowerment, technological optimism, and libertarianism through a series of other publishing projects such as the *Co-Evolution Quarterly* (1974).[52] Until the 1990s, all together 145 publications were produced from Brand's Whole Earth publishing activities.

Important in the context of this book is, that in the beginning of the 1970s, Brand moved his focus decidedly towards advocating the power of personal computing. He later mentioned in several interviews that psychedelics as well as the back-to-the-land communes had failed to bring about the expected widespread social change, however, while 'the drugs didn't get any better, ... computers never stopped getting better'– and he figured a community could also be formed sharing only a virtual space.[53] Networked personal computing was now meant to fulfil the goals of the *Catalog* with other means. And the new social group, that Steward Brand expected to bring change after the Communards had failed, were the 'Hackers'.

This playful and anarchic subculture had emerged at MIT and a few other US-American computer research labs already in the early 1960s. During the nightly off-hours in these institutions, a new generation of young programmers, who were assistants during the day, had started to experiment with writing their own code on the expensive mainframe computers.[54] They called themselves 'hackers' not in a

---

51 *The Last Whole Earth Catalog* had 452 pages, a circulation of 1.5 million and won a US National Book Award.

52 Stewart Brand distanced himself from libertarianism: 'I want to disavow libertarianism as something that has much to offer to the world at this point. [...] It is a simplistic set of algorithmic notions that do not fit with reality and actual governance. [...] Admire libertarianism for its elegance – and pay no further attention to it!' From a 2006 panel discussion at Stanford Library, min. 105, available on YouTube.

53 Cadwalladr, 'Stewart Brand and the Whole Earth Catalog, the book that changed the world', *The Guardian* (2013).

54 The terms 'hacker' and 'hacking' are used here in the positive sense as defined by Richard Stallman: 'Everything you do with a spirit of playful cleverness and intense joyous commitment is hacking.' (Stallman at the Hackers' Conference in 1984). The mischievous and destructive breaking into computer systems is understood as 'cracking'.

derogative way, but as a proud description of their very special attitude towards technology. They hacked together software for fun, out of curiosity, or to test, hone, and show off their mastery over the technology among like-minded experts. You became a true hacker if other respected hackers called you that.[55]

Over time, the playful misuse of the military-funded hardware not only made the hackers better and more motivated programmers: it also led to a lot of innovation. The hackers self-evidently shared their computer code freely in order to be able to build on the work of others and to get feedback and recognition, just as it was practiced in academic research. The contributors had well-paid engineering jobs in the labs, there was as yet no market for software and so it never occurred to them to charge each other for their hacks and programs.

The best example for this early hacker 'gift culture' is Spacewar, one of the first computer games developed in its earliest version in 1962 by Steve Russell at MIT. The code for the game circulated freely from the mainframe systems of one research centre to another and everywhere young computer scientists added to the code and further developed the game. They practiced a free-software or open-source culture without yet calling it that. In 1962, during a visit to the MIT, Stewart Brand had already seen an early version of Spacewar. In 1972, after the demise of the *Catalog*, he picked up that lead again to write an article for *Rolling Stone* magazine. Brand visited the Stanford Artificial Intelligence Laboratory, where Spacewar was still a big hit during night hours and he also went to Xerox PARC, where researchers were developing the ideas of Douglas Engelbart into an early desktop personal computer. In his article, Brand described what he had seen at the labs and suggested that the hackers he had met represented the continuation of the counterculture spirit, just with other means. He announced: 'Ready or not, computers are coming to the people. That's good news, maybe the best since psychedelics'.[56]

The hackers that Brand encountered in 1962 and 1972 were still a tiny and reclusive priesthood of young and mostly male, white, middleclass engineering experts working in the military-academic research complex. But it turned out that Brand was right: computers were actually coming to the people. In 1972, Dennis Allison, Bob Albrecht, and George Firedrake launched the *People's Computer Company* newsletter, in Menlo Park. The first edition had a hand-drawn cover that read in hand-written letters: 'Computers are mostly used against people instead of for people; used to control people instead of to free them; Time to change all that – we need a ... People's Computer Company.'[57] In a 1975 edition of the newsletter, the counterculture activist and electrical engineer Lee Felsenstein outlined his concept

55 According to another hacker speaking at the Hackers' Conference. From: Fabrice, *Hackers: Wizards of the Electronic Age* (1985), TV documentary, available on YouTube.
56 Brand, 'Spacewar', *Rolling Stone Magazine* (1972).
57 'People's Computer Company/Homebrew Computer Club', Cheung, Stanford University Libraries (2014); a scan of the 1972 newsletter is available in Stanford's digital repository: (purl.stanford.edu/ht121fv8052).

for the 'convivial design of cybernetic devices'. Felsenstein, who was strongly influenced by the book *Tools for Conviviality,* wanted to transfer Ivan Illich's ideas to the creation of personal computers. The sub-heading of his newsletter contribution read: 'design so that the user controls the tool, and not the reverse'.[58]

In the short text, that was essentially a hardware hacking manifesto, Felsenstein echoed Illich in arguing that the drive for profit maximisation and the industrial approach to production was 'chewing up not only our physical world, but also our ways of working with our tools and with each other.'[59] In order to enable people to understand the software and hardware they use, these tools should be designed in a way that users could repair and alter them at their will. In order to foster such convivial design, Felsenstein came to the conclusion that 'the computer must grow a club around itself'.[60] Gordon French and Fred Moore, two like-minded spirits from Menlo Park had the same idea and in March 1975 they founded the Homebrew Computer Club in one of the legendary garages of Silicon Valley. Its members wanted to build their own machines and were very exited about the arrival of the Altair 8800, the first affordable microcomputer.[61] The machine was launched in January 1975 as a do-it-your-selfkit for 439 US dollars and attracted a lot of attention: many technology amateurs and would-be hackers (like Steve Wozniak, another early member of the club) ordered it right away and a scene of hobbyists tinkering with the technology started to emerge – within just a few years, this evolved into a consumer market for personal computing hardware.

The fundamental shift that happened between 1964 and 1975, from the perception of computers as tools for oppression to tools for individual empowerment is impressive, and the hands-on approach of building and maintaining personal digital tools is compelling. But this attitude also has problematic limitations. In a 2006 panel discussion at Stanford University, with Fred Turner, Kevin Kelly (*Whole Earth Review*, the WELL, *Wired*), and Howard Rheingold (the WELL, *Virtual Community, Smart Mobs)*,[62] Stewart Brand recalled Buckminster Fuller's attitude 'Don't try to change human nature, don't bother with politics' as an important inspiration for the *Catalog*.[63] Kevin Kelly calls this 'the tool view of the world', an ideology according to which 'tools are more powerful than politics'. He argues that 'the way you

58 Felsenstein, 'Tom Swift Lives! & Convivial Design', *People's Computer Company* (1975); see also: Felsenstein, 'Convivial Cybernetic Devices', *The Analytical Engine* (1995).
59 *Ibid*. (Felsenstein, 1975).
60 Felsenstein, 'Social Media Technology', leefelsenstein.com (undated).
61 Fred Moore was another influential counterculture figure, member of the People's Computer Company and connected to Stewart Brand.
62 'From Counterculture to Cyberculture: The Legacy of the Whole Earth Catalog', Panel discussion with Brand, Turner, Kelly and Rheingold at Stanford library (2006), available on YouTube.
63 Two sentences frequently ascribed to Fuller in this context: 'If you want to teach people a new way of thinking, don't bother trying to teach them. Instead, give them a tool, the use of which will lead to new ways of thinking.' & 'You never change things by fighting the existing reality. To change something, build a new model that makes the existing model obsolete.'

change science, the way you change culture, the way you change politics through the tools, is one of the overarching connections between the Hippies and the Web 2.0'.[64] The libertarian 'tool view of the world', has been continuously propagated by the group around Brand, especially by Kelly and *Wired* magazine, as well as by many Silicon Valley-based tech-companies. A present day version is Kelly's on-going project *Cool Tools,* in which he reviews a new tool every week, under the premises of being 'always useful, always positive'.[65] Kelly neither wants to be bothered with politics nor with bad tools. What he leaves unanswered is: how to deal with tools that are not cool that do have negative effects, not just on the individual but on society, for example because they spy on citizens or exploit users? The answer of the 'electric communards' is to simply drop out of such systems and use different tools – which is indeed an empowering solution for the adequately skilled individual. However, not bothering with politics can't obviously be a solution to deal with pervasive, invasive, and exploitative digital tools and platforms on the level of society. To reject any political control or regulation of such 'non-convivial' tools that have become the de-facto standard is in itself a highly political stance. If tools and platforms transform society, their development and use has to be subjected to a broad democratic deliberation and decision-making process. It is the companies producing the tools that have to be subordinated to the needs of society, not the other way around. As the mostly Silicon Valley-based corporations, that currently provide the digital tools for literally billions of users, grew over time, the world view that politics and tool design should best be kept apart is increasingly misused by these companies to create the false impression that politics and government interventions only hold back the 'inevitable' and 'natural' progress of high-tech tools – that the companies who produce them are best left unregulated. Over the last decades, digital tools have grown in to supra-national platforms so powerful that only politics can ensure that the users' rights are protected. This is also why Ivan Illich's call to design *Tools for Conviviality* (as outlined in the introduction) is so important. What is needed are standards beyond what is profitable or technically feasible and according to which new tools can be evaluated. The individual user has become increasingly powerless.

64 Kelly in the panel discussion at Stanford Library (2006) min. 18.
65 Kelly, 'The Tools of Cool Tools' (2008). Kelly also publishes a slightly anachronistic book that mimics the style and format of the original *Catalog*: Kelly, *Cool Tools* (2013).

FREE SOFTWARE HACKER ETHICS

If the users don't control the program, the program controls the users. A non-free program is a yoke, an instrument of unjust power.
Richard Stallman

This section is about the philosophical roots of the Free Software Movement, which
is based on the Hacker Ethics, first made explicit in 1984, and eventually transformed into the depoliticised Open Source Movement in the 1990s. This is relevant
for today's discourse on crowdsourcing and digital labour platforms for a number
of reasons: First, because it was the first fundamental critique of the power asymmetries that arose from the proprietary ownership-model of software platforms.
Secondly, because it was the first successful attempt to redesign the system from
the ground up to create digital tools and platforms that were truly owned and controlled by their users only. Thirdly, because the development of open-source software is often named as a key precursor to crowdsourcing in the sense of a widespread division of labour between self-assigned individuals via the internet. It was
the proof of concept that people across the world who only knew each other's online
persona were able to design a complex product together, outside the confines of a
conventional company but still competitive with commercial products. Finally, it
touches on the problem of free labour in the production of immaterial, easy to copy
goods, which leads to a hard-to-solve conflict between two different ethical arguments – that work should be paid for and that one should be free to share non-rival
goods with whomever one wants.

The common representation of crowdsourcing as a continuation and advancement of open source principles is highly problematic, tragic even, when one considers the originally highly political motivation of this mode of production, outlined
in the first two points above.[66] Which is why it is necessary to have a closer look at
the origins of Free Software. Against this backdrop, the outlines of today's commercial crowdsourcing become far more visible. This chapter of web-history also offers
potential solutions to our contemporary challenges regarding ownership and pow-
er-asymmetries on digital platforms.

In 1975, when the Altair came out and 'the computer started to grow a club
around itself', a twenty-year-old Harvard student called William Henry 'Bill' Gates III
started to adapt the programming language BASIC (Beginner's All-purpose Symbolic Instruction Code) to make it run on the hobbyist machine. The program had

---

66 As already mentioned in the introduction, one of the two definitions of crowdsourcing that Jeff Howe
    provides is: 'The application of Open Source principles to fields outside of software.' See front page of
    Howe's blog: crowdsourcing.typepad.com.

already existed since 1964 and was circulating as a *free* piece of software for teaching programming to students. Bill Gates was the first person to realise that selling software to end-users could be a business in its own right. He dropped out of university to become the first software-entrepreneur and with his colleague Bill Allen he founded Micro-Soft in April 1975. Before that, the computer industry consisted only of hardware manufactures such as IBM, who created large machines for business, administrative, and research purposes: the software had been a complementary service to make the hardware usable. Private users were not at all part of this world. In order to establish an end-user market for software, the common culture of sharing computer code had to be reframed as a culture of stealing. In 1976, Bill Gates wrote 'An Open Letter to Hobbyists':

The feedback we have gotten from the hundreds of people who say they are using BASIC has all been positive. Two surprising things are apparent, however, 1) Most of these 'users' never bought BASIC (less than 10% of all Altair owners have bought BASIC), and 2) The amount of royalties we have received from sales to hobbyists makes the time spent on Altair BASIC worth less than $2 an hour. Why is this? As the majority of hobbyists must be aware, most of you steal your software. Hardware must be paid for, but software is something to share. Who cares if the people who worked on it get paid? Is this fair? [...] Who can afford to do professional work for nothing? What hobbyist can put 3-man years into programming, finding all bugs, documenting his product and distribute for free? [...] Most directly, the thing you do is theft.[67]

Bill Gates' Open Letter from 1976 marks a crucial schism in computing culture caused by the conflict between the ideal of the *free sharing* of knowledge, as in academia, and the expectation of *fair pay* of those who created immaterial goods as freelancers and entrepreneurs.

In 1984, when the hacker scene was already about twenty-five years old, the American technology journalist Steven Levy published a seminal book called *Hackers: Heroes of the Computer Revolution*.[68] It was the first comprehensive account of the history of this scene, its value system, and inherent conflicts. A core part of the book was the so-called 'Hacker Ethic', a previously implicit code of honour that Levy had made explicit in his book. It reads:

1. Access to computers – and anything which might teach you something about the way the world works – should be unlimited and total. Always yield to the Hands-On Imperative!
2. All information should be free.
3. Mistrust Authority – Promote Decentralization.

---

67 Gates, 'An Open Letter to Hobbyists', *Computer Notes*, 1976.
68 Levy, *Hackers* (1984), citations from the 2001 edition.

4. Hackers should be judged by their hacking, not bogus criteria such as degrees, age, race, or position.
5. You can create art and beauty on a computer.
6. Computers can change your life for the better.[69]

When Levy's book came out, Stewart Brand and Kevin Kelly were intrigued and decided to host the very first 'Hackers' Conference'. They invited 400 handpicked hackers to a three-day-event near Sausalito, north of San Francisco. At the event, a heated discussion unfolded among the high profile hackers about the conflicting interests that had emerged between the academic tradition of freely sharing computer code and the rapid development of a highly commercial software industry. In the debate, Steve Wozniak, at that time already a (hardware) multi-millionaire, complained about the practice of companies keeping code proprietary even when they had no intention of using it: 'That is a hiding of information and that is wrong.' To that, Stewart Brand replied:

On the one hand information wants to be expensive, because it's so valuable. The right information in the right place just changes your life. On the other hand, information wants to be free, because the cost of getting it out is getting lower and lower all the time. So you have these two fighting against each other.[70]

Wozniak countered 'Information should be free, but your time should not.'[71] This paradox and especially Wozniak's reply is insightful for the discussions about today's crowdsourcing and commons-based peer production: how can labour time be reimbursed when the fruits of labour are offered for free? *Information wants to be free* became 'a mantra, an ideology, a religion' for technology activists.[72] The slogan is now commonly attributed to Brand, although he had only rephrased a point that Steven Levy had distilled from his in-depth study of hacker communities. Remarkably, the first half of Brand's reply, that 'information wants to be expensive', has been forgotten.

What made – and still makes – things complicated, is the ambiguity of the word *free*. It can be interpreted technically, politically, ethically, and economically: *free* as in unrestricted access; *free* as in free speech; and *free* as in free beer. Levy writes of the first type of interpretation: 'The belief, sometimes taken unconditionally, that information should be free was a direct tribute to the way a splendid computer [...] works – the binary bits moving in the most straightforward, logical path necessary

69 *Ibid*. p. 40–44.
70 Brand, 'Hackers' Conference 1984 – Keep Designing', *Whole Earth Review* (1985): p. 49.
71 Ironically, the recordings of the conference are not free but owned by Getty Images. They can be watched for free, but with a huge branding watermark of the company across the faces of the interviewed hackers.
72 As the science literary agent and founder of *The Edge*, John Brockman, who was present when the famous words were said, confirms. See: Brockman, John, 'Edge@DLD – An Edge Conversation in Munich', edge.org (2011).

to do their complex job. [...] In the hacker viewpoint, any system could benefit from that easy flow of information.'[73] This belief was then transformed into a moral and political imperative, which in turn was (and still is) at odds with commercial interests in the information economy. Brand's famous quote is only concerned with the economic paradox of free information. Notably, he changed the sentence from an ethical guidance according to which information *should* be free into a form of technological determinism in which information *wants* to be free. Human agency is transformed into the agency of an immaterial and inanimate entity.

The debate at the 1984 Hackers' Conference was the first time that the conflicting technical, ethical, and commercial interests of producers in the information economy were brought to the awareness of a larger public outside the hacker community. Thirty years later, the debate has not lost its relevance. Among those involved in the discussions at the 1984 Hackers' Conference was also Richard Stallman, described by Steven Levy's as 'the last of the true hackers'.[74] Born in 1953 in New York, Stallman studied physics at Harvard from 1971 to 1974 and graduated magna cum laude.[75] At the same time he excelled as a hacker at the nearby MIT Artificial Intelligence Lab (A.I. Lab), where he worked during the night. Even by the high standards of these two elite institutions, Stallman was regarded as exceptionally bright. After 1974, he stayed at Harvard as a post-graduate student and continued to work at the A.I. Lab. During this phase, he experienced the slow demise of what he saw as the original hacking culture – caused by the advent of proprietary software as a big business. Code became 'closed-source', a well-kept trade secret. In reaction to the new development of *not* sharing code freely among peers any longer, of 'hiding information', Stallman made it his life's mission to fight for what he now called 'Free Software' – *free*, not as in free beer but as in *free speech*.

In an interview at the Hackers' Conference in 1984 Stallman said: 'If I were offered a chance to use a piece of software provided I would agree not to share it with anyone, I feel that it would be wrong – it would spiritually hurt me to agree.'[76] At that point he had already started writing what he would publish in 1985 as the 'GNU Manifesto'. In the same year he also initiated the Free Software Foundation, which still operates today.[77] Stallman furthermore developed the concept of 'copyleft', which cleverly uses (*hacks*) legal code that was originally meant to protect intellectual property, in order to permanently prevent proprietary ownership of software under the GNU Public Licence (GPL). Stallman had realised that in order for the user to be free,

73 *Ibid*. p. 41.
74 Levy, Steven, *Hackers* (2001).
75 *Ibid*. p. 416.
76 Richard Stallman at the first Hackers' Conference at Sausalito, California. Getty Images Archive Films, clip # 146485179 (online).
77 Stallman, 'The GNU Manifesto', Free Software Foundation (1985). 'GNU' is a recursive acronym meaning 'GNU is not UNIX'. See also: Stallman, Free Software Foundation mission statement: 'The Free Software Foundation (FSF) is a non-profit with a worldwide mission to promote computer user freedom and to defend the rights of all free software users'.

the software had to be free. Stallman's goal was to create a non-proprietary software platform from the ground up. To achieve this, UNIX, the standard operating system of the time, had to be replaced with a version that was free of all intellectual property claims. He published an open call on the internet to find volunteer collaborators with whom he could successively replace the modular building blocks of UNIX with *free* pieces of code.[78] In the GNU Manifesto, Stallman explained his motivation:

I consider that the Golden Rule requires that if I like a program I must share it with other people who like it. Software sellers want to divide the users and conquer them, making each user agree not to share with others. I refuse to break solidarity with other users in this way. [...] So that I can continue to use computers without dishonor, I have decided to put together a sufficient body of free software [...] Everyone will be permitted to modify and redistribute GNU, but no distributor will be allowed to restrict its further redistribution. That is to say, proprietary modifications will not be allowed. [...] I have found very many programmers eager to contribute part-time work for GNU. For most projects, such part-time distributed work would be very hard to coordinate; the independently written parts would not work together. But for the particular task of replacing Unix, this problem is absent.

Once GNU is written, everyone will be able to obtain good system software free, just like air. This means much more than just saving everyone the price of a Unix license. It means that much wasteful duplication of system programming effort will be avoided. This effort can go instead into advancing the state of the art.[79]

On the one hand, this open call can bee seen as the start of the first self-organised large-scale crowdsourcing endeavour, as this was the outsourcing of work previously done by highly skilled, paid employees to an undefined and large group over the internet. On the other hand, there was no specific brief, no time frame and, most importantly, no privatisation of the results, quite the contrary. Despite some similarities to today's crowdsourcing, the differences are more striking. Stallman was guided by a Kantian ethic of reciprocity (which he refers to as the Golden Rule). Seeking to defend people's dignity and freedom, he decided to fight for values beyond the profit margin and, important as a contrast to crowdsourcing, he wanted to prevent the wasteful duplication of effort.

The actual process of creating GNU was laborious and took several years. Until the early 1990s, Stallman and his collaborators had managed to re-engineer free versions of all UNIX components except the kernel. This last but pivotal component of the operating system was particularly hard to program. Eventually, it was a twenty-

78 UNIX was developed in a public private partnership by the telephone company AT&T/Bell and several universities such as MIT and Berkeley. The intellectual property rights were in the hands of AT&T. However, because of anti-trust laws, the company was restricted to its telephone business and had to provide anyone who was interested with a copy of UNIX without charge. UNIX was not created by the free marked but to a great deal through government funding.

79 Stallman, The GNU Manifesto (1985).

two year old Finnish software engineer called Linus Torvalds who provided the last piece of the puzzle in the 1991. Via a news board on the Usenet he humbly announced his achievement:

Hello everybody out there using minix [a Unix like operating system ...] I'm doing a (free) operating system (just a hobby, won't be big and professional like gnu) [...] This has been brewing since april, and is starting to get ready. I'd like any feedback [...] I'd like to know what features most people would want. Any suggestions are welcome, but I won't promise I'll implement them :-)[80]

At this point Linus Torvalds saw his contribution still as a hobbyist side-project to GNU. Like Richard Stallman, he also reached out to potential collaborators in an open call via the internet, first only for feedback and suggestions and later to delegate the myriad tasks that were necessary to further develop the operating system. It turned out that Linus Torvalds was not only exceptionally good at programming, but also at distributing and coordinating tasks across a global community of like-minded volunteers. The first entirely *free* operating system that he had been 'brewing' attracted a great number of supporters and evolved under his guidance into the famous Linux, which as Stallman insists, should correctly be called GNU/Linux.

Eric S. Raymond, a programmer and outspoken libertarian became an influential advocate and analyst of this new mode of production. In his famous essay *The Cathedral and the Bazaar* from 1996, he compares the top-down planning and execution of proprietary software companies such as Microsoft with the construction of cathedrals and the self-organised, decentralised bottom-up way of producing *free* and *open* software with the complexity of a bazaar.[81]

Linux is subversive. Who would have thought even five years ago (1991) that a world-class operating system could coalesce as if by magic out of part-time hacking by several thousand developers scattered all over the planet, connected only by the tenuous strands of the Internet? Certainly not I. [...]Linus Torvalds's style of development – release early and often, delegate everything you can, be open to the point of promiscuity – came as a surprise. No quiet, reverent cathedral-building here – rather, the Linux community seemed to resemble a great babbling bazaar of differing agendas and approaches [...] out of which a coherent and stable system could seemingly emerge only by a succession of miracles.[82]

Raymond tried to demystify this 'miracle' by explaining the previously implicit rules that made it possible. The best known of these he dubbed 'Linus' Law'. It states that

80 Torvalds, 'LINUX's History', 'a collection of various artifacts from the period in which Linux first began to take shape' (1992).
81 Raymond characteristically kept on re-writing and re-releasing his texts. Years of release and page numbers are therefore somewhat in flux. Raymond, Eric S., *The Cathedral and the Bazaar* (1997).
82 *Ibid*. p. 1.

'given a large enough beta-tester and co-developer base, almost every problem will be characterized quickly and the fix obvious to someone.' The law became famous in the form of a slightly weird mix of metaphors: 'Given enough eyeballs, all bugs are shallow.' This is a crucial aspect of both commons-based peer production and crowdsourcing. The idea is that every problem is trivial when the community (or crowd) trying to solve it is large enough. Such an approach goes against the grain of corporate practice, where managers assign tasks to employees and control the execution. Advocates of open-source development and crowdsourcing often point to the huge savings that can be made when people self-assign to tasks they enjoy doing and thus don't need a management to chose for them and control them.

Before the widespread dissemination of networked computers it would not have been technically feasible to coordinate the feedback of so many 'eyeballs'. But it also needed the compelling vision of a *free* operating system, a tool that would be useful for the contributors to capture the imagination of such a large community of experts and make them pool their resources. Many other projects followed the success of GNU/Linux. In 1998, Netscape announced that it was going to make its web-browser freely available as open-source software. The company explained in a press release that 'this aggressive move will enable Netscape to harness the creative power of thousands of programmers on the Internet by incorporating their best enhancements into future versions of Netscape's software.'[83] As Christopher Kelty notes: 'One of the selling points of Free Software, and especially of its marketing *as* Open Source, is that it leverages the work of thousands or hundreds of thousands of volunteer contributors across the Internet.'[84]

It turned out that the free software systems that were hacked together in a modular way by a distributed crowd of volunteers were often on par with their commercial competitors. But the success of the non-proprietary and distributed mode of production also aggravated the schism between Stallman's camp and the many new stakeholders with business interests. A vocal part of the community started to reject Stallman's 'Free Software' label because of the confusion the double meaning of the word *free* caused. As already mentioned in the introduction, it was Tim O'Reilly who played an important role in this rebranding as did Eric S. Raymond. The proponents of the term 'open source' were eager not to scare off business partners with an anti-capitalist and moral rhetoric and instead preferred to emphasise the pragmatic technical advantages of being able to read and modify the code. Despite Stallman's protest, the original term was successively replaced by 'Open-Source Software', which was regarded as less ambiguous and less ethically and ideologically loaded. Also Linus Torvalds distanced himself from Stallman's agenda: 'I don't want people using Linux for ideological reasons. I think ideology sucks. This world would be a

83 'Netscape Announces Plans to Make Next-Generation Communicator Source Code Available Free on the Net' (1998), archive.org.
84 *Ibid*. p. 105.

much better place if people had less ideology.'[85] As with the rebranding from GNU to Linux, Stallman lost the fight, and the commonly used term is now open-source software. The politically correct term, however, at least in the eyes of Stallman and his camp is Free/Libre Open Source Software (FLOSS). For many people today, Linux is the paragon of open-source software, and while the charming Linus Torvalds became famous and successful, Richard Stallman became a fundamentalist outsider, a travelling evangelist for the gospel truth of Free Software.

Stallman's foresightedness can hardly be overestimated and he is still valued by many in the hacker scene for recognising the importance of free software, but he is also often sneered at for his dogmatism. However, events such as the revelations by Edward Snowden about the massive spying operations undertaken by the American National Security Agency (NSA) and the British Government Communications Headquarter (GCHQ), that occurred in close cooperation with all major computing firms, have given Stallman's hardliner position new relevance. Stallman's argument is simple and I agree with him on this point:

If the users don't control the program, the program controls the users. With proprietary software, there is always some entity, the developer or 'owner' of the program, that controls the program – and through it, exercises power over its users. A non-free program is a yoke, an instrument of unjust power.[86]

I have included this section on the roots of the Open Source Movement in the Free Software Movement to show two things: Technically, it would be justified to regard the creation of the first *free* operating system as the first successful large-scale crowdsourcing project, initiated through an open call via the internet. Philosophically, however, the two approaches could not be further apart. The *free labour* the people contributed to create *free software* was motivated by an ethic that categorically valued interpersonal relationships, sharing, and individual autonomy much higher than any corporate commercial interest. The contributors were not treated as a source for cheap labour, as a crowd that can be harnessed for commercial gains. Stallman was the first among equals collaborating on a project with other experts that had an immediate use-value to them and that could not be privatised by anyone (thanks to Stallman's copyleft GNU GPL), and thus the fruits of the collective free labour remained freely available and useful to everyone (also outside the group of experts). In short, they became part of the *commons*. By putting values such as reciprocity, sharing, friendship, self-help, self-learning, autonomy, decentralisation, and dignity decidedly above corporate interest, Stallman fostered the creation of Tools for Conviviality in a form that Illich could only have approved of.

85 Kelty, *Two Bits* (2008): p. 233.
86 Stallman, 'Free Software Is Even More Important Now', gnu.org (2013).

RECURSIVE PUBLICS

The book *Two Bits,* published by anthropologist Christopher Kelty from UCLA, is an extensive study of *the cultural significance of free software.*[87] Since the 1990s, Kelty had immersed himself as a participant observer into what he calls geeks culture and studied the practices of these groups for over a decade. During this time he experienced the rapid growth and transformation of that culture from a frontline position. In order to capture what he regards as the core characteristic of the communities he studied, he introduced the useful concept of *recursive publics.* 'A recursive public is a public that is constituted by a shared concern for maintaining the means of association through which they come together as a public.'[88] In his analysis, he shows that 'geeks' form a public by creating a technological infrastructure that is at the same time medium, subject, and goal of their interactions. In other words, they meet via a free software platform they have created, to discuss on that platform how they want to further develop it. Based on a rough consensus they modify the platform, to then again discuss the new direction the platform will take – and a new iteration of the recursive cycle starts.

Kelty's concept of the recursive public makes it possible to draw the line between the methods of the Free Software Movement and the practices in crowdsourcing even more clearly. Kelty writes that in the last few years, 'the circuit of geek and entrepreneur conferences' has been dominated by talk of 'social software' or 'Web 2.0' concepts that are inspired by the Free Software Movement and take advantage of voluntary, self-directed contributions by 'leveraging and coordinating massive numbers of people'.[89] But they do this along restricted lines and are thus not what he would define as recursive publics.

Most of them are commercial entities whose structure and technical specifications are closely guarded and not open to modification, [...] few are interested in allowing strangers to participate in, modulate, or modify the system as such; [...] they want information and knowledge to be free, [...] but not necessarily the infrastructure that makes that information available und knowledge possible. Such entities lack the 'recursive' commitment.[90]

Ultimately, Kelty sees Free Software as a form of critique to question illegitimate, unaccountable, and unjust forms of governance, as well as a toolset to experiment collectively with modifiable infrastructures that allow for true participation and just forms of governance. And Free Software, Kelty emphasises, does not belong to

---

87 Kelty, *Two Bits* (2008).
88 *Ibid.* p. 28.
89 *Ibid.* p. 303.
90 *Ibid.* p. 303.

geeks alone. The recursive publics that Kelty analysed are close to what Pierre Lévy imagined Collective Intelligence would be like back in the 1990s.

At first glance, the culture that Kelty describes seems to offer an intriguing way of redesigning exploitative platforms – shouldn't all users of platforms be able to constantly modify their virtual playgrounds and workplaces? Theoretically, everyone can participate in such a recursive public. Yet practically, the level of programming skills necessary to meaningfully participate still creates a high entry barrier.

This is why the media scholar Jodi Dean heavily criticises Christopher Kelty's concept of recursive publics.[91] In her book *Blog Theory* she accuses him of glorifying the anarchic spirit of a self-organised, tech-savvy elite as generally the best way to solve the problem of governance. The same trap that Stewart Brand and his colleagues arguably stepped into: a libertarian understanding of politics that regards formal governance – as in representative democracies – as inefficient, hindering, and inferior to clever socio-technological, entrepreneurial hacks. Dean argues that this approach inadvertently ushers in most extreme forms of neoliberalism. How can it be that Kelty and Dean look at the same culture and come to such different conclusions? While he is looking at a tiny group within society for whom this form of enlightened anarchism, or techno-libertarianism works perfectly, she worries that this mode of production also affects everybody else.

In the scenario Kelty describes, the builders of communication networks are governing the rest of us (proceeding without our consent and generally beneath our awareness). They are a technocratic elite unburdened by constraints of representation or oversight. The programmers don't just build software; they act for the people – although this acting is itself formatted in terms of communicative capitalism's merging of markets and governance.[92] [...]

Kelty presents 'geeks' as outside government and industry even as they work within them, as outside of politics even as they endeavor to serve and enhance capitalism.[93]

Although I have great sympathy for the culture Kelty describes, I partly agree with Jodi Dean on this point. I write *partly* because I would not accuse the geeks living in a recursive public of wanting to govern everybody else, but I also think that this self-determined way of dealing with the digital infrastructure 'does not scale' to include the larger population. Recursive publics are ideal configurations only for skilful members (the type of user willing to invest years in learning the programming language of a system Douglas Engelbart also imagined). To become an active participant, one has to be able to program in order not to be programmed. Effectively, this means that only a tiny elite is capable of using and modifying the technological

91 Dean, *Blog Theory* (2010).
92 *Ibid*. p. 24.
93 *Ibid*. p. 25.

infrastructures in a self-determined way. If every citizen was a 'geek', this system would be perfect, but this will obviously never be the case in a society based on a division of labour – being a 'geek' in the sense of Kelty is a fulltime job. So where does that leave everybody else? There needs to be some system of representation through which the majority of participants who are less tech-savvy can have an influence on the rules of the platform it has to abide to.

THE SOURCE OF THE WELL

What will on-line interactive communities be like? In most fields they will consist of geographically separated members, sometimes grouped in small clusters and sometimes working individually. They will be communities not of common location, but of common interest.
J. C. R. Licklider and Robert Taylor, 1968[94]

In the of summer 2012, when Facebook had almost reached a billion users, one of the oldest *social networks* on the internet, 'the WELL', was on sale. The time-honoured community of, at that point, 2,693 subscribers who, at the time of writing, still pay \$15 per month, wasn't lucrative enough for its then-owner, the Salon Media Group.[95] The 'most influential online community' (according to *Wired*) seems tiny by today's standards, but the WELL never had the goal to be for everyone. In 1989, when the *New York Times* already regarded it as influential, it only had 2,600 members.[96] The platform had always been an exclusive club for the tech savvy elite, the so-called 'Digerati' or 'WELLbeings', as they liked to call themselves, for whom membership was a badge of honour.[97] Even today, the front page of the WELL promises potential subscribers: 'No more wading through endless dreck to find a few morsels of insight or wit.'[98] In September 2012, the site was eventually bought by a group of long-time members for 400,000 US dollars.[99] Launched in 1985 by Stewart Brand and Larry Brilliant, the WELL, an acronym for Whole Earth 'Lectronic Link, was the continuation of the *Whole Earth Catalog* by digital means. As Kevin Kelly, long-time editor of *Wired*, wrote in 2008:

This I am sure about: it is no coincidence that the Whole Earth Catalogs disappeared as soon as the web and blogs arrived. Everything the Whole Earth Catalogs did, the web does better. But by the same equation, much of what the web is doing now, Whole Earth was doing then. Those folks who subscribed to the 'feed' of CoEvolution Quarterly, the Whole Earth Review, and the WELL, got the blogosphere and user-created content 30 years early. Living on the web decades before the internet was born; now that was a strange trip.[100]

94 Licklider/Taylor, 'The Computer as a Communication Device' (1968), republished in *In Memoriam J. C. R. Licklider* (1990).
95 Wingfield, 'The Well, a Pioneering Online Community, Is for Sale Again', *The New York Times Bits Blog* (2012).
96 Markoff, 'Whole Earth State-of-Art Rapping', *The New York Times* (1989).
97 Brockman, *Digerati* (1997).
98 Landing page of The WELL (well.com).
99 The Well Group, 'Salon Media Group Sells The WELL to The Well Group', Press Release, 20 September 2012. See also: Grossman, 'Salon Sells The WELL to Its Members', *The Guardian* (2012).
100 Kelly, 'The Whole Earth Blogalog' (2008).

7 A collage by the WELL's community manager John Coate from 1986.[101] One of the earliest established uses of the term 'online community'.

This is type of myth-making is partly what made Brand and his colleagues so influential – the ability to always surf on the crest of what is cool and to connect the developments of seemingly remote communities and developments with a strong narrative of inevitable progress through technological tools. But the WELL is important for the historic dimension of crowdsourcing for a variety of reasons: it was the first internet platform that was described as a 'virtual community' or 'online community' and, in this form it now serves as a good contrast to today's notions of what a virtual crowd is. It was also the first online platform that made a profit from selling its users access to their own user-generated content and as such it is a business model related to, but not interchangeable with crowdsourcing. Already the *Catalog* frequently published content that came from its readers but the WELL took this approach much further by letting its users provide the entire content of the platform through their conversations. The communication of the community became the crowdsourced product. And the site had a pivotal function in transforming and transferring the social-liberal values of the 1960s back-to-the-land Communards to the economic-liberal and even libertarian values of 1990s computer culture that is today more dominant than ever through the tremendous reach of Silicon Valley-based platform corporations.

The WELL of the 1980s is the crucial link between the *Whole Earth Catalog* of the late 1960s and *Wired* magazine founded in 1993. The counterculture idea of a grassroots social utopia in the physical realm had failed in the early 1970s. But in the 1980s some of the old communards started to re-establish some of their core ideas in the digital realm, where they eventually merged with neo-liberal ideas of radical deregulation, individualist entrepreneurial spirit, and free market ideology. The WELL stands for the perpetuation of the vision of *saving the world, not through*

101 From John Coate's personal website (cervisa.com). According to him, he designed the image as a poster for the West Coast Computer Faire in San Francisco (1986).

politics but through smart digital tools in a decentralised, unregulated, self-organised manner. Today, advocates of crowdsourcing sometimes echo this rhetoric while ignoring the fact that the social utopia of self-reliant communities existing outside of capitalism was somehow lost along the way.

With the change of the medium from paper catalogue to online platform, the focus also shifted, from providing the Communards with 'access to tools' towards providing distributed PC-users with access to a refined social network of individualistic professionals. The members shared information and opinions on the platform, they experienced a sense of community, but without the harsh sacrifices and commitments that the communes demanded from its members. In that sense it was the 'light' version of the communes, offering the intellectual stimulation without the hard labour and responsibility for others required by collective subsistence farming.

In principle, the WELL was open to everyone who believed enough in computers as a social medium to overcome the technical hurdles and who was also affluent enough to buy a PC, pay the subscription fees (originally eight dollars per month plus three dollars per hour), and the high costs for internet connectivity. The exclusivity created by the comparatively high technical, social, and financial entry barriers was an important factor for its influence. In effect, the site became a haven for early adopters of personal computers, many of whom resided in California's Bay Area and had a connection to the cosmos of ideas that Stewart Brand had promoted during the previous two decades. The site was organised around discussion forums, so called 'conferences' on a wide range of topics – in that sense it was more similar to Reddit than to Facebook. The WELL offered its members instant access to like-minded experts and through them to exclusive information and insights but also gossip, counselling, consolation, and friendship. Many of the WELL's members worked in the computer industry, in research, or in journalism – and many had a background in the Californian counterculture. Like Brand, co-founder Larry Brilliant also had his roots in the scene around the Merry Pranksters and he was also part of an influential commune project called 'Hog Farm'.[102] Even the first three directors and community managers that Brand installed at the WELL were former back-to-the-land communards.[103] Together with their families they had tried to live an experimental and self-sufficient life but had 'returned to civilisation' out of disagreement and weariness. One of the community managers, John Coate, who freely admitted that he had little experience with computers, stated that his central

---

102 Rheingold, *The Virtual Community* (1995): p. 40.

103 The three were Matthew McClure, Cliff Figallo and John 'Tex' Coate from the commune 'The Farm' in Tennessee. John Coate was the second employee of the WELL, instrumental in founding *Wired*, and development director for the Electronic Frontier Foundation. For Coate's own account of this succession see his personal website (cervisa.com).

insight early on was that 'this is not the computer business – this is the relationship business – this I do know something about.'[104]

Even though there was no explicit agenda, Brand and the early members of the WELL shared the belief that the platform, while being a for-profit endeavour, would also become a vehicle for social change. The idea was that this change would emerge spontaneously through the specific bottom-up community structure of the WELL. As Kevin Kelly recalls it, the community was supposed to be 'self-governing', it would be a 'self-designing experiment. [...] the early users were to design the system for the later users. The usage of the system would co-evolve with the system as it was built.'[105] The founders of the WELL were 'in the business of selling the customers to each other and letting them work out everything else.'[106] Initially this sounded like an astute description of today's business model of social networking and crowdsourcing in the wider sense, but there were important differences: members paid with cash, not with their personal data and they proudly embraced the motto 'YOYOW – *You own your own words',* introduced by Brand. It meant that members were in full control but also had to take full responsibility of their data, their actions, their opinions, and their cognitive output. Also, users had to ask for permission if they wanted to use someone else's words. They could even retract their contributions entirely. By decree of Brand, anonymity was not an option. The platform owners took the members seriously as individuals with respective rights and obligation and the members were expected to influence and take responsibility regarding the structure of the system – but Brand always remained present in the background as a sort of benevolent dictator who only rarely but decidedly weighed in when it came to political decisions such as the question of anonymity. The 'WELLbeings' were not a sprawling, interchangeable mass or crowd but a community of people who took care of each other, who developed a code for social interaction, and who built a network of strong and weak social ties, at times overlapping with their circles of friends and family in the physical world. They also met on a regular basis for parties at the office of the WELL.

Howard Rheingold, tech-journalist and yet another veteran from the West Coast psychedelic counterculture had already joined the WELL in the autumn of 1985 and he became the first person to use the term 'Virtual Community' in print, in a *Whole Earth Review* article published in 1987.[107]

---

104 In a talk John Coate gave at the SWARM Conference for Community Management in Sydney on 18 September 2013.

105 Kelly after Rheingold, p. 43.

106 *Ibid.*

107 Rheingold, 'Virtual Communities – Exchanging Ideas through Computer Bulletin Boards', *Whole Earth Review*, Winter 1987. Eventually turned into the book *Virtual Communities* (1995).

Dreamers in the Artificial Intelligence research community are trying to evolve 'software agents' that can seek and sift, filter and find [...] specific knowledge [...] buried in 15,000 pages of related information. In my virtual community, we don't have software agents (because they don't exist yet), but we do have informal social contracts that allow us to act as software agents for one another. If, in my wanderings through information space, I come across items that don't interest me but which I know one of my group of online friends appreciate, I send the appropriate friend a pointer to the key datum or discussion. This social contract requires one to give something, and enables one to receive something. I have to keep my friends in mind and send them pointers instead of throwing my informational discards into the virtual scrap-heap. [...] I find that the help I receive far outweighs the energy I expend helping others: A perfect fit of altruism and self-interest.[108]

What Rheingold describes here could be called 'community-sourcing', a form of reciprocity among peers that can only work in small groups where people trust and know each other and work in similar fields – as hunters and gatherers within the fledgling information economy.[109] It is very similar to what Vannevar Bush had in mind when he envisioned the Memex in 1945: intellectual 'trailblazers' in an information space, making their trails of knowledge accessible to selected peers. A platform that functions this way is invaluable for knowledge workers and having this opportunity at one's fingertips is a great social and technological achievement. Yet, compared to the utopian ambitions that the communards originally pursued, this is a stripped-down vision of what a community is or can achieve. The perfect fit of altruism and self-interest that Rheingold raved about is reduced to only one strata of life, the Noösphere of information as a non-rival good. The members of such a virtual community can share their information freely without loosing anything, especially the type of information that would have otherwise landed on the 'virtual scrap-heap'. It is important to keep in mind, however, that the socially much more ambitious vision of sharing other resources such as food and housing and (physically) caring for the weaker members in a community has been relinquished. All members of the virtual community are now responsible for their own livelihood, their physical needs, and security. While the conversations might take place in a virtual space outside of conventional society, the bodies of the virtual communards are still trapped in the physical world. In the virtual community, the utopian idea of conviviality and altruistic sharing is limited to the top layers of Abraham Maslow's 'Pyramid of Needs'.[110]

---

108 *Ibid.* p. 4.
109 Special interest groups within Facebook as well as networks of 'followers' on Twitter can to some extent function in a similar way; people can create communities based on reciprocity and trust within much larger 'social networks' (that through their sheer size can't be regarded as a community anymore).
110 Maslow, 'A Theory of Human Motivation', *Psychological Review* (1943).

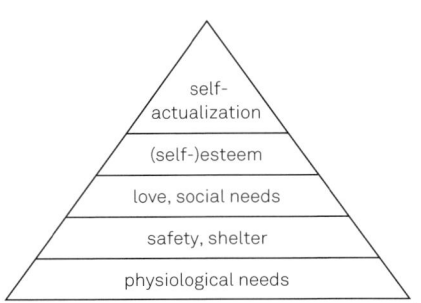

8 Maslow's hierarchy of needs, represented as a pyramid with the more basic
needs at the bottom.

self-
actualization

(self-)esteem

love, social needs

safety, shelter

physiological needs

The Communards of the 1960s had the ideal of changing society by sharing all levels of the pyramid, starting at the very bottom, by buying land, digging wells, growing food, building Fuller domes, and practicing free love. The members of the virtual community, however, must have already mastered the lower levels of the pyramid on their own before they can participate in the digital gift-economy that is only taking place on the top levels. They have become individualist agents, freelancers *within the system* of neoliberal capitalism, trading information to be more success-ful in their jobs.

My point here is not to discredit the sharing culture at the top of the pyramid, as it is undoubtedly an important achievement. It should not be confused with the much more ambitious original approach to create communities of radical sharing outside the system with the goal to eventually topple the system. The goals of the Communards who became members and advocates of the virtual community had fundamentally changed when they switched to a *centralised* and *commercial* plat-form. Yet they continued to use their accustomed rhetoric, making it look like they were still on their original mission, just with different tools. Whether they them-selves actually believed this narrative is hard to tell from the outside, but their pub-lications up to this date indicate that they did. Users of commercial online plat-forms today continue to be confronted with this gap between lofty hippie rhetoric and hyper capitalist reality.

Most importantly, when even the workplace is migrating into the virtual space, as is the case with commercial crowdsourcing, it has to pay enough to secure the lower layers of the pyramid – if it does not, so called 'sharing' as in the 'sharing econ-omy' can quickly become exploitative. Older visions of online collaboration, from Bush, to Engelbart, to Brand, always imagined strong, self-determined savvy indi-viduals co-operating as peers. Users were first imagined and portrayed as academics and other creative knowledge workers, later as maverick hackers, anti-authoritar-ian pioneers building outposts on the 'Electronic Frontier'. The idea that someone could take commercial advantage of large groups of these free-spirited, networked computer users emerged relatively late. And yet, even though Howard Rheingold's 1995 account of the first *Virtual Community* was generally very optimistic, he finished his book with a warning in reaction to the first mergers of the large old economy media corporations with the new online platforms:

The Net these players are building doesn't seem to be the same Net the grassroots pioneers predicted back in the 'good old days' on the electronic frontier. [...] Those who are used to thinking of CMC [computer mediated communication] as largely anarchic, dirt-cheap, uncensored forum, dominated by amateurs and enthusiasts, will have to learn a new way of thinking. Electronic democracy is far from inevitable, despite the variety of hopeful examples [...].[111]

Already a year earlier, Carmen Hermosillo, a long time active member of the WELL and several other platforms, best known under her username 'humdog', had published her concerns about the downsides of social networking that had started to become apparent to her:

it is fashionable to suggest that cyberspace is some kind of 'island of the blessed' where people are free to indulge and express their individuality. some people write about cyberspace as though it were a '60s utopia. in reality, this is not true. major online services, like compuserve and america online, regularly guide and censor discourse. even some allegedly free-wheeling (albeit politically correct) boards like the WELL censor discourse. the difference is only a matter of the method and degree. [...] i have seen many people spill their guts on-line, and i did so myself until, at last, i began to see that i hac commodified myself. [...] i created my interior thoughts as a means of production for the corporation that owned the board i was posting to, and that commodity was being sold to other commodity/consumer entities as entertainment. [...] furthermore, i was paying two bucks an hour for the privilege of commodifying and exposing myself. worse still, i was subjecting myself to the possibility of scrutiny by such friendly folks as the FBI [...] the rhetoric in cyberspace is liberation-speak. the reality is that cyberspace is an increasingly efficient tool of surveillance with which people have a voluntary relationship.[112]

I consider Carmen Hermosillo's re-evaluation of the mechanisms at work behind platforms such as the WELL and the gap between the utopian rhetoric and the capitalist reality of the platforms very astute. The warnings of Rheingold and Hermosillo are the earliest examples I could find of users – insiders and experts – questioning the asymmetry of power between the users and the owners of a digital platform. Already in 1995, when only about 16 million people or 0.4 per cent of the world's population were online, the emancipatory dream of the internet as a bottom-up utopian communal place, detached from the hierarchies of real-world capitalism and bureaucracy in which all rules could be reinvented, showed its first cracks.

111 Rheingold (1995): p. 275.
112 Hermosillo, 'Pandora's Vox: On Community in Cyberspace', *The Alphaville Herald* (1994).

People slowly started to realise that the platform providers would gain enormous power through the content produced by and the communication exchanged between users on the infrastructure provided by corporations. The question at this point in web history is whether the users of the internet should be protected by government regulations against platform capitalists or if their freedoms should be protected against any form of regulation by the government in order to sustain the dream of a libertarian utopia?

In 1990, John Perry Barlow, former lyricist of The Grateful Dead, cattle farmer, and early member of the WELL, co-founded the non-profit digital rights group the Electronic Frontier Foundation (EFF), together with Mitch Kapor, a former teacher of transcendental meditation who had become a rich software mogul with the publication of the first commercial spread-sheet program Lotus 1-2-3 in the 1980s. In 1996, Barlow published *A Declaration of Independence of Cyberspace*.[113] It was a libertarian, techno-deterministic manifesto that vocally restated the ideology that his fellow 'WELLbeings' Carmen Hermosillo and, to a lesser extent, Howard Rheingold, had already started to question. For Barlow, the threat to freedom on the 'Electronic Frontier' didn't come from the corporate platform providers commodifying and controlling their users, but from 'Big Government', the entity which he addressed in a bold voice, seemingly speaking for all internet users, or with the voice of 'liberty itself' (as he himself suggests):

Governments of the Industrial World, you weary giants of flesh and steel, I come from Cyberspace, the new home of Mind. On behalf of the future, I ask you of the past to leave us alone. You are not welcome among us. You have no sovereignty where we gather. [...] I declare the global social space we are building to be naturally independent of the tyrannies you seek to impose on us. [...] Cyberspace does not lie within your borders. [...] It is an act of nature and it grows itself through our collective actions. [...] We believe that from ethics, enlightened self-interest, and the commonweal, our governance will emerge. [...] The only law that all our constituent cultures would generally recognize is the Golden Rule. [...] In our world, whatever the human mind may create can be reproduced and distributed infinitely at no cost. The global conveyance of thought no longer requires your factories to accomplish. [...] We will create a civilization of the Mind in Cyberspace. May it be more humane and fair than the world your governments have made before.

Barlow wrote the famous *Declaration* while being a guest at the World Economics Forum in Davos, mingling with some of the world's most powerful people. The text was a reaction to the US Communications Decency Act of 1996, with which the US Government wanted to censor pornography on the internet. Barlow's Declaration thus comes from a concern about freedom of speech online, not fair labour condi-

113 Barlow, John Perry, 'A Declaration of the Independence of Cyberspace' (1996).

tions. But it is still relevant in the context of this book, because it makes visible a strong belief in what is sometimes referred to as 'digital dualism' – the conviction that cyberspace is a place totally detached from the physical world. Nathan Jurgenson, who coined the term, argues that it is a fallacy to create a binary distinction between the 'virtual' and the 'real' because 'people are enmeshing their physical and digital selves to the point where the distinction is becoming increasingly irrelevant.'[114] The last two decades have shown that, in an unregulated cyberspace, 'enlightened self-interest' will not only foster the commonweal and structures of self-governance but also the emergence of global corporate monopolies taking advantage of the masses online.

114 Jurgenson, 'Digital Dualism versus Augmented Reality' & 'Digital Dualism and the Fallacy of Web Objectivity', both on *Cyborgology*, (2001); see also: Witten, 'The Digital Dualism Debate', *MePhiD* (2013); and Miller, *Tales from Facebook* (2011). Anthropologist Daniel Miller strongly emphasizes the continuity between social life in a physical space (Trinidad, in his ethnographic study) and the digital life of h s subjects.

Chapter Three: The Design of Crowdsourcing

9 Cover of *Time* magazine, December 2006.

In the last chapter, we have seen how the idea of personal computing and online collaboration has evolved throughout the twentieth century – from an early vision in the 1940s when only a handful of mainframe computers existed; via first steps to build such systems with an individual user in mind in the late 1950s and throughout the 1960s; via an appropriation of the technology by the counterculture in the early 1970s; via the development of the first truly user-controlled platforms in the Free Software Movement by highly skilled hackers in the 1980s; to the emergence of the first commercial online community of 'non-hacker' professionals and early adopters on a centralised platform – the WELL of the late 1980s and early 1990s.

This chapter will provide an analysis of what occurred after the crowds arrived online in the early twenty-first century, especially with regard to the narrative of the empowerment of the individual user, the rise of platforms to coordinate the masses and make a profit from their activities, and the design of commercial crowdwork as a new form of labour market. It is about this new division of labour, power, profits, and risks – and the design of new tools to manipulate and control the masses.

MAKING SMALL CONTRIBUTIONS MATTER

Buy it, use it, break it, fix it,
trash it, change it, mail – upgrade it,
charge it, point it, zoom it, press it,
snap it, work it, quick – erase it,
write it, cut it, paste it, save it,
load it, check it, quick – rewrite it,
plug it, play it, burn it, rip it,
drag and drop it, zip – unzip it,
lock it, fill it, call it, find it,
view it, code it, jam – unlock it,
surf it, scroll it, pause it, click it,
cross it, crack it, switch – update it,
name it, rate it, tune it, print it,
scan it, send it, fax – rename it,
touch it, bring it, pay it, watch it,
turn it, leave it, stop – format it.
Daft Punk, Technologic, 2005

Every day, we click our way through an endless succession of microtasks, often with-out even noticing that we are doing work. In their most fine-grained, infinitesimal form, these tasks are almost under the threshold of our perception. Yet, in aggre-gated form, they have become a valuable resource for companies: *Surf it, scroll it, pause it, click it*. The path of our attention online leaves a rich trail, the raw material for Google, Facebook & Co. to further hone their search algorithms and user pro-files and to sell personalised, targeted advertising to their clients. In recent years, we have seen the rise of new platform monopolies built from data mining our digi-tal exhaust. *Write it, cut it, paste it, save it*. Other tasks already demand more engage-ment; they not only create raw data but actual content, be it merely for the purpose of self-expression or as a deliberate service to others. Amateurs write online articles for Wikipedia, moderate help forums, debug open-source software, and make im-portant contributions as citizen scientists in fields ranging from astronomy to or-nithology. With increasing complexity, these tasks stop being micro and demand a high level of engagement and expertise. They eventually become indistinguishable from work – in the sense of having a job, providing labour for someone else, accord-ing to that person's specific brief and time frame.

The lines between amateur and professional, between consumption and pro-duction, use and creation, play and labour, have been continuously blurred in post-industrial production, not only, but especially, on online platforms. Portmanteaus such as *prosuming*[1] and *produsage*,[2] *playbour*[3] and *weisure*[4] or the *pro-am revolution*[5] have tried to express this weird new mix. Should we be cheerful because work has become more playful and consumers and end-users are more creative now? Or is it the other way around and capitalism has now even co-opted our recreational time? It all depends on who you ask. The discourse around so called 'digital labour' and when it should be remunerated continues. Should we, for example, join the New York based artist and curator Laurel Ptak in demanding 'Wages for Facebook'?[6] In her online manifesto it reads: 'They say it's friendship. We say it's unwaged work. With every like, chat, tag or poke our subjectivity turns them a profit. They call it sharing. We call it stealing.' With her demand, Ptak echoed a feminist, workerist (operaismo) campaign by Selma James from 1972 demanding wages for housework; and a 1975 manifesto by Silvia Federici called *Wages Against Housework*, which Ptak took as the basis for her critique of Facebook.[7]

They call it sharing. We call it stealing – What a curious inversion of roles since Bill Gates' Open Letter to Hobbyists. It was the founder of Microsoft, for many years now the richest man in the world, who in 1976 reframed sharing as stealing in order to be able to sell software to 'end-users', who, as a consequence, were not allowed to tinker with the product and modify it to their needs anymore. The users could no longer even see what a Software product actually did; not that it was closed source, they simply had to trust the company that released it. Nevertheless, Gates had a valid point back then when he argued that the labour of writing the software had to somehow be reimbursed. Today, social media users like Laurel Ptak direct the accusation of stealing against Mark Zuckerberg, because he is making a huge profit from their *affective labour* in *the social factory* that is Facebook – even though the use of the product is 'free' – as in without charge. It is of course paid for indirectly with private data and the uploaded user-generated content.

The collapse of boundaries between the two domains, between leisure and corporate value creation, is what makes the question of appropriate remuneration so tricky. We are confronted with a whole new spectrum of work-and-play-hybrids. The spectrum includes forms of digital labour that are predominantly fun to those that are predominantly work. Sure we can demand wages for Facebook, and maybe we should – but declaring all our activities to be a job doesn't leave us in a useful place – and neither does declaring everything as play. What we see instead is a continuum between work and play. I would argue that the more job-like an activity is –

1   Toffler, *The Third Wave* (1989).
2   Bruns, *Blogs, Wikipedia, Second Life, and Beyond* (2009).
3   Kücklich, 'Precarious Playbour: Modders and the Digital Games Industry', *The Fibreculture Journal* (2005).
4   Patterson, 'Welcome to the "Weisure" Lifestyle', *CNN.com* (2009).
5   Leadbeater and Miller, *The Pro-Am Revolution* (2004).
6   Ptak, 'Wages For Facebook' (2013); see also: Jung, 'Wages for Facebook', *Dissent Magazine* (2014).
7   Federici, 'Wages Against Housework' (1975); see also: Tortorici, 'More Smiles? More Money', *n+1*, 17 (2013).

in the sense of demanding a lot of effort to be invested into a specific task that we do primarily *for someone else*, who then makes a profit from that – the more pertinent is the demand for wages or some other form of fair share from the value that is being generated.

Probably the best illustration of the strange amalgam of work and play is 'gold farming', where the fun of playing an online game such as World of Warcraft is perverted into pointless 'point-and-click' virtual drudgery for real world currency – for some players, the game has become a full-time job, but not for the majority of them.[8] This shows that even one and the same action can be either work or play, depending on who is doing it in what context. But wouldn't it be absurd to demand wages for time spend in World of Warcraft, or demand regular players to pay taxes for the virtual riches they accumulate as a side effect of their hobby without planning to monetise them. Where does one draw the line?

Wages for value creation through the mere use of software, such as a fantasy game or a social network, is one of the aspects of the digital labour discourse that are harder to grasp. The immense productive force that masses of internet users can muster if given access to the right tools is more obvious when they actually create new and distinct media content, like videos on YouTube. User-generated content became the central idea of the so-called 'Web 2.0', a term popularised in 2004 by publisher Tim O'Reilly.[9] The new version of the internet, so it was said, had become more collaborative and participatory. After the burst of the 'dot-com bubble' in the spring of 2000, the enthusiasm for e-commerce had cooled down for a few years. What united most of the internet businesses that arose from the ashes of the new economy crash was that they all found ways to allow the newly arrived masses of internet users to produce content for each other. These companies had understood that they only had to provide the infrastructure – the tools for digital production and the platforms for the systematic orchestration of the efforts – to attract more users and, by proxy, big advertisement budgets. With the notion of 'Web 2.0', Tim O'Reilly delivered the narrative for this transformation. Of course this narrative was about the empowerment of the individual. But with the arrival of the masses online also came the revival of the notion of the crowd, which is strangely at odds with the image of the user as an individualist hero and 'micro-entrepreneur'.

In the case of Amazon, users had already contributed ratings, reviews, and recommendations for a while, but they did not create the actual products. With the launch of Second Life in 2003 and, most importantly, YouTube in 2005, the concept of user-generated content was elevated to new heights. Now, users also created the core product. Wikipedia had started in 2001, but it was between 2004 and 2006 that it grew exponentially. All this contributed to a great hype about the

---

8   Heeks, 'Current Analysis and Future Research Agenda on "Gold Farming"', University of Manchester (2008).
9   O'Reilly, 'What is Web 2.0', *O'Reilly Media* (2005).

empowerment of the user, which peaked in December 2006 when *Time* magazine made 'You' the 'Person of the Year', the cover featuring a mirror foil, framed by a YouTube browser window (fig. 9). Below it read: 'Yes, you. You control the Information Age. Welcome to your world'. In the corresponding article, *Time* continued:

This is not the Web that Tim Berners-Lee hacked together [...] and not even the overhyped dotcom Web of the late 1990s. The new Web is a very different thing. It's a tool for bringing together the small contributions of millions of people and making them matter. [...] It's about the many wresting power from the few and helping one another for nothing.[10]

As it turned out, this was largely an illusion. In hindsight, the *Time* cover is more revealing than was probably intended by the publishers at the time – a mirror image that catered to the narcissism of each individual reader/user, while actually being a product for the masses. If everybody is special, nobody is. While the *many* did indeed use their digital tools to help one another for nothing, the power today seems to be back firmly in the hands of the very *few* who own and control the digital platforms on which this exchange is taking place. Users had much more control over their data in the world wide web that Tim Berners Lee 'hacked together', before they handed over their most intimate personal data and user-generated content, which had previously been hosted on personal decentralised home pages, to the server-farms and platforms of a very small number of global content aggregators and social networks. Unsurprisingly, Tim Berners-Lee objected to the notion of a 'Web 2.0'. Asked in an interview in 2006 whether he would agree that 'Web 1.0 was about connecting computers and making information available' while 'Web 2.0 is about connecting people and facilitating new kinds of collaboration', Berners-Lee firmly disagreed:

Totally not. Web 1.0 was all about connecting people. It was an interactive space, and I think Web 2.0 is of course a piece of jargon, nobody even knows what it means. If Web 2.0 for you is blogs and wikis, then that is people to people. But that was what the Web was supposed to be all along.[11]

In the meantime, media scholars such as Trebor Scholz have shown that the proclaimed novelty of the 'Web 2.0' was deceptive.[12] It was just a clever marketing label from which even Tim O'Reilly distanced himself eventually. Still, something had changed on the internet around the time that 'Web 2.0' rose to fame. The naive hubris of the 2006 'Person of the Year' *Times* cover is reminiscent of Hunter S. Thomson's famous 'Wave Speech' from the novel *Fear and Loathing in Las Vegas*, published

10 Grossman, 'You – Yes, You – Are TIME's Person of the Year', *Time* (2006).
11 Berners-Lee, 'IBM Developer Works Interviews' (2006). Anderson, 'Tim Berners-Lee on Web 2.0', *Ars Technica* (2006).
12 Scholz, 'Market Ideology and the Myths of Web 2.0', *First Monday*, 13 (2008).

in 1971. Thomson was trying to grasp how the revolutionary zeitgeist of the 1960s counterculture had evaporated so quickly:

Five years later? Six? It seems like a lifetime, or at least a Main Era – the kind of peak that never comes again. San Francisco in the middle sixties was a very special time and place to be a part of. [...] There was a fantastic universal sense that whatever we were doing was right, that we were winning ... And that, I think, was the handle – that sense of inevitable victory over the forces of Old and Evil. Not in any mean or military sense; we didn't need that. Our energy would simply prevail. There was no point in fighting – on our side or theirs. We had all the momentum; we were riding the crest of a high and beautiful wave ...

So now, less than five years later, you can go up on a steep hill in Las Vegas and look West, and with the right kind of eyes you can almost see the high-water mark – that place where the wave finally broke and rolled back.[13]

A decade later, the *Times* cover of 2006 looks like another such high-water mark, a prominent display of the unabated belief in the web as a tool for good, a tool that was beyond politics, and that would inherently empower the masses and topple the forces of Old and Evil. It was yet another expression of utopian technological determinism, the belief that access to decentralised high-tech tools could replace or 'route around' politics and hierarchies. An ideology that first took shape in the scene around Stewart Brand, the *Whole Earth Catalog* and the WELL, that was later advocated by Kevin Kelly and his colleagues at *Wired* and that is still characteristic of today's Silicon Valley corporations, now more influential then ever. The promise is the empowerment of the individual, not through politics but through technology – fast, cheap, and out of control – but undoubtedly a force for good. The spirit of inevitable victory, so vividly described by Thomson, can also be found in John Perry Barlow's libertarian *Declaration of the Independence of Cyberspace* from 1995,[14] as well as in the consumerist *Cluetrain Manifesto* from 1999.[15] While reality seems to stubbornly insist on the fact that new tools can and will also be used by those already in power, as a means to defend their privileged position, the belief in utopian technological determinism continues to haunt the tech world. As in the 1960s, a wave originating from California's San Francisco Bay Area is rolling over the rest of the world, but this wave is not characterised by decentralised tools for individual empowerment but by monopolistic platforms and centralised control. It is a reversal of the counterculture ideals, piggybacking on the old and now-empty rhetoric of *power to the people*.

---

13 Thompson, *Fear and Loathing in Las Vegas* (2005): p. 66.
14 Barlow, 'A Declaration of the Independence of Cyberspace' (1996).
15 Levine/Weinberger/Locke/Searls, 'The Cluetrain Manifesto' (1999).

With regard to freedom of speech and the fight against despotic regimes, similar claims of empowerment were made in the context of the so-called 'Twitter Revolution' in Iran in 2009 and also later during the so-called 'Arab Spring'. The biased and often naive view of social networking as the sole force for good was debunked by Evgeny Morozov, Silicon Valley's most caustic critic, in his book *The Net Delusion*, published in 2011, and in the follow up, *To Save Everything, Click Here*, from 2013.[16] But the narrative that tools such as smartphone apps, the ubiquitous sensors of the 'internet of things', and social media platforms are better suited than politics to improve society continues to dominate. The Silicon Valley-based billionaire and venture capitalist Peter Thiel, co-founder of PayPal, early investor in Facebook and more recently Donald Trump, an outspoken and influential techno-libertarian, declares openly that he wants to replace politics with technology as the much better system to get things done.[17] In his world view, states should function like corporations in a radical, free market approach that reaches all the way up from individual to government and rewards bold, disruptive, innovative entrepreneurship alone, without having anything to offer to those who can't keep up with the rat race or find themselves in a less privileged position to begin with.

For the questions at the heart of this book, the high-water-mark of the 2006 *Times* cover is a good vantage point from which to acknowledge how much has changed in the interim. Seen through the eyes of Illich, 2006 could be described as the second watershed of online collaboration. It was a point in web history, where the new power of the masses online had become evident, but it had not yet been commercially exploited to the extent that we have become accustomed to subsequently. The coinage of the term crowdsourcing, marks a paradigm-shift – away from the empowerment of the individual user – towards the harnessing of the 'immaterial labour' of all internet users. It was a shift from commons-based peer production on the open web towards large-scale aggregation, privatisation, and value extraction from the contributions of the many. The ideal of *sharing* among peers was transformed into the business of *harvesting* the crowds – while continuing the pretence of sharing. The users do participate in sharing among one another, but what is happening on the systemic level is best described as 'sharecropping'. A poignant phrase introduced by internet critic Nicholas Carr to emphasise that the users now find themselves in deeply undemocratic feudal platform structures.[18]

---

16 Morozov, *The Net Delusion* (2011). Morozov, *To Save Everything, Click Here* (2013).
17 Meerman, 'Cybertopia: Dreams of Silicon Valley', VPRO Backlight, Dutch TV documentary (2015).
18 Carr, 'Sharecropping the Long Tail' (2006) & 'The Economics of Digital Sharecropping' (2012), both on Carr's blog *RoughType*.com. For a discussion of the return to feudal structures on digital platforms see also: Sterling, *The Epic Struggle of the Internet of Things* (2014).

It is noteworthy that the term 'user' already implies a certain hierarchy. A user is not the person who has created the tool or platform that he or she is using. The user typically only sees the front-end of the platform and is not meant to worry about the infrastructure, the administration, or the code behind it. Via the mandatory 'I agree' button, the user has to submit to the 'terms of use', the so-called 'click-wrap'. The user is theoretically free to create anything, but within boundaries, technical and legal ones, defined by the platform providers. On commercial platforms, there is a clear gap between those who make and enforce the rules and those who submit the content and their private data. We are certainly not talking about recursive publics here. Even though users can make suggestions through user-forums, they don't take part in the definition of the rules. They can however create what they like, for each other in their own time, without having to follow a brief or job description; they work for fun, reputation, maybe even for a share of the advertising money, if they are very successful, and they keep the copyright of their content.

In crowdwork, by contrast, the crowdsourcer wants to complete a specific job. To achieve this without paying the crowd, one can disguise the work, redesign it as a game, or convince the crowd that participation is an honour and serves a higher purpose. If one is willing to pay the crowd, one can either pay tiny amounts of money for every job done, or one can award a higher amount of money, but only to a small group or even just one individual who delivered the best result:

1. Unpaid Crowdwork
   a. Indirect Crowdwork (work done as side-effect, e.g. of gamification)[19]
   b. Volunteer Crowdwork (work donated for a perceived higher purpose)

2. Paid Crowdwork
   a. Microtasking Crowdwork (cognitive piecework done for micropayments)
   b. Contest-based Crowdwork (creative work done for prize money)

The two forms of paid crowdwork are by far the most consequential categories because they have created a new and global class of precarious workers: crowdworkers. Before analysing paid crowdwork in detail, I will briefly outline the first two categories.

19 With this categorisation I partly build on legal scholar and internet critic Jonathan Zittrain, legal scholar Alek Felstiner. What I define here as 'indirect crowdwork', Zittrain has called 'epiphenomenal work' and Felstiner has called this 'disguised crowdsourcing': Zittrain, *Ubiquitous Human Computing* (2008). Felstiner, 'Working the Crowd' (2010).

Indirect Crowdwork

Some crowdsourcing techniques make it possible to extract value from the behaviour of people without them even realising. An old, pre-digital form of this is the concept of the 'working customer', studied by the German industrial sociologists G. Günter Voß and the occupational psychologist Kerstin Rieder.[20] It is a type of work that we frequently do, often happily, obediently, sometimes while cursing under our breath: things like the self-assembly of IKEA-furniture and the self-service in fast food restaurants; but also online banking, installing mandatory updates to our devices, and giving advice on how to use products in online-forums. By externalising part of the labour to their customers, large companies can make enormous savings. Voß calculated that in 2013 IKEA saved 75 million euro through the self-assembly of the popular 'Billy' shelf alone.[21] McDonalds supposedly saves two billion euros per year by letting customers clean up after themselves.[22] It remains opaque from the outside to what extent the customers are compensated for their work with cheaper prices.

In the digital realm, it is even possible to passively extract value from user behaviour. This is sometimes referred to as 'Mobile Crowd Sensing', where environmental sensor-data is gathered from peoples' smartphones, for example to figure out in real time how crowded a place like a tourist attraction or a public event is.[23] In 2016 Google added such a feature to its search engine.[24] In these applications, the constant tracking of user behaviour, to which we have already grown accustomed online, is now extended to the physical world and researchers also want to acquire data about noise levels, traffic conditions, and pollution through these 'context-aware distributed systems', in which humans function as 'nodes'.[25] This is a form crowdsourcing, but it is not really work.

Volunteer Crowdwork

In this subcategory, people have to follow a specific brief and time frame, but they are aware that they are doing work for someone. They have no immediate personal use for what they are producing, it does not become part of the commons, and they don't get any monetary rewards. Instead, they are consciously donating their labour to a perceived greater cause. This type of work is probably best illustrated by the

---

20 Voß/Rieder, *Der arbeitende Kunde* (2005).
21 Calculated with 2.50 euros for the half hour of work the self-assembly of 'Billy' takes.
22 Günter Voß in the foreword to: Papsdorf, *Wie Surfen zu Arbeit wird* (2009): p. 16.
23 Guo et al, 'From participatory sensing to Mobile Crowd Sensing' (2014).
24 Carman, 'Google will tell you how crowded your favorite bar is in real time', *The Verge* (2016).
25 Ferraira/Alves, *Distributed Context-Aware Systems* (2014): p. 12.

story of Tom Sawyer getting his friends to paint Aunt Polly's fence.[26] Tom even made a profit because he managed to let the task of painting the fence look so honourable that his friends paid him with sweets. Volunteer Crowdwork is often used against perceived wrongdoing or even crime. In 2011, the initiators of the German project 'GuttenPlag' engaged the crowd to reveal plagiarism in doctoral dissertations of high profile politicians. Since 2014, the London Metropolitan Police tries to find suspects through a privately owned crowdsourcing app called Facewatch ID.[27] In 2010, the company Internet Eyes, also from the UK, crowdsourced and gamified the surveillance of shops through CCTV cameras; and in the US, also in 2010, a company called BlueServo experimented with real time crowdsourced surveillance of the Texas border to report illegal immigrants.[28] While crowdsourcing might be efficient to battle certain unwanted behaviour, this certainly brings up ethical questions regarding the motives of those doing the watching and reporting, the effect on those who are paid to do these jobs (the police), and the effect on those being named and shamed, potentially innocently, by a vigilant 'cyber-mob'.

26 Walker, 'Taking a Cue from Tom Sawyer', *Washington Post* (1999).
27 (facewatch.co.uk), accessed January 2017.
28 *Koskela, '"Don't mess with Texas!" Texas Virtual Border Watch Program and the (botched) politics of responsibilization' Crime Media Culture, Sage, 7 (2011): pp. 49–65.* Internet Eyes and Texas Border Watch have been discontinued, as of January 2017 Facewatch ID is still up and running.

GAMIFIED HARVESTING OF
THE COGNITIVE SURPLUS

Jeff Howe once described crowdsourcing as 'distributed labor networks [...] using the Internet to exploit the spare processing power of millions of human brains.'[29] Obviously, the tone here is a far cry from the claims of a sharing culture and the empowerment of the individual. Instead, it is more reminiscent of the network of human batteries in the movie *The Matrix*. In this dystopian fiction, the world as we know it is merely a 'screen saver' to keep human brains happy and entertained while their bodies are producing the energy needed by robot overlords.

When we leave the *virtual* reality of Hollywood behind to look at the *actual* reality of early twenty-first century digital platforms, it turns out that, instead of using the waste body heat of people to run machines, it makes much more sense to use their 'waste processing' power to augment machines with cognitive and creative skills they can't muster otherwise. It is the inversion of Engelbart's goal to augment the individual human intellect. Now humans augment the machine.

Since the widespread dissemination of networked computing made it feasible to harvest brainpower on a massive scale, people started thinking about how to put this new and renewable resource to good use – and centralised platforms play a key role in the management of the aggregation process. One of the most influential figures in this field is the Guatemalan computer scientist Luis von Ahn, now a professor at Carnegie Mellon University. In the year 2000, at the tender age of 21, von Ahn developed the technique of CAPTCHAs to prevent 'spam bots' from opening email accounts.[30] Since then, users have to decipher artificially distorted words, which computers are not able to read, in order to prove that they are humans.

[...] CAPTCHAs constitute a viable mechanism to harness large amounts of human mental effort. After exactly 1 year of running the system, humans had solved more than 1.2 billion CAPTCHAs, amounting to over 440 million suspicious words correctly deciphered. Assuming 100,000 words per book (400 pages, 250 words per page), this is equivalent to over 17,600 books manually transcribed.[31]

Within five years, about 200 million CAPTCHAs were being typed everyday and von Ahn 'started to feel bad, because each one was wasting 10 seconds of someone's time.' In a very clever twist, he therefore introduced reCAPTCHA in 2007. The new version of the program now showed the user two words, one to which the answer was already known (in order to test the trustworthiness of the user) and another one

29 Howe, 'The Rise of Crowdsourcing', *Wired* (2006).
30 CAPTCHA is an acronym of 'Completely Automated Public Turing Test to Tell Computers and Humans Apart.'
31 von Ahn et al. 'reCAPTCHA', *Science* Vol. 321, Issue 5895, (2008): pp. 1465–68.

10 Typical pop-up dialogue of reCAPTCHA, used to tell humans and computers apart.

to which the answer was unknown but sought after. If humans had to spend brainpower to solve CAPTCHAS anyway, it might as well be for something productive – in this case helping Google with scanning books, recognising house-numbers for Street View, or more recently, street signs for its fleet of self-driving cars.

While von Ahn's invention is a great example of 'wasted' human brainpower put to good use, it is problematic that most people don't even realise that they donate their cognitive capacities to Google. This form of *indirect crowdwork* shows that if work is broken down into tiny bits and distributed across the web, it is sometimes not even recognisable as work anymore. In 2005, von Ahn published his PhD thesis on what he now called 'human computation'.[32] In the introduction he wrote:

We focus on harnessing human time and energy for addressing problems that computers cannot yet tackle on their own. [...] In this paradigm, we treat human brains as processors in a distributed system, each performing a small part of a massive computation. Unlike computer processors, however, humans require an incentive in order to become part of a collective computation. We propose online games as a means to encourage participation in the process.[33]

And indeed, von Ahn created several such 'Games With a Purpose', as he called them that successfully motivated people to contribute their cognitive skills to solving tasks that could not be automated. One of them was the 'ESP Game', which in 2006 was acquired by Google and then continued under the name 'Google Image Labeler'.[34] The purpose of the game was to get people to provide descriptive labels for the content of images to make them accessible for search engines. It did that by randomly teaming up two volunteer players, showing them the same image at the same time and awarding them with points when they both quickly typed in matching descriptions. The game was quite popular and provided not only tags for images but also created data-sets for machine learning processes aimed at training algorithms to become better at image recognition. Von Ahn reported that as of July 2008,

32 von Ahn, *Human Computation* (2005).
33 *Ibid*. p. 11.
34 'ESP' stands for extra-sensorial perception, the so-called 'sixth sense'. The most popular of von Ahn's Human Computation applications is the language learning app Duolingo.

200,000 players had contributed more than fifty million labels.[35] They had contributed their time, not because of altruism or because of financial rewards, but because the researcher had taken his cues from video games and managed to make the work seem fun.

According to von Ahn, it took seven million human-hours to construct the Empire State Building and twenty million human-hours for the Panama Canal, while the time that people spend playing the Microsoft Windows embedded card-game Solitaire was estimated to be in the billions per year.[36] Such attempts to fathom the amount of 'wasted' brainpower, or the latent potential of 'spare cycles', with astronomic calculations are a reoccurring theme in crowdsourcing literature. Internet guru Clay Shirky wrote in his book *Cognitive Surplus* that it took 'only' about one-hundred million man-hours to create Wikipedia (as of 2009) while Americans alone watch two-hundred billion hours of TV each year.[37] In a TED talk from 2010, Shirky expressed this idea even more poignantly: 'There are a trillion hours a year of participatory value up for grabs.'[38]

The game-designer and author Jane McGonigal is juggling with equally mind-boggling numbers. According to her, the accumulated time that people played World of Warcraft reached 5.93 million years in 2011 – that is just for this one game alone – but people also spent 3.5 million years with the puzzle game Bejeweled and 250,000 years with Microsoft's ego-shooter Halo.[39]

From their description of this new resource, one has no reason to doubt that Shirky, McGonigal, and von Ahn only have the best of intentions. All three authors are concerned with putting the 'cognitive surplus' from gaming to good use for humanity, in one way or another. Shirky explicitly wants to funnel at least a fraction of the otherwise 'wasted' time in front of the TV into more productive, social, communal, and civic-minded projects such as the open-source, non-profit, activist, geospatial citizen journalist platform Ushahidi. McGonigal is radiant with optimism as well and wants to use the 'cognitive surplus' to 'fix a broken world' and 'make it into a better place' by tackling challenges in areas such as health and ecological sustainability.[40]

However, two things are striking, if not deeply worrying about this new paradigm. First of all, it introduces a macro-economic efficiency calculation into the private lives of people – the time during which they are not contributing to the GDP through conventional work, but recovering from it. Leisure time, formerly characterised by being free of the imperative to be productive, is now regarded as a waste for society when it is not contributing to 'world saving' crowdsourcing projects

35 von Ahn/Dabbish, 'Designing Games with a Purpose' (2008): pp. 58–67.
36 von Ahn, *Human Computation* (2005).
37 Shirky, *Cognitive Surplus* (2010): p. 10.
38 Shirky, 'How Cognitive Surplus Will Change the World', TED talk (2010).
39 McGonigal, 'Gaming Can Make a Better World', TED talk (2010).
40 McGonigal, *Reality Is Broken* (2012).

based on communal and civic-minded engagement. The question is: Do we really want to live in a society where every minute of free time that does not feed content back into a digital platform is regarded as being wasted? The second aspect that I find worrying is the question: Who is in the end actually going to 'grab' that participatory value? Furthermore, how can one ensure that the 'cognitive surplus' actually benefits social projects instead of profit-oriented digital labour platforms? The socially spirited harvesting of the cognitive surplus, so often advocated in management literature, sometimes seems to function like a Trojan horse, distracting one from the profit-orientated application of the same methods.

In his book *Cognitive Surplus* Clay Shirky builds on the work of Yochai Benkler's concept of 'commons-based peer production'. Benkler and Shirky both dismiss the classic economic model of the 'homo economicus', a human guided only by rational self-interest, as a short-sighted way to explain all that motivates humans. They both show that in many social contexts, money is not the best incentive to guide and reward human behaviour.[41] Shirky writes that instead of using extrinsic monetary incentives, systems to harness the cognitive surplus should be designed to appeal to intrinsic motivations, especially to the generosity of people. Shirky believes, and he offers many examples to support this view, that if people have the opportunity and the choice, they will generously contribute their free time to projects that are meaningful and social.

Luis von Ahn and Jane McGonigal don't believe that money is the best incentive to guide behaviour either. Instead of trying to convince people to do volunteer work, they employ game mechanics to motivate the crowd. In the face of more and more stakeholders trying to harvest the cognitive surplus, McGonigal predicted that '[T]he competition for participants will be fierce, and not all projects will thrive.'[42] The various projects will have to, as she argues, engage the crowds on a deep emotional level in order to make them not just passively watch but actively contribute in an engaged and persistent way. It is essentially the same problem that MIT's Thomas Malone is contemplating on with regard to 'collective intelligence' – 'how do you motivate people to do the things you want them to do?'[43] (see on p. 062 ff.)

The difference between McGonigal and von Ahn, who both design systems with *fun* as the core incentive, is that she hopes for real world changes in behaviour that are meaningful to the participants and persistent for companies and society outside of the game, while he primarily wants to 'grab' data that can only be created by human cognitive skills. That data is then made useful for the public and for Google, but is also used to train machines. While Shirky is an advocate of what I call

41 Benkler and Shirky both refer to a study that showed the adversarial effects of making parents pay a fine when they didn't pick up their children from day-care centres on time: Gneezy/Rustichini, 'A Fine is a Price', *The Journal of Legal Studies*, 29 (2000): pp. 1–17.
42 McGonigal, 'Engagement Economy', Institute for the Future (2008).
43 Malone, 'The Future of Work with MIT's Thomas Malone', interview with *The Economist* (2013), available on YouTube.

Volunteer-based Crowdwork, where people consciously donate their labour, von Ahn and McGonigal are proponents and active design practitioners of what I call *Indirect Crowdwork,* where people are not really aware that they are providing labour for someone else – or in fact that they are doing work at all. McGonigal and von Ahn both use *Gamification* as their method to enable and incentivise *Unpaid Indirect Crowdwork*.

Since its coinage in 2008, the term 'gamification' has quickly evolved from yet another internet buzzword into an influential and widely applied method. It results in the application of game design mechanics in non-game contexts in order to influence people's behaviour.[44] Something that was hitherto not a game is *'gamified'* through the introduction of various feedback mechanisms such as *points*, *badges*, *levels*, *achievements,* and *leaderboards*. The typically public comparison of *performance statistics* plays a crucial role in gamification, which is why the technique relies heavily on *big data* technology. In the words of German media scholar Niklas Schrape: 'While the big data techniques are the governor's tools to watch over their subjects, gamification mechanisms are the means to regulate their behaviour.'[45] All behaviour that is meant to be influenced through gamification first of all has to be automatically tracked through various sensors or through input devices fed by the users themselves. Thus constant feedback about their performance is analysed on the respective platform and signalled back to the users, together with information about how well they perform in comparison to their peers or their own previous records. Gamification aims to change behaviour not through punishment but through repeated positive feedback for every little increment of improvement. It can be seen as the modern-day digital application of B. F. Skinner's behaviourist set of methods, which were based on continuous positive feedback as a means of control through conditioning.[46]

Most people know from experience (or at least from observation) how addictive games can be, especially video games. The the astronomic hours of aggregated playtime listed above speak volumes. An important reason why games are so captivating, motivating, and satisfying is that they are very good at creating a state of constant *flow*, the peculiar state of mind that was extensively studied by the Hungarian-American Professor of Psychology Mihály Csíkszentmihályi.[47] The state of flow is characterised by an intense and focused concentration on the present moment, a merging of action and awareness, a loss of reflective self-consciousness, a sense of personal control or agency over the situation or activity, a distortion of temporal experience, and the experience of the activity as intrinsically rewarding. For Csíkszentmihályi, the state of flow is a key to happiness and it can be experienced in many

---

44 Deterding et al., 'Gamification: Toward a Definition', *CHI* (2011). See also: Bunchball whitepaper, 'Gamification 101' (2010).

45 Schrape, 'Gamification and Governmentality', *Rethinking Gamification* (2014): p. 34.

46 Catania/Harnad ed., *The Selection of Behavior: The Operant Behaviorism of B. F. Skinner* (1988).

47 Csíkszentmihályi, *Flow: The Psychology of Optimal Experience* (1990).

areas of life, in making music, juggling, drawing, programming, and especially in playing video games. On top of the characteristics above, computer games enhance the effects of flow with those of competition and perceived perpetual progress through 'levelling up' – quantified and expressed in points and shared with other players. Through various feedback mechanisms, gamers continuously have the feeling of getting better, of gathering more points, of climbing up the leaderboard, and thus of gaining a higher standing among their peers. In the parlance of gamers, an 'epic win' is always within reach. As J. C. Herz, the first game design columnist of the *New York Times,* had already observed in 2002, long before the term 'gamification' existed:

As in Slashdot's 'karma' system or eBay's reputation ratings, 'levelling up' is a big motivating factor for players: It's the game's way of validating their cumulative accomplishments with something quantifiable, if not tangible. [...] The accretion of value in persistent worlds changes the psychology of leisure: You haven't 'spent' 1,000 hours playing a game; you've 'built up your character'. You've made progress! Accretion transforms idle time into something that feels industrious. It turns spending into earning.[48]

Gamification has become a successful manipulation technique to motivate and control the masses; the frequent-flyer programs are the most common example, others are Nike+ and Foursquare. In many cases, gamification is used to foster loyalty between a brand and its customers: in the context of crowdsourcing, however, gamification is used to get the crowd to do work it wouldn't do otherwise, to do it more efficiently, and to engage with fellow crowdworkers in certain ways valued by the crowdsourcer. It has become a tool to keep workers highly motivated without having to pay them. Gamification propels competition and ambition among those at the receiving end of that method. It transforms the actual loss of time (and sometimes money) into a feeling of constant achievement and progress. But even if gamification is meant to serve a perceived higher purpose, like health and ecologic sustainability, it is still ethically problematic, because it does not appeal to reason but tries to nudge the masses in the perceived right direction (from the perspective of the crowdsourcer that is.) It is therefore closely related to (and a method of) the so-called Nudge Theory in behavioural science, political theory, and economics. 'Nudging' is a form of policy with which the state tries to influence its constituents not by appealing to their reason with good arguments but by employing psychological tricks, supposedly in the citizens' best interest.[49] The most prominent advocates of nudging, behavioural scientist Richard Thaler and legal scholar Cass

---

48 Herz, 'Harnessing the Hive', *Esther Dyson's Release 1.0* (2002).
49 In 2010, the coalition government under David Cameron set up a so-called Behavioural Insight Team (BIT), aka the 'Nudge Unit'. In 2014 also Angela Merkel started to build a nudge unit. See: Neubacher, 'Alchemie Im Kanzleramt', *Der Spiegel*, 36 (2014). Klug, 'Nudging: Wie Frau Merkel uns hilft, die bessere Wahl zu treffen', *Deutschlandradio Kultur* (2015).

Sunstein, have described the method as 'libertarian paternalism'.[50] The individual citizen retains its freedom of choice but is gently pushed into the 'right' direction by a caring state (or a platform provider).

Because of its manipulative power in the business context, media philosopher and games scholar Ian Bogost has suggested the substitution of the term 'gamification' with 'exploitationware'.[51] Evgeny Morozov said, when he was asked about gamification at a talk he gave at the LSE in London in 2013: 'We should not think about making gamification better, we shouldn't use it at all. I think it is evil.'[52] One of the most important arguments against gamification for social purposes is the same that is used by Shirky and Benkler against monetary incentives: The intrinsic motivation to do something out of social responsibility or altruism, for example donating blood or organs or voting in an election, is 'crowded out' – replaced – by extrinsic rewards, no matter if it is money or virtual points.[53]

Furthermore there is an element of deliberate deception involved when it comes to the profit-oriented applications of gamification. It is difficult not to side with Bogost and Morozov when reading what Gabriel Zichermann, a salesman of gamification, teaches on the topic in a management book published by O'Reilly Media:

That truism underlies the last basic lesson of games in the real world: no matter what the player thinks, the house will always win a well-designed game. Just as any honest casino manager will tell you, while the illusion of winning is vital to motivating use and play, actually winning is much harder than it seems. Broadly speaking, this has implications not only for players, but also for those of us charged with building and designing great user experiences. As markets gamify and consumer demand for fun, engaging, and creative experiences increases, you have a fundamental choice: either be the house, or get played. Trust us, you want to be the former.[54]

Zichermann – in contrast to McGonigal, von Ahn, and Shirky – is not at all bothered with socially beneficial ends of gamification. He openly promotes it as a technique to trick customers, to get them to spend more money than they intend to, or to work for free. He takes advantage of the effect that by replacing real money with virtual currencies, the crowd can no longer keep track of whether it gets a fair deal or not: 'If you don't have a ton of cash to give away as an incentive (who does?), status is an excellent alternative. It is a great driver of loyalty, not to mention a player's fiscal behavior (and, over time, you can bet it is a whole lot cheaper). A gamified program

50 Thaler/Sunstein, *Nudge: Improving Decisions about Health, Wealth, and Happiness* (2008).
51 Bogost, 'Persuasive Games: Exploitationware', *Gamasutra* (2011).
52 Morozov, 'The Folly of Technological Solutionism', London School of Economics (2013).
53 Frey/Jegen, 'Motivation Crowding Theory', Journal of Economic Surveys, 15 (2001): pp. 589–611.
54 Zichermann, *Gamification by Design*, (2011): p. 13.

with a status benefit needs far fewer monetary, physical, or even real-world-redeemable rewards.'[55]

Zichermann uses his book on gamification to promote himself as a marketing consultant specialised in this technique of crowd manipulation and in doing so, he follows the tradition of Bernays' *Propaganda* (see chapter one). Zichermann's approach to gamification, especially if applied in the for-profit work context, falls into what Matthew Fuller and Andrew Goffey have described as *Evil Media*.[56] It is a stratagem in the contemporary media landscape that uses the infrastructure of an online platform to cunningly take advantage of its users.

Zichermann's design philosophy (if we want to call it that) for developing gamified platforms is truly remarkable, at least in its blatant honesty – the goal to exploit one's users is rarely stated so explicitly in public. It is pertinent in the context of this book, because it ties into the ethics of designing crowdsourcing platforms for creative work in several ways. First of all, the platforms for creative crowdwork that I will discuss in chapter four use various gamification mechanisms to incentivise the crowd and influence its behaviour. Furthermore, creative crowdwork is typically organised in form of contests – thus, there is not just a layer of gamification woven into the platforms – these workplaces structurally take the form of gambling. When it is 'well-designed' in Zichermann's sense, 'the house', or the platform, always wins: for the individual workers, it remains a game of chance to actually get paid for labour undertaken in advance. Keeping up the 'illusion of winning is vital' for the platform, while 'actually winning' must be 'much harder than it seems'. Zichermann is clear about the fact that the platforms he has in mind are in the game to generate a profit while its users have to be fooled so they don't realise that the odds are stacked against them. This is what Zichermann frames as the 'fundamental choice': either exploit or get exploited. In Zichermann's worldview, those who design the system are the antagonists of those who are supposed to use it. Obviously, this is a far cry from the design ideals of system designers such as Douglas Engelbart, who wanted to augment the users' intellect and it adds weight to Stallman's argument that corporations cannot be trusted to act in the best interest of their users. If we recall the design ethics of Ivan Illich and especially Lucius Burckhardt (outlined in the introduction), design objects can be evil, especially 'when they foster our dependence on systems that ultimately pillage our resources.' In that sense, what Zichermann promotes, are systems that are indeed *evil by design*.

55   *Ibid*. p. 10.
56   Fuller/Goffey, *Evil Media* (2012).

MAPPING PAID CROWDWORK IN
THE PLATFORM ECONOMY

Over the last decade, since around 2005, platform-based business models have permeated many areas of society and commerce, from retailers of physical goods, via streaming services for music, film and video, to dating sites and apps. Digital platforms make the lives of millions of people easier and we can hardly imagine modern life without them any longer. The platform providers are proud to cause 'disruptive' change in many industries and they can satisfy consumer demands more efficiently and conveniently – but they also pose a serious challenge, not only for established, supposedly ossified 'brick and mortar' businesses. Now that labour markets are also increasingly organised via digital platforms they are challenging the social state and its welfare systems. The platforms foster the transformation of regular employment into new forms of precarious self-employment, and the political implications of this shift can hardly be overestimated.

The new platform-based labour markets portray themselves as the future of work and political terms such as 'Arbeit 4.0' (literally: 'Work 4.0', a term used frequently by German politicians) support this spirit of progressiveness. Nonetheless, with regard to workers' rights and social security, it seems that the new platforms instead represent a regression to the era of the early Industrial Revolution. The development gives employers access to a huge on-demand workforce and is leading to a shift in the structure of labour markets. The emerging business models of what is best described as the 'platform economy' rely on private individuals who, as independent contractors, carry out small jobs in their free time; an army of more or less precarious workers who can be hired or fired in an instant. Literally thousands of digital platforms for the commercial coordination of digital labour have emerged in recent years. Many of them are very small and short-lived, while others have millions of users. It is still uncertain how many of them are economically viable in the long run, and to what extent the new types of jobs will replace more conventional forms of employment.

The potentially destructive force of the new platforms is partly rooted in the fact that they can be used to circumvent national laws for consumer protection, workers' rights, minimum wage regulations, and social security contributions. Since the web-based platforms for cloudwork and crowdwork have evolved into the smartphone-based platforms for local gigwork, the disruptive change is now also becoming visible in the physical world. Digital platforms for the outsourcing of labour are of particular relevance because, on one hand, they allow for more flexible sources of income beyond conventional employment, while on the other hand, they seem to be fostering a new class of precarious workers, a so-called 'Cybertariat'.[57]

---

57 Huws, 'Capitalism and the Cybertariat' (2015); See also Strube, 'Crowdwork: Vom Entstehen der Digitalen Arbeiterklasse' (2015).

However, it is important not to look at the labour platforms in isolation but to see them as part of the larger platform economy. Therefore the following analysis first describes the functionality and structure of the platform economy in general (see figure 11) before it focuses on the categorisation of digital labour platforms in particular (see figure 12). The categorisation offered here is a tree typology that makes it possible to locate the specific opportunities and risks of certain branches in the platform economy, as well as particular points where it is necessary to tackle these structures with political measures.

The term 'platform' proves to be particularly useful in this context because it points to the crucial structural similarity of various new digital business models and methods and directs the focus to the mechanics of the infrastructure in the background. Unfortunately, the discourse on platform-based digital labour often suffers from inconsistencies in the use of terminology and confusion in the categorisation of different platform types. In order to address at the appropriate level the multiple challenges our labour markets are faced with, it is important to differentiate between the new business models and the use of a terminology that reflects this differentiation. The problem is not only a confusion of the different methods used by the digital labour platforms, but also the fact that the language used to describe them is dominated by marketing terms. People in the field commonly speak of 'Turkers', 'HITs', 'awards', and the 'cloud' instead of independent contractors, jobs, payment, and someone else's data centre. However, it doesn't seem practical to avoid the neologisms entirely. In the following I rather organise the free-floating terminology in a mapping diagram in order to distinguish between cloudwork, crowdwork, and gigwork as the three most important categories of digital labour. In order to understand the shifting labour landscape and to take an active role in designing the future of work, it is necessary to look at these phenomena, not in isolation but in the context of other platform-based business models. It is also necessary to recognise them as just the latest digital stage in a long, on-going development towards more flexible, temporary, and tentative forms of labour with analogue predecessors in outsourcing companies and temporary employment agencies.

Commercial or Commons-based?

In order to categorise the vast number of digital platforms, the first distinction that has to be made is between commercial and non-profit, commons-based platforms. On platforms for commons-based peer production, collaboration is more important than competition and the fruits of labour are freely shared with everybody, including people outside the platform. Such many-to-many platforms are part of the commons and it is crucial to distinguish them from the majority of platforms in the so-called 'sharing economy' that are misleading and pretend to be about sharing, while actually being about rent extraction or wage labour. In contrast to commercial platforms, the roles and interests of platform providers and users are not strictly separated within commons-based peer production. Users who are engaged in commons-based peer production projects can gradually gain influence over the structure of their platform and have a say in the rules that coordinate the collaboration between the different stakeholders.[58] Platforms such as Wikipedia, OpenStreetMap, and CouchSurfing should therefore be politically protected and supported as an important alternative to commercial platforms. However, they are beyond the scope of this book.

Two questions are essential for the categorisation of digital labour platforms: are the services and tasks coordinated via the platform bound to a specific location? And are these services and tasks bound to a specific person? Both aspects have far-reaching implications for how the platforms operate, the situation of the independent contractors, the legal framework that applies, and potential regulatory measures. The taxonomy suggested here is as follows: if the task is not location-based and can be done remotely via the internet, it is regarded as cloudwork. If the task is not assigned to a specific individual but to an undefined group of people online, it is crowdwork. If the task is further subdivided into tiny units for piecemeal work, each paid for with an equally tiny amount of money, it is microtasking crowdwork. If in contrast the task cannot be subdivided but is solved in a redundant fashion, in parallel, by an entire crowd, while in the end only one result being used and paid for, it is contest-based crowdwork. However, when a task has to be undertaken at a specific location and time, by a specific person that is responsible for task, it is gigwork. These location-based services are further differentiated by the degree of personal involvement necessary and the degree of opportunities and risks they entail for the independent contractor. As a result, one arrives at the following six basic types of digital labour platforms.

Cloudwork (web-based digital labour)
(i)   freelance marketplaces
(ii) microtasking crowdwork
(iii) contest-based creative crowdwork

Gigwork (location-based digital labour)
(iv) accommodation
(v)   transportation and delivery services (gigwork)
(vi) household services and personal services (gigwork)

In practice, there are many hybrid platforms and further subcategories. The categorisation suggested here is as simple as possible and as differentiated as necessary.

---

58 See: Kelty (2008).

The order of the six platform types listed above roughly represents the historical succession in which they have emerged. Within the first three categories, a substantial market consolidation has already occurred and a lot of research has already been done. The last three categories are more recent and especially the last one is still being developed and, as yet, is not well understood. More research is needed, especially on the newer types of digital labour platforms and a more refined differentiation of the types that might become necessary in the future. All six categories pose political challenges with regard to issues such as privacy, data protection, labour laws, fair pay, and the mechanisms of 'algorithmic management' (the automated rating and tracking of independent contractors).

Three-sidedness and Power Asymmetry

Economists define the structures under discussion here as two-sided markets or multi-sided platforms.[59] This means that there are always at least two other parties between which the platform-provider functions as intermediary. Thus, in these systems there are always three groups of stakeholders. In order to emphasise this crucial aspect, I refer to them as three-sided platforms. The platform owners provide the infrastructure that mediates between supply and demand provided by the other two parties. When analysing a particular platform, one has to look closely at whether the platform provider facilitates the exchange between the other two stakeholders merely on a technical level – therefore serving as nothing more than a software company or infrastructure provider, as these companies often claim – or if they actually control the interaction between the other two parties, as is often the case with digital labour platforms. In the latter case, the question is whether these platforms effectively operate as temporary employment companies. This is relevant to the employment status of the workers and to the question of whether they might have been misclassified as independent contractors, while in fact being employees.

Typically, the software behind the commercial platforms runs in rented data centres ('the cloud') and has three sides of access. The users are divided into two opposing groups for supply and for demand, and both groups see different and very limited front-ends of the platform: small windows on the data and the processes of the system. The platform providers, however, have access to a back-end that gives them a comprehensive big-data overview of all the interactions between the two user groups, and they furthermore have the power to influence the exchange between the other two parties and potentially do this in real time. The platform providers control who sees what and when, what interactions between the other two are possible and under what conditions, and they wield this control technically,

59 Hagiu/Wright, 'Multi-Sided Platforms', *Harvard Business School Working Paper Series* (2015).

			Amazon.com
		tangible, for sale	eBay
			etsy
	goods	tangible, for rent	Airbnb*
			leihdirwas.de
		intangible, for sale	App-Store
			iTunes
		intangible, for rent	Spotify
			Netflix

			Upwork
		cloudwork (web-based)	Amazon MTurk
commercial digital platforms in general	services (digital labour)		99designs
			Uber
		gigwork (location-based)	Airbnb
			Helpling

			Indiegogo
	money	crowdfunding	Kickstarter
	communication	dating	Tinder
	entertainment	social media	Facebook
			YouTube
	information	news	Google News
		search	Google Search
		reviews	Yelp

11 Important factors across all platform types are the emergence of monopolies, network effects, biased terms of service, lack of transparency, permanent tracking and rating of user behaviour, and lack of data protection – all of which have problematic consequences for digital labour platforms in particular. (*Because of its many structural similarities Airbnb is treated here as part of gigwork, even though the role of labour is secondary on this particular platform.)

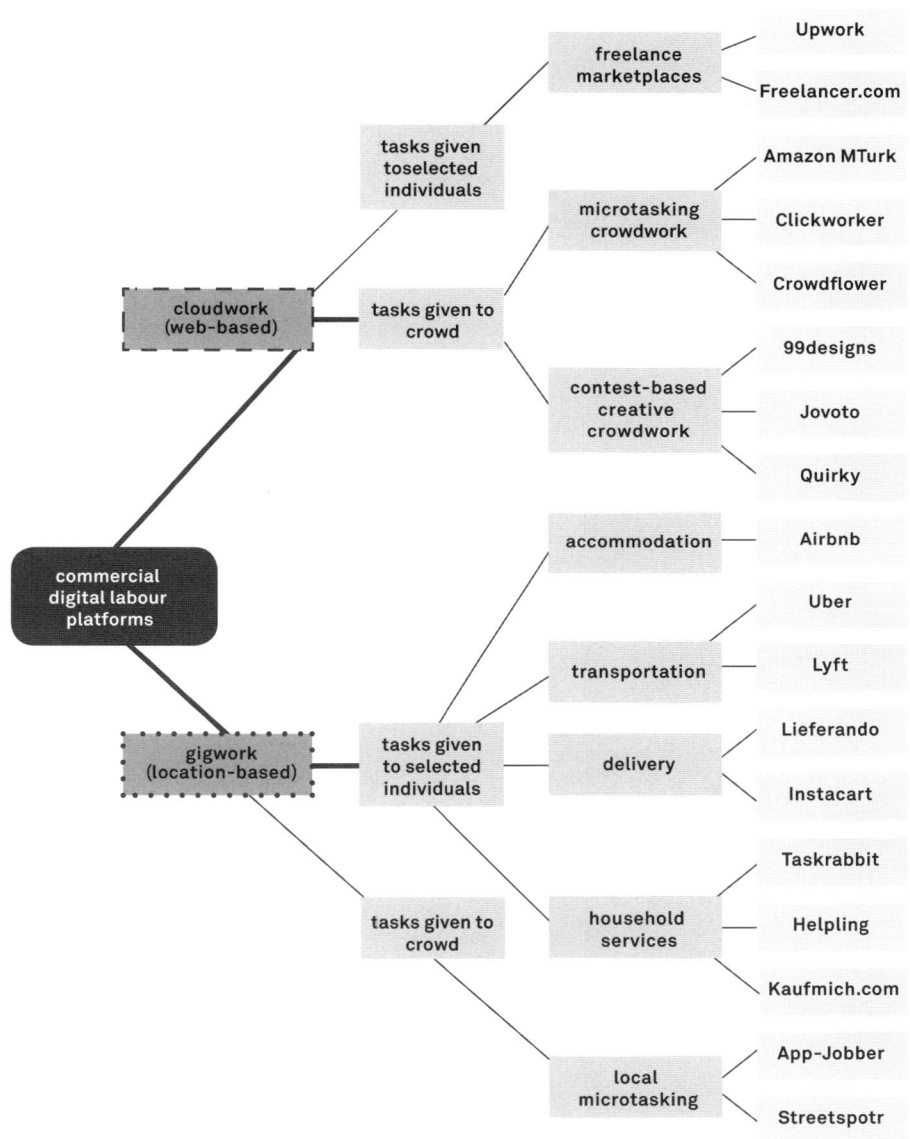

12 To differentiate between digital labour platforms one has to ask: Is the work bound to a specific place and is the work bound to a specific individual? If it can be done from everywhere, it is cloudwork. If it can be done by anyone and is given to an unspecific group, it is crowdwork. Freelance marketplaces are therefore cloudwork but not crowdwork. If the work has to be done at a specific location and is given to one selected individual, it is gigwork. Local microtasking is the only form of gigwork given to a crowd.

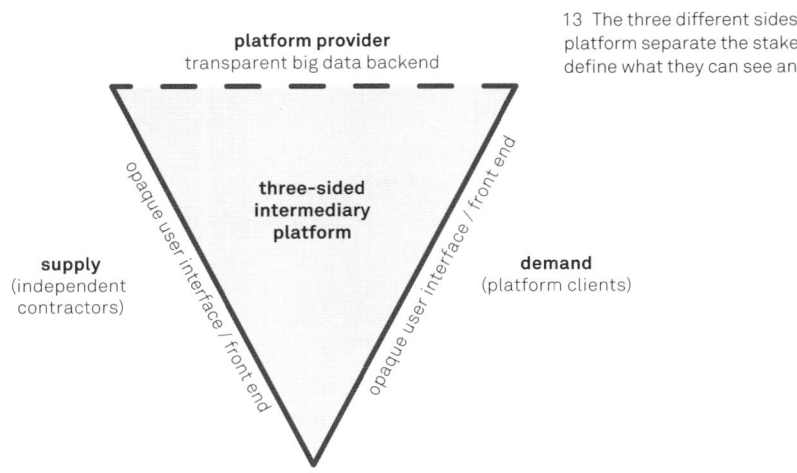

platform provider
transparent big data backend

three-sided
intermediary
platform

opaque user interface / front end

opaque user interface / front end

opaque user interface / front end

supply
(independent
contractors)

demand
(platform clients)

13 The three different sides to a digital platform separate the stakeholders and define what they can see and do.

legally, and via the design of the interface. Therefore, the typical platform is characterised by a systemic information and power asymmetry in favour of the platform providers. This structural imbalance in the architecture of the system could only be countered by decentralisation; a change that seems feasible for gigwork but much less so for cloudwork and crowdwork.

The three-sidedness is also important because it allows the platform-providers to shift entrepreneurial risks, legal liabilities, the cost of labour, and the means of production to the other two parties. The platform itself is an immaterial software product and as such it can potentially grow (or scale) exponentially without the providers having to spend proportionally more on staff or other costs of production (very low marginal costs). Depending on the area or industry in which the platform operates, it can often provide its service to one of the two user groups for free, as long as one group is willing to pay for the access to the other. This is the case, for example, with social networks and search engines.

Disruption, Economies of Scale, and the Rise of Monopolies

It holds true for most platforms that the more people participate, the more useful they become for all users. These so-called network effects foster the rise of monopolies, or at least oligopolies, because from the perspective of the users, it is advantageous to opt for just one search engine, one social network, one online retailer, and one online auction house. The result is a strong accumulation of power in the hands of only a small number of corporations.

The tendency towards power asymmetries and the emergence of oligopolies – rooted in network effects and the centralised, three-sided software architecture – is further enhanced by the role of venture capital. To attract investors, the platforms have to be 'disruptive', meaning that they have to break up an established business model or industry and funnel its profits into the platform economy; the platform also has to be able to 'scale' indefinitely. To achieve the exponential growth expected by the investors, the marginal costs of the product must be as low as possible, which in turn means that the product must be mainly virtual. This allows the platform providers to outsource the physical infrastructure and operate with a comparatively small staff. A few hundred employees are often enough to facilitate the business exchange between millions of users, taking a cut of typically 20 to 30 per cent from every transaction between them.

Platforms for the mediation of paid services (digital labour) that are web-based and not bound to a specific location (cloudwork) make their profit mainly from the labour of their independent contractors (even though these workers still have to pay for their computers and access the internet as means of production). Platforms for the mediation of location-based tasks and services (gigwork) – especially in the sectors of accommodation and transportation – integrate not only the labour of their independent contractors into their own value chain, but also their capital in the form of cars and homes. This is partly the reason why investments in gigwork platforms, as well as the valuations of these companies, are so much higher than in the crowdwork sector. Airbnb and Uber can challenge conventional companies in the hospitality and transportation industries, respectively, without having to own real estate for accommodation or a fleet of taxis, without having to pay for the maintenance of these capital goods, and without being liable for the safety of the guests, the drivers, or the service personnel. Only when seen from this perspective do the astronomical valuations, as of 2016, of Airbnb (US$ 25.5 billion) and Uber (US$ 62.5 billion) begin to make sense.

The huge amounts of venture capital that the platform companies have raised are often used to finance an aggressive growth strategy that entails buying competitors and selling one's service under value for a while, in order to reach a critical mass of users before anybody else. The goal is a market penetration with network effects strong enough to keep the users on the platform even when, in order to break even, the terms of service are eventually changed to the disadvantage of the users. Pertinent examples are the changing privacy settings on Facebook (affecting 1.8 billion users as of early 2017), or the changing rates for fares of Uber rides, which over time have become significantly less favourable for the drivers in order to benefit the platform.

Overreaching Terms of Service

While it is typically the case that centralised, multinational, venture capital–funded corporations control the back-end of a commercial digital platform, the two parties at the front-ends are compartmentalised, fragmented, and disorganised. Hence they have to negotiate from a position of weakness and this shows in the terms of service. The venture capital allows the platform providers, who are operating at an international level, to risk lawsuits at a national level – for example when being sued by workers, consumer advocates, or the government for violation of local labour laws and regulations (Uber is the best example here). The problem of overreaching terms of service occurs in all areas of the platform economy. They are sprawling in terms of the sheer amount of text (with 55,000 words, Airbnb's terms of service have almost the length of a novel), they are often strongly biased against the users, and they are supposed to apply to more and more areas of life. Contracts that formerly only applied to the relationship between a software product and its individual user now also apply to the interactions between the users, and to their private and business relationships. This continuous expansion of the terms of service becomes particularly problematic in the domain of digital labour platforms, where the software licencing contracts have effectively evolved into work contracts. In the case of cloudwork, the situation is further complicated by the fact that potentially all three parties of the platform triangle can – and often do – reside in different countries. The place of jurisdiction is usually the city in which the platform provider is registered, and the terms of service are usually written in an all-encompassing way that is supposed to be binding for millions of users across the globe. Obviously, this wholesale approach frequently collides with the national jurisdiction of the states in which the users reside.

Algorithmic Management through Ratings and Tracking

It is one of the fundamental principles of the platform economy that production itself is not undertaken by the platform provider, but by one of its two groups of users. To accomplish this, a lot of coordination is required from the platform provider, especially in order to sift through the flood of heterogeneous contributions on the supply side, and in order to orchestrate the interactions of the users. To keep the marginal costs of production close to zero and ensure that the platform can grow exponentially, it is imperative for the platform providers to automate as many of these processes as possible. With only a small number of employees, they could not possibly deal with the millions of users personally. It is at this point where the interplay between 'big data' and 'algorithmic management' is activated;[60] some

60 Lee et al., 'Working with Machines' (2015).

researchers also call this form of control 'algocracy'.[61] Algorithms now do jobs previously performed by middle managers, accountants, and customer service representatives. In the case of the digital labour platforms, even 'human resource management' is outsourced to the users – especially in crowdwork, where the individual workers self-assign to their jobs. If the results do not match the clients' expectations, the independent contractors are algorithmically rejected from future jobs, either entirely or from those above a certain threshold of quality or pay. This is achieved by blocking their account or by making certain jobs invisible to them at the front-end of the platform interface.

For many people, Amazon and eBay were the first places on the internet where they made business deals with strangers and afterwards publicly rated their satisfaction with their counterparty by awarding one to five stars. This method has become ubiquitous and is now also used for the management of the workforce on digital labour platforms. These ratings create trust between users who know nothing about each other. They also make qualitative judgements between humans quantitative and thus machine-readable. Amazon and the users of its online warehouse heavily rely on the detailed product reviews written (without compensation) by its users. But only by reducing these judgements to five-star-ratings can they be sorted effectively by the platform. And it is this method that has become the standard for evaluating the performance of crowdworkers and service personnel in the gig economy, too.

Ratings require the active participation of the users in an act of mutual evaluation that takes place after each completed interaction. *Tracking* in turn refers to the passive but continuous recording and evaluation of all user interactions, even very small ones. With its search engine, Google has shown how the tracking of user behaviour can be turned into a highly profitable business model. In a similar fashion, the detailed data that the platform providers continuously collect about the performance of their workforce – the knowledge about individual worker's thoroughness, industriousness, and error rate – becomes an important asset; part of the capital of the platform providers.

Thanks to smartphones, the *tracking* and *rating* of customers, service personnel and independent contractors can now occur on the spot, face to face, and in real time.[62] People assess each other's performance in the physical world immediately through actively rating the other.[63] Furthermore, the platform providers can expand the tracking of the individual worker's efficiency on the platform itself to tracking their movements in space. On digital labour platforms, the aggregated ratings of workers de facto become their employment reference, while the constant tracking of their performance can amount to a fully automated curriculum vitae – a personal

61 Aneesh, 'Global Labor: Algocratic Modes of Organization', *Sociological Theory* (2009).
    Danaher, 'The Threat of Algocracy', *Philosophy & Technology* (2016).
62 Dzieza, 'The Rating Game', *The Verge* (2015).
63 Reisinger, 'The Terrifying 'Yelp for People' App Is Now Available', Fortune (2016).

big-data sheet. This development creates a number of tricky questions regarding the fairness and accuracy of these evaluations and it challenges the right to informational self-determination. Who should be allowed to access these big-data résumés? And is it – from the workers' perspective – worth striving for the possibility of making the personal big-data sheets transferrable from one digital labour platform to another, in order not to lose their hard-earned reputation when jumping platforms? Or would that be disadvantageous, because it would create the pressure to fully reveal one's complete data set when looking for a new platform provider or employer, even if the data might contain unfair or faulty evaluations? On digital labour platforms such as Amazon Mechanical Turk it has been a known problem for years that there is no proper dispute resolution policy if workers think either man or machine has rated them unfairly. In order to ensure informational self-determination, workers would need a tool to monitor their big-data résumés and the heterogeneous digital labour platforms would have to agree on transferable standards or protocols, for example in the evaluation of reliability. The alternative would be to collect less data in the first place.

Gamification

As already outlined above 'gamification' is an important mechanism for the automated coordination of large groups of users, or workers, in the case of digital labour platforms. It has become a tool of algorithmic management that is made possible with data from ratings and tracking. It's a technique that allows platform providers to reward favourable user behaviour by awarding virtual credit points and by ranking the users' performance on public leaderboards. The awarded points often serve as a pseudo currency within the reputation economy of one platform, but they cannot be transferred to another. Gamification transforms wage labour into a game, in an often manipulative, behaviouristic manner. The basic principle is not new, analogue precursors of gamification include military medals or employee-of-the-month schemes. What is new is that, through rating and tracking on digital labour platforms, even the tiniest actions and utterances, down to the level of single mouse clicks, key strokes, and scrolling behaviour, can be monitored and influenced through gamification. In contemporary video games, such as Grand Theft Auto V, one can already get a glimpse of how this development could play out for the workplace and the résumés of the future. Menus list hundreds of categories with statistical data on how often, how long, how fast, and how accurate the player has solved specific tasks. Even the minutest actions are rewarded with 'awards' and 'achievements' and have their own leaderboards to compare the performance of different players. This type of data not only serves to motivate gamers or workers, respectively, but it is also a treasure trove of information for the digital labour platforms. What's more, the

Chinese Government in collaboration with the Chinese shopping platform Alibaba is currently launching a project that shows how serious and politically relevant the role of gamification is in the platform economy. Under the name 'Sesame Credit', it has introduced a public, individual 'citizen score', based on factors such as shopping behaviour, credit history, and social circles of individual citizens, in order to reward political obedience and publically shame potential deviants. From 2020 onwards, China plans to make participation in the scheme mandatory for its citizens.[64]

Flexibilisation and Atomisation of Labour

The most important promise that digital labour platforms make to their workforce, as well as to their clients is flexibility. Independent contractors are available 'on-demand' as a 'contingent workforce'; they are hired for specific tasks only and are dismissed as soon as the job is complete.[65] In return, the independent contractors can work whenever, however, for whomever, and as much or little as they want, as long as there are enough suitable tasks available and there are not too many competitors trying to do the same jobs. The entry barriers for cloudwork, crowdwork, and gigwork are extremely low, so that even marginalised groups can potentially find work immediately; the only prerequisites are that they accept the terms of service and have a fast and stable internet connection. This is a huge opportunity for people outside conventional career paths, without certain qualifications, with little education or work experience; but also for people who cannot hold a full-time job because of personal health issues or because they have to take care of a family member; and, in the case of cloudwork, also for people who either live in regions without jobs, or choose to work as 'digital nomads' from abroad while travelling. There were (Txteagle) and are (Samasource) even attempts to hire people in refugee camps in the Global South as translators, who are asked to translate texts line by line via text messages on mobile phones.

Digital labour's enormous flexibility is partly enabled by the Tayloristic breakdown of what were once occupations into their smallest possible components. Jobs become projects, then gigs and tasks, and eventually microtasks. The units of time and payment are broken down into seconds and cents and the independent contractors switch from one client to another with ever-higher frequency. The fine granularity of tasks causes both groups to be willing to take more risks with regard

---

64 Hatton, 'China 'social credit': Beijing sets up huge system', BBC News (2015).
65 In the words of Lukas Biewald, CEO of CrowdFlower: 'Before the Internet, it would be really difficult to find someone, sit them down for ten minutes and get them to work for you, and then fire them after those ten minutes. But with technology, you can actually find them, pay them the tiny amount of money, and then get rid of them when you don't need them anymore.' Cited after: Marvit, 'How Crowdworkers Became the Ghosts in the Digital Machine', *The Nation* (2014).

to the likelihood of getting paid and the quality of the results respectively, because when one microtask in a succession of microtasks goes wrong for either side, the damage that such an individual incident can cause is negligible. The aggrieved party has merely lost a tiny amount of money or time. In the aggregate, however, these losses become a problem, especially when the uncertainty of getting paid for work already done becomes the new norm. The tiny values in dispute also have the effect that workers on digital labour platforms are usually unwilling to go to court to sue the other party for compensation (or the platform providers for their legally questionable terms of service, or for the misclassification of workers as independent contractors).

The question is, how established standards of labour law and social security can be sustained if what constitutes a job is divided into ever smaller tasks with uncertain pay? What is the legal status of people working under these conditions? Almost all platforms for digital labour state in their terms of service that the workers are independent contractors, as well as that, because they are 'self-employed', it is also their responsibility to take care of all social security contributions. But is that a realistic description of those cases in which, although the clients might change from minute to minute, the independent contractors work continuously for the same platform provider, which in turn exerts strong influence over how exactly the work must be done and what is paid for it? Here the question is whether the independent contractors are in fact misclassified employees of the platform. So far there have been a number of class action lawsuits, mainly in the United States, in which crowdworkers and gigworkers have sued their platform providers in order to retroactively demand the minimum wage they would have been entitled to as regular employees. In the context of crowdwork, there was a prominent lawsuit against CrowdFlower and, in the context of gigwork, against Uber.[66] For the platform providers these class action lawsuits pose an imminent threat to their business model, but to-date they have been able to resolve them through multi-million dollar settlements. That also means that the legal situation remains unresolved.

Cloudwork on Freelance Marketplaces

Freelance marketplaces (sometimes also referred to as online outsourcing, outsourcing marketplaces, or the online staffing industry) transfer the principle of outsourcing from the level of companies to that of individuals. Clients can find independent contractors abroad via these platforms and the latter can in turn bid for the advertised jobs. In principle, all three parties in the platform triangle can be based

---

66 Cherry, 'Beyond Misclassification' (2016). Seiner, 'Tailoring Class Actions to the On-Demand Economy' (2017).

in different countries across the world, which as mentioned earlier, is a tricky complication with regard to the applicable legal jurisdiction.

Upwork, one of the largest platform providers in this area, explicitly advertises its service within the framework of the lifestyle choice of becoming a 'digital nomad', a creative, well-educated online worker travelling the world, able to earn money at the beach or from the pool side. All it takes is a laptop and a fast internet connection, 'work is no longer a place' and 'every day is an exiting new adventure'.[67] This type of digital labour platform always falls into the category of cloudwork, but it is typically not crowdwork.[68] The important difference is that on the freelance marketplaces clients handpick independent contractors based on their skills; the payment is negotiated individually; and only one person eventually does the job. Freelance marketplaces have millions of independent contractors as users, huge revenues, and have been in existence for over a decade: eLance was founded as early as 1999, oDesk in 2003, and Freelancer.com in 2009. In 2013, the former two merged into eLance-oDesk, and since 2015 they have traded under the name 'Upwork'. The Silicon Valley–based company now claims to have nine million registered freelancers, four million clients, and a turnover of US$ 1 billion per year. After merging with several smaller providers, Freelancer.com, Upwork's biggest competitor, now claims to have twenty million registered workers, who so far have finished nine million jobs (which also means that the majority of registered contractors have never been assigned a job via the platform). It must be noted that the user numbers published by platform providers are generally not very reliable; the platforms typically publicise only the total number of people who have ever registered in order to appear larger than their competitors. The number of active users is always much smaller and follows a 'long tail' or Pareto distribution – only a small number of 'power-users' (between one and ten per cent) accomplishes the majority of all jobs on the platform. Most users who create an account are only active sporadically or not at all. In order to evaluate the size of a platform, revenue figures or the number of finished jobs are much more significant.

The types of jobs mediated via freelance marketplaces are very heterogeneous, but in contrast to microtasking (which will be discussed in detail in the next section) the tasks are relatively complex, demanding, specialised, technical, and are often relatively well paid. In 2013 oDesk published a graph that showed the distribution of job types on offer.[69] Search engine optimisation (SEO) was in the lead, followed by jobs in software and web development; but also jobs in marketing, design, writing, legal services, and engineering were featured in the spectrum.

For mediating between supply and demand, freelance marketplaces typically charge a fee of ten to twenty per cent from the independent contractors. For clients the service is often free. Even though the available data on the subject is limited, it

67 See: (upwork.com/blog/category/digital-nomads) and: oDesk promotional video: 'Digital Nomads: Goodbye Commute, Hello World' (2014), available on YouTube.
68 Although some freelance marketplaces also offer crowdwork as an alternative mode to outsource work.
69 See: https://content-static.upwork.com/blog/uploads/sites/4/2013/08/LongtailSkillsChart.jpg.

seems that the freelancers on these platforms are comparatively satisfied.[70] In contrast to the neighbouring fields of crowdwork and gigwork, there is no larger debate around the potential exploitation of workers in this area of the platform economy. It seems that there has been little demand for political regulation so far. However, there are two critical aspects in the functionality of freelance marketplaces that are of great relevance for all digital labour platforms.

First, on these outsourcing sites individual contractors have to compete with each other globally, and through the practice of bidding there is the danger of entering a race to the bottom for common tasks. How cheaply one can offer a service depends partly on one's cost of living but more importantly on one's degree of specialisation. The more specialised a skill is, the less it is in danger of a deterioration in prices caused by global competition. For freelancers in the Global North, it will be less and less profitable to offer services that can be done just as well via the internet by people from the Global South. This development also affects skilful but routine tasks, such as the analysis of medical X-ray imagery.

Secondly, the freelance marketplaces are characterised by a relatively high level of surveillance. Upwork, for example, uses a software application called 'Work Diary' to allow clients to virtually look over the shoulders of their independent contractors. In the words of oDesk: 'This handy-dandy tool captures work-in-progress snapshots of your freelancer's screen.'[71] Six times per hour and at random intervals, the software takes a screenshots of the freelancers' computer. In this way the client can ensure that the contractors stay on task, instead of, say, checking in on Facebook while being on the clock. Furthermore, the Work Diary also tracks the number of mouse clicks and keystrokes and even makes webcam photos of the independent contractors – who can, however, refuse clients the permission to use this feature.[72] In addition, Upwork states in its terms of service: 'We will share information contained in Work Diaries with the relevant client and with any manager or administrator of any applicable Freelancer Agency.' It is made clear that as a freelancer, one has little control over the data gathered on one's work behaviour. The extraordinary degree of freedom on digital labour platforms such as Upwork is accompanied by an extraordinary degree of control. Interestingly, industrious workers often welcome this form of surveillance, because it allows them to demonstrate their reliability and therefore justifies their comparatively high hourly rates. People who decide to work under these conditions agree to an ambivalent trade-off. They are free to work from any place they want but must endure being constantly monitored.[73]

---

70 Leimeister et al. 'Crowd Work im Netz' (2016).
71 (odesk.com/info/howitworks/client).
72 See: https://www.upwork.com/legal/privacy/#work-diaries.
73 For a conversation about the monitoring among Upwork workers see: (https://community.upwork.com/t5/Freelancers/Disabling-screenshots/td-p/119616) accessed January 2017. For the surveillance of the workers, the platform won the critical 'Big Brother Award by the German data protection activists Digitalcourage in 2015 (bigbrotherawards.de/2015).

THE COGNITIVE PIECEWORK OF
THE MECHANICAL TURK

[Mechanical Turk] gives us a snapshot of a depressing future in which legions of click-slaves toil away at identifying duplicate Web pages for less than minimum wage. Amazon says it hit on the idea for Mechanical Turk when it realized that there were some tasks that even the smartest computers couldn't perform. I've got an alternate theory: Maybe the computers just didn't want to.[74]
Jeff Howe, 2006

In the eighteenth century, the Hungarian nobleman Wolfgang von Kempelen toured from court to court across Europe to baffle aristocratic audiences with a miraculous machine – the Mechanical Turk – which is said to have earned him a small fortune. 'Der Schachtürke', as it is called in German, appeared to be a chess-playing automaton in the guise of an oriental-looking wooden robot, residing over a cabinet full of cogs, wearing a turban and smoking a pipe. 'The Turk' was an extraordinary chess player who won nearly every match and was even able to checkmate the likes of Edgar Allan Poe, Charles Babbage, and Napoleon Bonaparte. As part of his performance, Kempelen opened the various doors of the cabinet to show the audience that there was nothing but machinery inside. How the machine worked remained a well-kept secret. The original Turk was eventually destroyed in a fire, and not until years later was it revealed that Kempelen had relied on a small human chess master hidden inside the machine, operating the Turk through an intricate system of levers.

In 2005, Amazon decided that this story would make a great metaphor for a new service machine it was building. The online warehouse has to manage a database with millions of products, and being a platform-based business model, the product descriptions and photos come from countless external retailers. Amazon has to constantly detect and merge duplicate entries of products. Computers are not very good at this because it requires, for example, advanced image recognition capabilities to understand whether a product on two differently taken photos is actually the same. The company had already had good experience with letting its working customers create product reviews and so it created a mechanism for outsourcing these small, repetitive data processing tasks as well. What makes things interesting is that Amazon then built a platform to allow its business clients to access this new external workforce as well; it created an API, an application programming interface, through which the clients can assign tasks to the crowd directly, in return for a fee payable to Amazon. It advertised this new service as '*artificial* artificial intelligence'.

---

74 Howe, 'Crowdsourcing: Taking Measure of Mechanical Turk', Crowdsourcing.com blog (2006).

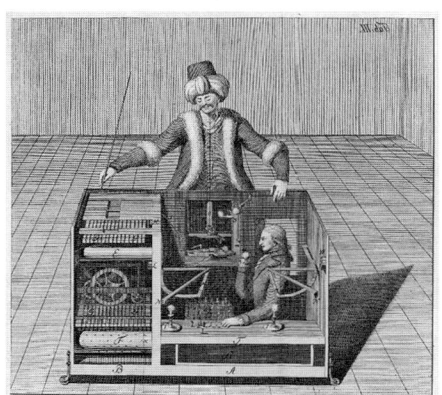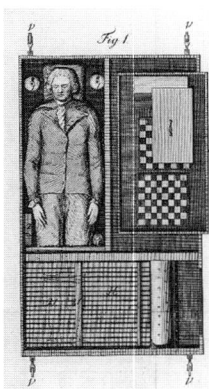

14 The Mechanical Turk, invented by Wolfgang von Kempelen in 1770, depicted here in two copperplate prints from 1789 by Joseph Friedrich Freiherr zu Racknitz, who reverse-engineered the original machine to reveal that it was a hoax.[76]

In doing so, Amazon applied an old trick, known in the field of Human Computer Interaction (HCI) as the Wizard-of-Oz technique. It is a prototyping method in which humans 'impersonate' parts of the operating system that the prototype itself cannot yet perform.[76] Design researcher Nigel Cross already described the basic idea of such 'human-behind-the-scene' prototypes in 1977. In order to be more flexible in the design process and to save costs, he suggested devising 'a suitable simulation of a computer-aided design system':

All that the user perceives of the system is this remote-access console, and the remainder is a black box to him.

[...] one may as well fill the black box with people as with machinery. Doing so provides a comparatively cheap simulator, with the remarkable advantages of the human operator's flexibility, memory, and intelligence, and which can be reprogrammed to give a wide range of computer roles merely by changing the rules of operation. It sometimes lacks the real computer's speed and accuracy, but a team of experts working simultaneously can compensate to a sufficient degree to provide an acceptable simulation.[77]

The novelty was that Amazon transformed the prototyping technique into the real product. Now the *black box* was permanently filled with people, crowds of them. To be able to provide the necessary speed and accuracy, these humans were treated just like processors in a system of distributed computing. In contrast to Luis von Ahn's

75 Racknitz, Über den Schachspieler des Herrn von Kempelen und dessen Nachbildung (1789).
76 Green/Wei-Haas, *The Wizard of Oz: A Tool for Rapid Development of User Interfaces* (1985).
77 Cross, *The Automated Architect* (1977): p. 107.

concepts of 'games with a purpose', where fun is the key incentive, and reCAPTCHA, which is based on *indirect crowdwork*, Amazon offered the crowdworkers in the black box tiny amounts of money for every task solved. (Arguably because these tasks are so dull that people wouldn't do them for free, as they did with writing book reviews). The Mechanical Turk (MTurk) became part of Amazon Web Services, a portfolio of various on-demand, scalable, 'cloud-based', data storage and processing services – virtual infrastructure rented out to developers. In addition to software-as-a-service, Amazon could now also offer 'humans-as-a-service'. From the company's perspective, an on-demand cloud-labour service seemed like the logical next step. From the perspective of internet users wanting to earn something on this side, this represented access to a new labour market with very low entry-barriers. Finally, from the perspective of Amazons business clients, this meant access to a completely unregulated workforce.

Amazon's MTurk is not the only platform for paid microtasking crowdwork. And with about 500,000 workers it is not even the largest. There is also the platform microWorkers from Dallas, with 850,000 workers, Clickworker from Essen, with 800,000 workers, and meta-platforms like CrowdFlower that are even larger and used to partly build on MTurk. I will focus my observations here on MTurk as it is the most prominent, prototypical, and best researched example of microtasking crowdwork.

When entering the Mechanical Turk, visitors are confronted with a crossroads typical for digital labour platforms: they can either 'make money' or 'get results', depending on whether they want to be an employer (a 'requester' in Amazon's parlance) or a worker (called a 'provider' or 'contractor' on the platform). The language is important here because in most countries employees would be entitled to various benefits such as minimum wage. New crowdworkers must agree that they are 'independent contractors', freelancers not under the protection of conventional labour laws.[78]

Curiously, almost twelve years after the launch of MTurk, the platform still claims to be in 'beta' mode.[79] Yet, it has become the workplace for half a million people from 190 nations who refer to themselves as 'Turkers'. In times of highly advanced web-services with user-friendly intuitive interfaces, the design of MTurk seems like a relic of a prehistoric time of the web. If Amazon.com is the inviting front of a huge department store, MTurk is its shabby delivery entrance, located in a dark alley behind the warehouse. The platform does not only feel user-unfriendly – its surface is indicative of its deeper structure: It is a machine within which the

---

78 In 2013, CrowdFlower, which built its service partly on top of MTurk, had to fend off a class-action lawsuit by crowdworkers in the US suing for misclassification, based on the Fair Labor Standards Act (FLSA), which entitles employees to minimum wage. CrowdFlower prevented a ruling by paying a settlement. Since 2014, CrowdFlower is not using MTurk anymore. Schmidt, 'For a Few Dollars More – Class Action Against Crowdsourcing' (2013). Cherry, 'Beyond *Missclassification' Comparative Labor Law & Policy Journal* (2016).

79 As of January 2017, the word 'beta' is still included in the MTurk logo.

people working have to adapt, not vice versa. The platform can do without even a veneer of human-centred design, it doesn't want to look attractive but instead tries to blend into the background as just a piece of technical infrastructure of the web.[80] The workers don't have names but numeric IDs and the employers hide behind pseudonyms. Amazon is keen to emphasise its status as a 'neutral' platform provider that just creates and maintains the infrastructure for a marketplace and can therefore not be held responsible for the relationships between the buyers and sellers of labour – neither legally not with regard to providing proper services in the form of employees from Amazon. There is no accessible service team and employers and workers are left to their own devices.

The lack of support is most likely a strategy of Amazon to avoid class-action lawsuits for the misclassification of workers – as experienced by competitors like CrowdFlower who provided more service, but of course it also saves a lot of money to run this labour market practically automatically. And yet, the platform is not at all neutral – it clearly favours one class of 'users', the employers, over the other class of 'users', the workers. In its Terms of Use, Amazon explicitly gives employers the right to reject work without having to give the workers any reason. If a HIT done by a worker gets rejected, she or he will not get paid and will get a lower approval rate. In such a case the employer still has the right to use the results of the rejected work; critics call this an invitation to wage theft.[81] The power to reject work without explanation is a function meant to sanction fraudulent, sloppy, or incompetent workers, who are either not willing or not able to deliver good results. Since the workers are anonymous to the employer, they might indeed be tempted to aim for speed rather than quality. So there needs to be some form of protection for the latter not to fall prey to a crowd of scammers and dabblers.

Through the workers' qualification level and country of origin, employers can exclude certain groups of workers based on demographics (and individuals through their ID number after they have done a job). Amazon advises the employers: 'If you don't want to use Workers who just registered this morning and have no work history, we recommend that you require Workers to have a 95% Approval Rate and 1,000 Approved Assignments to work on your project.' Since 2011, the better paying jobs can usually be done only by MTurk 'Masters' who have already provided a lot of work with a high HIT-approval-rate. If their approval rate is too low, the interface hides the better-paid tasks from them.

The workers can choose from a list of a few hundred thousand 'human intelligence tasks' or HITs: recognising, describing, or tagging content in images to make them digitally searchable, transcribing video or audio recordings, categorising

---

80 Irani/Silberman, 'Turkopticon: Interrupting Worker Invisibility in Amazon Mechanical Turk', *CHI '13* (2013): pp. 611–20.
81 Irani/Silberman, 'From Critical Design to Critical Infrastructure' (2014): p. 33. Irani, 'Difference and Dependence among Digital Workers' (2015): p. 227.

15 The crossroads users
are confronted with
on the landing-page of
Amazon Mechanical
Turk (2017).

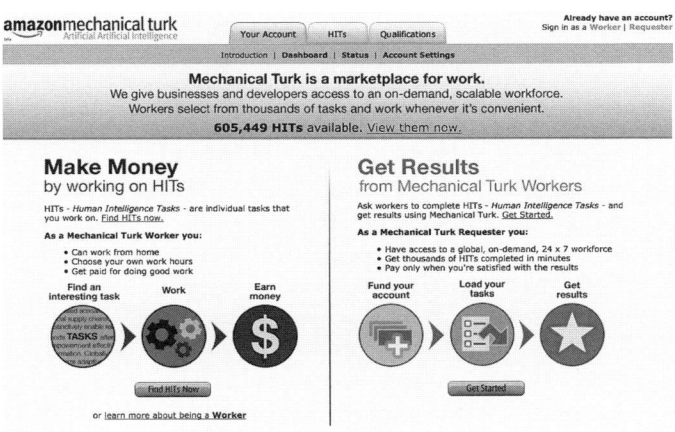

content, moderating user-generated content, filtering out pornography, finding addresses of people or checking them for their validity, cleaning up databases, translating texts, writing copy, or filling out scientific surveys.[82] What unites the huge variety of tasks is that they are broken down into tiny bits, paid for with tiny amounts of money, and later aggregated to become more than the sum of the parts. The briefs for the requests are written on a strict 'need to know basis'. Usually, the workers don't learn anything about the employer, the context of the job, or what they might contribute to on a larger scale.

A typical task reads like this: 'You are shown a set of images and you must determine which ones contain a naked vagina.' Fifteen minutes are allotted for this specific task by the requester 'mirador-tech', who pays $ 0.04 for each completed set of images.[83] On one of the external MTurk worker forums, someone who had done this task wrote that one set contains about 50 images. The worker willing to click through all available 3,409 sets of images could earn about $ 136 ... for looking at probably 170,000 images of nudity of various degrees. The task of separating nudity from legal pornography and from child pornography, as well as fictional violence from the depiction of real violent crimes is a psychologically very burdensome and damaging task that can't be properly done by computers. This type of work is not only outsourced via MTurk, but also to companies specialised on such 'moderation' of user-generated content. A lot of this work is done in the Philippines, and according to journalist

82 For many academic researchers MTurk has become a crucial resource to conduct surveys and psychological studies across the globe easily; this has lead to concerns that universities are taking advantage of the underpaid workers and treat them as ‚lab rats'. See: 'Experimental Psychology: The Roar of the Crowd', *The Economist* (2012). Workers now offer guidelines for researchers: 'Guidelines for Academic Requesters', Dynamo, (2014).
83 The company Mirandor Technologies was using the Turkers to train an algorithm to detect nudity for real-time content moderation.

16 Two screenshots of typical 'HIT' descriptions on Mechanical Turk from 2014.

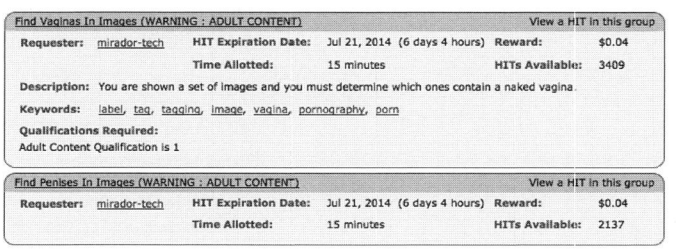

Adrian Chen, the workers often suffer from post-traumatic stress syndrome after being continuously exposed to gruesome pictures.[84]

Most tasks are more boring than shocking. Between 2011 and 2014 one of the largest employers on MTurk was LinkedIn, hiding behind the pseudonym 'Oscar Smith'. Via a smartphone-app called CardMunch, LinkedIn users uploaded photos of business cards and got them transcribed seemingly automatically, while in fact crowdworkers transcribed them manually – between 45,000 and 50,000 per day, millions all together.[85] LinkedIn provided the service to its users for free; the crowdworkers were paid $0.02 per card. It took on average a minute to do the task, depending on the worker, amounting to an average hourly wage of about $1.20.[86] Since 2014, these 'HITs' are discontinued, partly because the algorithmic text recognition (OCR) has significantly improved over the years.

84 Chen, 'The Laborers Who Keep Dick Pics and Beheadings Out of Your Facebook Feed', *Wired* (2014). For the technological struggle to algorithmically detect 'assholes and other undesirable body parts' see: Steyerl, 'Proxy Politics: Signal and Noise', *e-flux* (2014).
85 'LinkedIn Scales Business Card Transcription with Mechanical Turk', *The Mechanical Turk Blog* (2013). Lunden, 'LinkedIn Gives Up The Ghost On CardMunch', *TechCrunch* (2014).
86 In 2013, LinkedIn had a revenue of about 1.5 billion US dollars.

MICRO-TASK MANAGEMENT

In many respects, the division of labour on MTurk is reminiscent of the efficient design of a pin factory as Adam Smith described it in 1776, and especially of Frederick Taylor's *Principles of Scientific Management,* published in 1911.[87] The mechanical engineer and management consultant developed a set of methods that increased the efficiency of workers tremendously by breaking large tasks into the smallest possible 'microtasks' and by letting the workers do the same task repetitively ad infinitum – a technique that later became infamous as 'Taylorism'. The management defined the ideal pace of the workload, based on scientific studies and, in the case of the conveyor belt, the machine enforced it.[88]

The work of every workman is fully planned out by the management [...] and each man receives in most cases complete written instructions, describing in detail the task which he is to accomplish, as well as the means to be used in doing the work. [...] This task specifies not only what is to be done but how it is to be done and the exact time allowed for doing it. And whenever the workman succeeds in doing his task right, and within the time limit specified, he receives an addition of from 30 per cent, to 100 per cent, to his ordinary wages.[89]

In addition to the brief, each worker received a second sheet of paper each day, giving him quantified feedback on how well he or she achieved the previous tasks and how high his or her bonus was. When the sheet was yellow, even an analphabetic worker knew immediately that he or she had failed.

For Taylor, the biggest problem of his age was that the interests of the workers and the employers were seen as antagonistic, leading workers to deliberately slack off on the job to evade the increasing pressure. He saw 'natural laziness' as a problem, but the 'greatest evil' for him was 'systematic soldiering', the collective and intentional slowing down of the workforce. Taylor's goal was to eliminate this behaviour by measuring precisely how small a task would have to be to enable the worker to work continuously without getting exhausted while also rewarding him with higher wages for the increased effort and efficiency.

The principal object of management should be to secure the maximum prosperity for the employer, coupled with the maximum prosperity for each employé. [...] prosperity for the employer cannot exist through a long term of years unless it is accompanied by prosperity

---

87   Smith, *An Inquiry into the Nature and Causes of the Wealth of Nations* (1776). Taylor, *The Principles of Scientific Management* (1911).

88   The assembly line was introduced by car manufacturer Ransom Olds in 1901 and then significantly improved by Henry Ford with the introduction of the conveyor belt in 1913.

89   *Ibid.* p. 39.

for the employé, and vice versa; and that it is possible to give the work-man what he most wants – high wages – and the employer what he wants – a low labor cost – for his manufactures.[90]

Taylor had ample data to support his claim that task management based on the scientific quantification and optimisation of all movements would be so much more profitable that both parties could benefit from it financially. He also believed that not all workers were fit for this type of microtasking, that they should be chosen and trained by management, and that their capabilities would grow within the company, making them less replaceable. Something that in today's management jargon would probably be called 'an investment in human capital'. To align the interests of employers and employees and to distribute the gains from more efficient methods is the crucial challenge in the new world of digital labour – so far they do indeed seem antagonistic and the workers have a very weak negotiating position.

Today, Taylor's method of constant quantification and feedback loops has gained new relevance, now that every mouse-click of an online worker can easily be tracked, aggregated, and algorithmically analysed. Interestingly, in stark contrast to current gamification tendencies, Taylor also said that: 'It is a matter of ordinary common sense to plan working hours so that the workers can really "work while they work" and "play while they play," and not mix the two.'[91] The problem with piecemeal task work in general is that it deskills the workers, who in turn become exchangeable and therefore have very little negotiating power regarding their working conditions. They also become alienated from their work by losing any connection to the thing they are producing a tiny part of.

One matter that makes things more complicated today is that there is now a third party, the platform provider, who has become increasingly influential and also wants a share of the benefits. Furthermore, in contrast to what Taylor had in mind, the workers don't enjoy the legal protections of employees anymore. They are contract workers spread across the globe, they self select the tasks and are not bound to a specific factory anymore, where they could congregate as a physical crowd and for example block the factory entrance with picket lines. They have become *free to* choose what they want to work on and for how long, but they are also *free from* any protection by the company or by labour laws. By becoming a virtual crowd, the workforce has become more contingent than ever, because the employer doesn't invest in the abilities of individual workers anymore and they can easily be replaced not only by other workers in the vicinity of the factory but by anyone with a computer and a reasonably fast internet connection. As Taylor wrote in 1911: 'A great deal has been [...] said about "sweat-shop" work and conditions. The writer has great sympathy with those who are overworked, but on the whole a greater sympathy for those

90 *Ibid.* p. 9.
91 *Ibid.* p. 87.

who are *under paid*.'[92] More than a hundred years later, we are still discussing what constitutes a sweatshop and what should be a fair payment for piecework. MTurk has not only been called a virtual assembly line, but is also frequently described as a sweatshop, though one without a physical location – a sweatshop 'in the cloud'.[93]

In 2010, Michael S. Bernstein, an influential human-computer-interaction (HCI) researcher and crowdwork pioneer published a report about a special crowd-sourcing tool he and his colleagues had developed and tested: 'Soylent: A Word Processor with a Crowd Inside'.[94] The tool was designed as a plug-in for Microsoft Word that connected to the 'human API' of MTurk and added yet another layer in the process of hiding the workforce in the machine. The idea was to enable one class of users to outsource tasks such as the shortening of paragraphs, spell checking, and the formatting of citations to another class of users, the crowd, without having to leave the interface of the word processor or personally interact with the other humans doing the minor tasks. The crowdworkers were embedded as a feature into the interface. The name of the prototype was derived from the dystopian science fiction film *Soylent Green* from 1973, in which the protagonist tries to survive in an overcrowded and impoverished world. At the end of the film, the hero finds out that Soylent Green, the nurturing snack everybody eats, is actually made out of humans. It is hard to tell whether Bernstein's choice of name is an expression of cynicism or just distasteful nerd humour, but it definitely brings across the core idea. The user is buying a packaged product and is supposed to forget that there is not just 'Intel Inside', but humans.

As for all designers of crowd-powered systems under scientific management, quality control is a big issue for Bernstein and his colleagues. Under the sub-heading 'programming the crowd', they write that in their experiments, about thirty per cent of the results provided by the crowd were poor, an error rate unacceptable for the end user. In search for the 'nature of unsatisfactory responses' the authors identify two problematic groups within the workforce:

We might characterize two useful personas at the ends of the effort spectrum, the *Lazy Turker* and the *Eager Beaver*. The *Lazy Turker* does as little work as necessary to get paid. [...] *Eager Beavers* go beyond the task requirements in order to be helpful, but create further work for the user in the process. For example, when asked to reword a phrase, one *Eager Beaver* provided a litany of options [...]. Without clear guidelines, the *Lazy Turker* will choose the path that produces any signal and the *Eager Beaver* will produce too many signals.[95]

---

92 *Ibid*. p. 17.
93 Cushing, 'Amazon Mechanical Turk: The Digital Sweatshop', *Utne Reader* (2013). Uddin, 'The Dystopian Digital Sweatshop That Makes the Internet Run', *AlterNet* (2012).
94 Bernstein et al., 'Soylent: A Word Processor with a Crowd Inside' (2010).
95 *Ibid*. p. 4.

Again, the language is remarkable, not only with regard to what the workers are called.[96] From the perspective of the system designer, the results of the workers are merely signals (and noise) emitted from the machine. Problems like these are typical in human computation. They emerge because the time of the person in front of the interface is so much more valuable than that of the people hidden inside the machine. Therefore interpersonal communication between employer and employee is to be avoided, which in turn leads to misunderstandings and bad results. For the same reasons, conflicts caused by this then have to be resolved algorithmically too, which leads to even more grievances among the workers. 'Eager Beavers' don't understand why their results are rejected, their payment withheld, and their approval rate lowered – with grave consequences for the chances to get good jobs on the platform in the future. But they have nobody to appeal to because everything is automated. Bernstein et al. conclude their 'vision of interface outsourcing' from 2010 with the suggestion that 'it may be possible to transition from an era where Wizard of Oz techniques were used only as prototyping tools to an era where a "Wizard of Turk" can be permanently wired into a system.'[97] Yet, the wizardry looses its power as workers can contact the end-user to complain about unfair treatment.

Soylent remained a prototype and only three years later, in 2013, Bernstein, together with a number of other high profile crowdsourcing engineers, co-authored an influential and extensive paper titled 'The Future of Crowd Work'.[98] In this roadmap for future crowd research, the authors ask the crucial ethical question: 'Can we foresee a future crowd workplace in which we would want our children to participate?' Obviously a fundamental shift in perspective had taken place, from being primarily concerned with the efficiency of the system and the convenience of the better-off class of end-users in front of the interface to being concerned with the life of the people hidden behind it.

This leads to the question: who are the crowdworkers, why do they put up with these work conditions in the first place, and what can be done to improve their situation? The US-American computer scientist Panagiotis Ipeirotis has been tracking the demographics of MTurk for many years and since 2015 he has been providing daily updates to this data (gathered by asking workers about their background in the form of a paid microtasks) on a special website.[99] The proportions of nationalities fluctuates with the time zones, but in 2015 'approximately 80% of the Mechanical Turk workers are from the US and 20% are from India'; the gender participation is balanced; 'roughly 50% of the workers are born in the 1980s and are

---

96 To German ears, Lazy Turkers sounds very offensive, given Germany's history with Turkish working-class immigrants (Gastarbeiter).
97 *Ibid*. p. 9.
98 Kittur et al. 'The Future of Crowd Work' (2013).
99 Ipeirotis, 'Demographics of Mechanical Turk', (2010); and Ipeirotis,'Analyzing the Amazon Mechanical Turk Marketplace', *XRDS*, 17 (2010): 16–21. For the constant tracking of the demographics see Ipeirotis: demographics.mturk-tracker.com.

around 30 years old. Approximately 20% of the workers are born in the 1990s, and another 20% are born in the 1970s; The median household income is around US$ 50,000 per year for US Turkers, which is on par with the median US household income. Indian workers have considerably lower household income, with most of them being around US$ 10,000 per year.'[100]

Workers from outside the US and India had been disadvantaged for a long time because they are not paid in cash but in Amazon vouchers (which means that Amazon profits a second time when they redeemed their wage vouchers to shop at the company store). Between 2012 and 2016, Amazon did not accept any new international workers.[101] The number of international workers seems to increase since that time; according to Ipeirotis' MTurk tracker, seven to ten per cent of the workforce in 2016 came from countries other than India and the US.

The main reasons for people becoming a microtasking crowdworker are the following: they can work from their home, even if they live in a remote area, without having to commute. They can work as much or as little as they want, in short intervals and at odd hours, some even do the tasks as a diversion or while watching TV. More importantly, the work can be done while taking care of children or the elderly at home, it can thus be used as a secondary income to complement traditionally female, unwaged housework.[102] The crowdworkers don't need any formal qualifications like academic degrees, they don't have to comply with a corporate dress code, get involved into office politics, communicate with others, follow orders, or do anything they don't want to do. Thus, while being tremendously precarious, the work also offers a lot of freedom.

Because MTurk provides no support, workers' protection, or communication structure for its vast workforce, the crowdworkers have to self-organise outside of the platform in dedicated workers' forums, the most well-known of which is 'Turker Nation'.[103] Most Turkers looking for advice on how to navigate Amazon's workplace, as well a most researchers in the field, had at some point or other an encounter with 'Spamgirl', who for many years had been the community manager of Turker Nation. Little was known about her, except that she had been a Turker right from the beginning of the platform, that she was very articulate and opinionated, and that she ruled over her Turker Nation with vigour, banning unwelcomed researchers from the forum without hesitation. She also was in contact with the elusive MTurk staff,

---

100 Summary from Ipeirotis' blog: www.behind-the-enemy-lines.com/2015/04/demographics-of-mechanical-turk-now.html (2015).

101 I tried to become a Turker but was rejected: 'Greetings from Amazon Mechanical Turk, We have completed our review of your Amazon Mechanical Turk Worker Account. We regret to inform you that you will not be permitted to work on Mechanical Turk. Our account review criteria are proprietary and we cannot disclose the reason why an invitation to complete registration has been denied. If our criteria for invitation changes [sic], you may be invited to complete registration in the future.'

102 Compare: Federici, 'Wages Against Housework' (1975).

103 Hits Worth Turking For (hitsworthturkingfor.blogspot.de); MTurk Forum (mturkforum.com); MTurkgrind (mturkgrind.com); CloudMeBaby (cloudmebaby.com); Turker Nation (turkernation.com).

which allowed her to occasionally make an appeal for fellow Turkers who had had their HITs unfairly rejected or who had been banned for no apparent reason. Spamgirl could sometimes convince the platform providers to reverse such measures.

In an interview from 2010, she revealed that she is a married mother from Toronto in her thirties with a degree in web-design who had already been moderating online forums for ten years. She also disclosed that she had to work from home because of a medical condition and that she had to spend her life in front of the computer doing microtasking to keep the family afloat, since her husband had lost his job.[104]

I love mTurk, and I love the work I do, and I appreciate everything they have done for me, but I have to work so hard to make enough just to EAT ... I can't wait until the debt is paid off, hubby gets a job, and I can spend some time with my family. I'm a little burnt out.[105]

Spamgirl (mockingly) described herself as being 'the Hoffa of the Turkers! Trying to help the people.'[106] Curiously, she was not only defending the workers against Amazon but also the other way around. Despite her own grave criticism of the work conditions, she frequently pointed out that MTurk is an operation separate from Amazon.com and that the platform simply doesn't have the means to improve the service for the workers. Even though Spamgirl identified with a union leader, she was not exactly fond of unions or of any involvement from the outside into the relationship between the Turkers, the platforms providers, and the employers. In May 2013, the following post appeared on Turker Nation:

Hi, I am [K.], I study Graphic Design in Holland and I am currently working on a project about Mechanical Turk. I am trying to design a union for turkers. Turkers work from their home and therefore don't really have the community of an office and colleagues around them that turk. I want to give the divided community of Turkers a unified, online voice, so that it's not just individuals, but a group. This group would then for example be able to contact requesters directly and to find out more about the community of workers as a whole. As a group you have a louder voice than you would as an individual. I was wondering what your views on this are, and if people would be interested, since I am only new to turking. Thanks in advance, [K.] :)[107]

---

104 Milland, 'Spamgirl Speaks! An Interview', *BrokenTurk* (2010)
105 *Ibid.*
106 *Ibid. Part 2*; James 'Jimmy' Hoffa, born 1913, was an influential American labour union leader who disappeared in 1975 and had been involved with organised crime before.
107 Forum thread on a potential 'Turker Union' (2013) turkernation.com/showthread.php?18874-Turker-union, accessed 5 January 2017. The post by K. was also mentioned in a radio feature: Strube; 'Crowdwork: Vom Entstehen der digitalen Arbeiterklasse' (2014).

K.'s suggestion was met by a wave of comments by Turkers, ranging from scepticism to strong objections and sarcasm. The Turkers questioned her motives and her knowledge of the problem, with her being an outsider and not an experienced crowdworker. 'Did a group of workers come to you and ask you for help?' asked one Turker, 'Because there are already plenty of academics who are currently sticking their noses into our business and claiming to speak for us on this issue. They are calling for boycotts of specific companies, regulation of the crowdsourcing industry and other changes that most workers do not care about.' They pointed out that a lot of the crowdworkers have become Turkers precisely 'BECAUSE they don't want to be part of a group thing', because they are individualists, and that Turker Nation would already provide everything K. suggested for them. Some Turkers found the idea interesting but impractical. However, most of the commentators reacted with hostility to the mere mention of the word 'union' and feared that such move would destroy their workplace. One Turker wrote that 'unions ultimately become parasitic to the host they invade and end up sucking the vitality out of it.' Finally, also Spamgirl weighed in:

Unions are a way for greedy people to take advantage of companies. As a person who rallies against corporations who behave in just that manner, I would *never* become a part of any other organization which plans to do the same. As a group, Turker Nation can fight its own battles. We can choose when to fight back and when not to individually. No union speaks on our behalf as no one can truly stand up and speak on the opinions of each individual. We're good, thanks, and I wish all of these knights on white horses would just back off and leave us alone. If we wanted help, we'd ask for it. We don't. So please go away.

The debate petered out after this post, followed only by a few snarky remarks claiming that 'the liberator' had quit the board instead of 'defending her position' and 'engage in the discussion'. When I contacted K. a year later via email, she told me that she had been immediately banned from the Turker Nation forum, right after posting her suggestion. She only learned from the debate that she had tipped off in the forum through me. K. explained: 'My idea was way more open source, and social media oriented than the top heavy structure they have in mind, so I would have very well been able to participate in their discussion.'[108]

Since 2014, Spamgirl has become publically much more visible and has started to contribute to different research projects and the academic discourse under her real name, Kristy Milland and was about to finish a Psychology major at Ryerson University in Toronto.[109] In May 2014, I had the chance to interview her, ironically for a book on crowdwork by IG Metall, one of the world's largest labour

108 Quote from an email exchange that I had with K. in February 2014.
109 Milland, 'A Mechanical Turk Worker's Perspective' *Journal of Media Ethics*, 31, 4 (2016): pp. 263–64.

unions.[110] In the interview, Milland identified three distinct categories of Turkers: those who Turk as a hobby in their spare time to earn an extra income whenever they like; those who Turk out of desperation because they can't find another job in the then on-going economic recession after 2008; and those who can't do another job because of disabilities, mental illness, other health issues, or for legal reasons.

The third group contains people who can either be vulnerable or predators [...]. For people who are in the sexual offender database, have a felony on their record, or can't bring themselves to leave the house, mTurk is also a new opportunity to do something with their life. This is one use of mTurk we must embrace as it provides an opportunity for these lumpen-proletariat to adhere to social or criminal requirements upon them as well as giving them the ability to rebuild their lives and not have to live off government hand-outs.

The fact that the crowd is so heterogeneous, not only on MTurk but in crowdwork in general, makes it so difficult to tackle the hardship that this type of work means for some of the workers. People who do crowdwork as a hobby obviously have totally different needs and expectations from those who have no other choice because they are part of a new digital 'lumpen-proletariat'. The wide variety of motives partly explains the hostility of some Turkers against attempts to regulate or organise the workforce from the outside, even though this would seemingly be in their best interest.

Milland thus argues that the best approach to improve the situation is to educate the employers that paying better for tasks will improve not only the self-image of the workers but also the speed and quality of the work – essentially, she says that one should appeal to the self-interest of the requestors and create a higher segment of well paid crowdwork. And indeed, for certain types of more complex tasks where quality is more important than price, this strategy might well work. But if we recall the earlier mentioned example of LinkedIn using the crowd for the unskilled labour to transcribe business cards, it is questionable if such a company can be 'educated' to pay more than two cents per card, as long as some people are willing to accept an hourly wage of US$ 1.20 – a price of labour so cheap that it allowed LinkedIn to give away the fruits of this labour to its customers for free. Milland argues, that journalist and researchers do the crowdworkers a disservice by reporting about the abysmal low rewards that some requesters pay and some crowdworkers are willing to accept, because it attracts even more cheapskates. But I am sceptical that the situation can be improved in the long run by hiding these facts. Especially with regard to the potential misclassification of workers as independent contractors, and for any attempts to regulate the platforms on the political level, it is important to point out the huge gap between the legal minimum wage and the low hourly wages in

110 Interview conducted together with Vanessa Barth from IG Metall: 'We have been sold as nothing more than an algorithm', *Crowdwork – zurück in die Zukunft?* (2015). In November 2014, I met Milland at the Digital Labor conference at the New School in New York, and again in May 2015 at the conference Circuits of Struggle in Toronto.

microtasking, even if professional and experienced Turkers such as Kristy Milland easily make ten times that much by choosing their tasks and the requesters they work for wisely. But even if workers like Milland can generate a higher income on MTurk, this doesn't alleviate the indignation of being forced, by economic hardship, to be treated as a dehumanised machine part:

We have been sold as nothing more than an algorithm. Requesters don't realize that there is a living, breathing human on the other end of the connection who needs to feed their children, pay medical bills or ensure their home doesn't go into foreclosure. No matter what you work on mTurk, you obviously don't have the resources to be doing something that pays better, but that is no excuse for paying unfairly.[111]

In 2008, the HCI design activists Lilly Irani and Six Silberman collaborated with crowdworkers from MTurk to find out how the situation could be improved. They entered into a conversation with the Turkers through paid microtasks, using Amazon's infrastructure as a means to analyse and eventually improve its systemic problems. Together with the microtaskers they developed a Workers Bill of Rights based on the most common grievances brought forward by the workforce. Remarkably, only 7 out of the 67 crowdworkers they talked with thought that a minimum wage for crowdwork would be a good idea.[112] Irani and Silberman located eight areas of conflict that the workers were worried about: 'uncertainty about payment; unaccountable and seemingly arbitrary rejections (i.e., non-payment); fraudulent tasks; prohibitive time limits; pay delays; uncommunicative requesters and administrators; costs of employer errors borne by workers; and low pay.'[113]

Irani and Silberman went on to develop Turkopticon a browser plug-in that serves as a critical design intervention into MTurk. The name is an allusion to Jeremy Bentham's infamous Panopticon and the plug-in counters the information asymmetry on Amazon's platform by giving workers the possibility to rate the behaviour of employers, not just the other way around.[114]

Because Amazon's platform only watched and quantified the workers, Irani and Silberman, in accordance with the Turkers, built a worker-controlled platform on top of the existing infrastructure so that workers can now watch out for and avoid exploitative employers. Fig. 17 shows Turkopticon in action with the example of the nudity image classification task that was already shown in the previous section. A drop down menu shows how requesters score in the categories 'communicativity', 'generosity', 'fairness', and 'promptness'. In this particular example, the evaluation

---

111 From the interview with Kristy 'Spamgirl' Milland I conducted in May 2014.
112 Irani/Silberman, 'Turkopticon: Interrupting Worker Invisibility in Amazon Mechanical Turk' (2013): pp. 611–20.
113 Irani/Silberman, Stories We Tell About Labor: Turkopticon and the Trouble with "Design" (2016): p. 3.
114 (turkopticon.ucsd.edu).

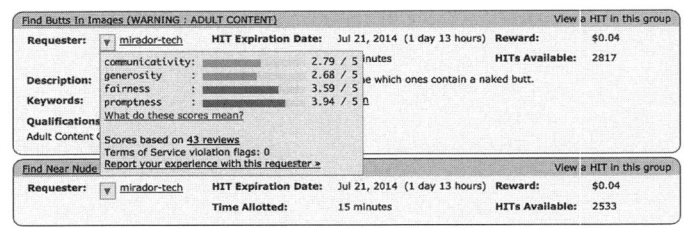

17 A screenshot of the browser plug-in Turkopticon – the drop-down menu – which allows workers on MTurk to access and provide evaluations of the behaviour of employers/requesters, in this case 'mirador-tech'.

of 'mirador-tech' is based on the feedback of 43 Turkers who have worked for this requester, who scores comparatively low in generosity but seems to at least pay promptly.

In 2016, Turkopticon had reached 'over 55,000 registered users, 287,000 reviews of 42,000 employers, and a steady flow of 20,000 unique visitors per month' – as Irani and Silberman put it, the plug-in had become part of the 'ecology infrastructure' of MTurk.[115] Which also meant for the two initiators of the project that 'we, as designers, have become ordinary parts of Turking life through maintenance, repair, and ongoing communication with Turkopticon's users.'[116] Turkopticon is an important example in the history of digital labour platforms and Human Interaction design because it came out of a course on tactical media led by artist Beatriz da Costa (a student of Donna Haraway) in the Arts Computation Engineering (ACE) program at the University of California, Irvine. Throughout the various influential papers by Irani and Silberman and ingrained in the architecture of the Turkopticon project one finds the influence of Donna Haraway, Judith Butler, and Michel Foucault, scholars concerned with structures of power and the perspective of the disenfranchised – a political stance all too often absent from engineering and programming projects, typically only concerned with technical efficiency and easily co-opted or infused by a managerial perspective.

The success of Turkopticon shows how crucial it is to combine engineering, the arts, and critical social theory in education, instead of artificially keeping these domains apart. But for Irani and Silberman, it also led to a number of dilemmas: their intervention into MTurk was originally meant as a form of 'adversarial design' (Carl Di Salvo) or 'critical design' (Antony Dunne & Fiona Raby); 'What design can do about these complex issues', write Irani and Silberman, 'is to shift the debate by changing the interfaces, maintaining refusal, and articulating the critique.'[117] But because Turkopticon became a fully functional tool, widely adapted by the community of crowdworkers Irani and Silberman cared about, they understandably felt obliged to continue to develop and maintain it (at their own cost and that of their

115 Irani/Silberman, 'Stories We Tell About Labor' (2016).
116 Irani/Silberman, 'From Critical Design to Critical Infrastructure' (2014).
117 Ibid.

university) – thus they effectively provided Amazon with a missing but important feature for their infrastructure that the huge corporation didn't bother to provide, but accepted into its platform ecology. To put it polemically, the lesson for Amazon and similar companies could very well be: Why waste time and money on such social features, if anyone really needs them, some design activist will surely come along and fix it for us. The other dilemma that the initiators of Turkopticon ran into is that their prime goal was to counter the invisibility of the crowdworkers and give them a voice – without the Turkers input and support on various levels, Turkopticon would not be possible; yet all reports about the tool (and this one here is no exception) put the role of Irani and Silberman centre stage. In their 2016 paper 'Stories We Tell About Labour: Turkopticon and the Trouble with "Design"', the two authors demonstrate an extraordinary degree of reflexivity, showing that one can read the origin of the design profession as the split into workers of socially higher-status doing the creative planning and those seemingly exchangeable workers occurring in higher numbers doing the mass manufacturing.[118] 'We are not simply Herbert Simon's designers in pursuit of preferred states, but privileged economic actors. These stories of economic and social progress sustain us institutionally, but they also become complicities and liabilities for those who wish to redistribute power through design practice.'[119]

By tackling the inequalities of one system they entered as outsiders, that of microtasking crowdwork, Irani and Silberman became aware of the inequalities inherent in their own system, that of the design profession and, more importantly, that the privileged position and high social status they enjoyed through their special skill set as being both designers and engineers to some extent perpetuated the problem they wanted to solve, at least in the perception of the wider public. In this later phase of the Turkopticon project, Irani and Silberman try hard to work against this reading of their work by emphasising the various important contributions by the Turkers, by cooperating with community leaders such as Kristy Milland and Rochelle LaPlant, a moderator on the Turker forum MTurkGrind, and by bringing crowdworkers as experts to high profile HCI conferences – but in the end, all these measures cannot overcome the fundamental characteristic of the crowd: the individual that joins it becomes by definition exchangeable. Individuals can stand out from the crowd through their achievements, be it as critical designers or as community managers, but they are inevitably the exception that proves the rule.

118 Irani and Silberman build their argument on: Forty *Objects of Desire: Design and Society from Wedgewood to IBM* (1986).
119 Irani/Silberman, 'Stories We Tell About Labor' (2016).

Chapter Four:
The Crowd-
sourcing
of Design

CREATIVITY CONTESTS

In his book *The Invention of Creativity* the German sociologist Andreas Reckwitz argues that being creative has turned into a cultural imperative.[1] He writes that in our contemporary economic and cultural climate, it has become unconceivable not to wish to be creative. *Not being able* to be creative is problematic, but this sad short-coming can be overcome by enough special training and effort – *not wanting to be creative*, however, is as shocking today as it would have been in other times to not wanting to be moral, normal, or autonomous. This holds true for individuals, cor-porations, and cities alike. The phenomenon Reckwitz describes has wide-ranging implication for the economics of the creative industry in general and the platform-based outsourcing of creative tasks in particular, because there now seems to be an unfathomable supply of creatives and would-be creatives trying to work in this field, even if this means working without hardly any remuneration. There is not another sector of the economy, where the lines between amateur and professionals have been so completely blurred.

Strikingly, a very large proportion of the platform-based outsourcing of crea-tive tasks is organised in the form of contest-based crowdwork and hardly ever in the form of microtasking crowdwork, which lends itself more to 'uncreative', repet-itive tasks with a predictable outcome that can be evaluated algorithmically. What are the reasons for this correlation? What are the consequences of organising de-sign work in this way? What does it say about creative work and about design as a practice that it lends itself so much to the contest model? And could the crowd-sourcing of design also be organised differently, in order to be fair and sustainable for all stakeholders?

It is a slippery slope to define what exactly is creative and what not. But some distinction is necessary: to recall a few examples from the last section on microtask-ing crowdwork, most people would agree that transcribing business cards or recog-nising genitals in pictures is not at all creative, while some might already see the description of content that is depicted on a photo as a potentially creative act. Trans-lating an isolated sentence from a manual would probably not be regarded as crea-tive, while translating a haiku might very well be. Writing a search-engine optimised product description that is also understandable for a human reader might be consid-ered creative but is certainly less so than writing a short story.[2] Creativity demands some level of originality, individuality, and freedom to find an innovative solution to a problem, one that also touches on hard-to-define aspects of aesthetics and quality.

---

1   Reckwitz, *Die Erfindung Der Kreativität* (2012): p. 9.
2   Kenneth Goldsmith argues that what is taught today as 'creative writing' is so riddled with clichés that it is more creative to be uncreative and let an algorithm write a story by cutting, pasting and randomising found footage; see: Goldsmith, *Uncreative Writing* (2011).

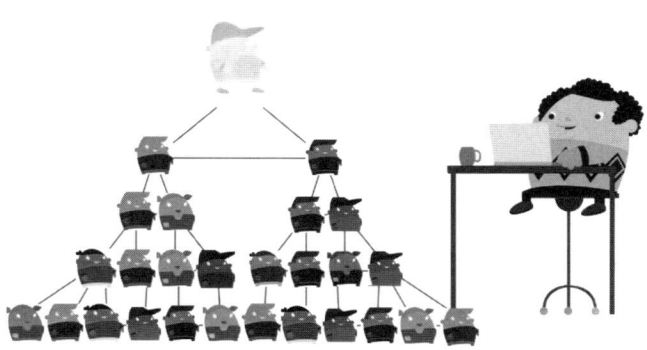

18 Illustration of how *contest-based creative crowdwork* is organised; from a promotional video by the logo platform MycroBurst, 2011.

The tricky thing about innovation or novelty, especially of the ideal aesthetic type for marketable design innovations once described by industrial designer Raymond Loewy as 'most advanced but yet acceptable' (MAYA), is that nobody knows beforehand what the result will look like and whether it will actually turn out to be acceptable.[3] What's more, value judgements about aesthetics are never entirely objective but, at least to some extent, lie in the eye of the beholder. Simply being 'new' is not enough. Whether or not an aesthetic innovation turns out to be acceptable will only be found out after the creation has come into being. In the field of user-generated content, people have learned that this is not necessarily a problem. It has become a truism that ninety per cent of everything is crap (Sturgeon's Law),[4] but the good stuff bubbles to the surface anyway, thanks to the free labour of ranking, rating, linking, liking, tweeting, and so on. So, for those content aggregators who want to skim the cream of social production, the problem of quality is much less of an issue than was originally thought in the early days of the so-called 'Web 2.0'.[5]

Yet, seen from the perspective of someone who wants to get someone else to solve a particular problem that demands a creative solution, according to a specific brief and within a predetermined timeframe, this proves to be a difficult challenge. The traditional model is to hire a carefully selected person based on previous creative work, credentials such as a portfolio, academic degrees, work experience with previous employers, and personal recommendations. One agrees on a price, either per result or per hourly or daily rate, and hopes that in the end the previously creative person will continue to be creative. But this entails the risk of buying a pig in a poke, of having to pay a substantial sum for (and therefore then being stuck with) something that one doesn't like in the end. This uncertainty is happening on all

3   Loewy, *Never Leave Well Enough Alone* (2002): p. 277.
4   Prucher, ed., *Brave New Words: The Oxford Dictionary of Science Fiction* (2007): p. 224.
5   Keen, *The Cult of the Amateur* (2007).

levels of the creative industry and often stifles creativity, because the party paying for an innovative solution often steers the creative process towards solutions proven to be successful in the past, thus stifling the chance for a genuinely new idea to minimise the risk of financial failure (Hollywood blockbuster remakes and epigones are the most prominent example of how this conundrum plays out when huge budgets are involved). But the same problem also exists on the (budget-wise) lowest level of the creative industry, especially when private individuals who are not used to hiring creatives have to take a leap of faith and agree to pay for something in the end, when they don't know how it will turn out, whether they will like it, how their peers will see it – and who don't have command of the necessary language (or even imagination) to express what they want, and to steer the creative process. This can be nerve-wracking for both the person paying the bill and the creative freelancer doing the job.

Contest-base creative crowdwork seems to offer the perfect solution to that problem. From the client's perspective: why tie yourself to the creativity of just one person when you can hire hundreds? And from the perspective of the creative: why tie yourself to a nervous and unarticulated client who nips every truly innovative idea in the bud and then demands an endless array of changes that only make the result worse? Obviously, until recently, hiring so many people would have been forbiddingly expensive and the orchestration of their work incredibly time-consuming. But now that the costs of communication and labour have dwindled, and so many people want to have a go at trying creative tasks, the outsourcing of creative work has become a whole new world, full of possibilities and complications.

The use of competitions to find creative talent and innovative solutions is a very old method, especially in the field of architecture. The history of architectural design contests stretches all the way back to ancient Greece and the reconstruction of the Parthenon in 500 BC. In the Renaissance, Filippo Brunelleschi designed the Dome of Florence as the result of a competition; and the method really started to flourish shortly after the French Revolution. The end of the eighteenth century saw dozens of architectural competitions with hundreds of contributions.[6] Over the centuries, architectural competitions have evolved into very complex practices with different rules, regulations, and procedures in every country.[7] Since the late twentieth century, they have become a field of research in their own right, especially in Scandinavia.[8] A detailed discussion of this area is beyond the scope of this book because there is neither a crowd involved nor usually an online platform, nevertheless, I would briefly like to point out some of the similarities and differences.

---

6   Chupin/Cucuzzella/Helal, eds., *Architecture Competitions and the Production of Culture, Quality and Knowledge* (2015).

7   Jong/Mattie, *Architectural Competitions, Vol. 1&2* (1994).

8   Kreiner, 'Architectural Competitions', *Nordisk Arkitekturforskning*, 21 (2009). Andersson et al., eds., *Architectural Competitions: Histories and Practice* (2013).

The rise of competitions as a method in architecture was to some extent an expression of the shift towards democracy in the nineteenth century. At the time the decision about what to build in a city ceased to be the prerogative of the church or the patron. Architecture affected many stakeholders and so the large building projects became part of a public debate and were subjected to the judgement of juries – comprised of politicians, artists, and scientists. The French architectural critic Quatremère de Quincy wrote in his *Encyclopédie Méthodique* (1788–1825): 'The competition's main purpose is to remove from the ignoramus the choice of the artists who are responsible for public works and to prevent that scheming does not usurp the work due to talent.'[9] Aesthetic decisions that affected the whole city were not to be left to the 'ignorance' of the client alone, but also favouritism among artists should be prevented through a public and transparent selection process. These competitions were not about saving the cost of labour – they were emancipatory and participatory devices to restrict nepotism and to bring forth beauty and innovation in the interest of the public. As the editors of one of the most recent books on architectural competitions emphasise: 'Every competition remains a world of possibilities: an intermediary space-time locus for the search for excellence in architecture. In some ways, competition projects function like utopias!'[10] And yet, they are not without controversy. In the documentary *Urbanized* from 2011, Dutch star architect Rem Koolhaas bemoaned the problem:

There is an incredible amount of wasted effort in the profession. A fair amount of it is generated through the procedure of competitions, which is a complete drain of intelligence. I don't know of any other profession that would tolerate this. At the same time you are important, we invite your thinking, but we also announce that there is an eighty per cent chance that we will throw away your thinking and make sure that it is completely wasted.[11]

Architectural competitions are labour-intensive, fiercely competitive, and subject to some of the same criticisms as crowdsourcing. The waste of labour created by letting people work on the same task in parallel but separately, when ultimately only one solution is needed, is the inherent, unsolvable problem of organising work in the form of a contest and not collaboratively or cumulatively.

As discussed in the previous chapter, people in *microtasking crowdwork* typically work on tiny fractions of much larger tasks. There is also systemically redundant work done there as a form of quality control. The same task is given to a handful of people to allow an algorithm to compare and evaluate the result. But in principle, the work of every participant is meant to become part of the greater,

9   Quoted after Chupin et al. (2015): p. 14.
10 *Ibid.* p. 12.
11 Hustwit, *Urbanized*, PlexiFilm (2011), quote at min. 51:50.

unified result of the distributed *microtasks*. In contest-based crowdwork, however, the goal is to find that *one* best solution, a synthesis of the many contributions can happen under certain circumstances, but is highly unusual. This is why from the perspective of creative people the great majority of work done for a competition is wasted (although there is also the argument that they can build up a portfolio this way; I will come back to that). For the party conducting the contest, however, the many 'bad' solutions are necessary to be able to identify the 'best' solution. By only looking at one solution in isolation, it would be much harder to evaluate it.

Despite the similarities, there are also important differences between architectural competitions and the crowdsourcing of design work. The most important one is that in architecture, the studios do not finish the complete project beforehand; they are instead competing with *proposals* for a complex job for which they will eventually be properly remunerated. Furthermore, architectural competitions are prestigious events that create a lot of publicity for the studio that wins, but also for those who are short-listed. The designs of the contestants are discussed in architectural magazines and this contributes to the reputation of the architects and can be transformed into the acquisition of new clients and the recognition of peers. As in platform-based crowdwork, there are also three main parties involved, but in architecture these are the client (typically municipalities or governmental agencies), a jury (typically a group of high profile experts and stakeholders), and number of invited architecture studios.

The client doesn't want to outsource the labour of production to the crowd but the decision-making process to a public jury of experts: the jury contributes to the prestige of these contests and raises the bar with regard to professionalism and innovation in construction and artistic expression. The studios are invited based on their qualification, experience, and merits; sometimes they even get paid for their participation. So in contrast to a crowd, which is by definition open to everyone, the entry barriers for the architecture profession, as well as its competitions, is high. Everybody can declare himself a designer, while the architecture profession is protected (for the obvious reason that an amateur architect can cause great damage).

As a result, the dynamic of contests in the two fields is very different. I don't want to lessen the problematic of the free labour in architectural competitions, especially because the effort by professional studios over many weeks is much more labour intensive and expensive than that of an individual designing a logo at home with a laptop. But on platforms for contest-based creative crowdwork, especially in the field of graphic design, hundreds of designers complete the entire job simultaneously and in advance. Because there is no pre-selection, the number of participants is higher, which means the chances to win are lower, and who wins is subject to arbitrariness, because typically, there is no jury involved (it is again the 'ignoramus' who decides).

What's more, to win a logo-contest on a platform of industrial size like 99designs, where there are thousands of open contests in any given moment, the incentive is not to win the appreciation of professional peers, critics, or affluent clients. Even if one gains new clients through such a contest, as many participants hope for and the platforms promise, it is a hard sell for the designer to convince the new client that he or she now won't get 99 designs for free anymore by only paying for one.

Contest-based creative crowdwork today is particularly strong in the area of logo design, and also here we find historic precursors. In 1936, the Japanese car manufacturer Toyota organised a large crowdsourcing competition to create its new logo. The company received some 27,000 entries and the winner was awarded 100 Yen. Toyota took the input of the crowd seriously and the logo that emerged as a winner from the contest was registered as the company's new trademark in 1937.[12] Two years later, Toyota built on this success with a 'a public contest to compose a song for an automobile convoy [and] a contest to design the name, body color, and mascot for a mid-sized passenger car' – this time, the company received 600,000 entries'.[13] Also the Procter & Gamble Ivory Soap carving contests, orchestrated by Edward Bernays throughout the 1920s and 1930s (see chapter one), can be regarded as an early example for the large-scale application of contest-based creative crowdsourcing, although in this case, the company was not looking for a particular solution to a creative problem. The customer input was not valued in the same way as it was at Toyota, and it was not 'work' in the sense of having to follow a specific brief. There was the additional benefit for Procter & Gamble that the crowd had to buy copious amounts of its exclusive white soap as working material; the participants essentially stayed consumers.

What unites these two historic examples is that the main motive was the marketing of products, not the harvesting of cheap labour. For Toyota it was certainly much more expensive to advertise the campaign through newspapers across the country and then handle between 27,000 and 600,000 design suggestions in analogue form, than it would have been to simply hire a professional designer. These are clever publicity campaigns, forerunners of a branch of crowdsourcing for marketing purposes that finds wide application today, with the crowd being asked to contribute mottos, names, and label designs for limited editions of products – and even ideas for prominent TV commercials. Sometimes, these campaigns backfire and the crowd decides on funny and puerile or even hostile solutions that can damage a brand.[14] Toyota also had to learn this lesson when in 2009 the company organised a pitch with five advertising agencies to come up with a TV-spot for a new car. One of them, Saatchi & Saatchi, sub-outsourced the job to the crowd and the clip

12 '75 Years of Toyota – Advertising and Publicity: 1935–1945', Toyota company website (undated).
13 *Ibid.*
14 In 2016 in the UK, Natural Environment Research Council (NERC) asked the crowd to come up with a name for a new polar research ship. The crowd voted for 'Boaty McBoatface', but officials eventually named the ship 'RRS Sir David Attenborough', overruling the crowd.

19 Toyota logo from 1936, result of a crowdsourcing contest.

that was produced based on this process turned out to be 'degrading to women and having incestuous overtones'.[15] While also being profit orientated, crowdsourcing for marketing is usually a one-off PR stunt between companies and their customers, there is now third party platform provider involved and precarious labour is not an issue in this area. With platform-based creative crowdwork, this is a totally different matter.

15 Tice, 'Crowdsourcing is Great – Except When it Fails', *Entrepreneur* (2009).

LET THEM DESIGN LOGOS

In early 2008, several now very large platforms for crowdsourced logo design were launched independently of each other, but almost at exactly the same time and with the identical business model. In short, a client posts a design brief on the platform and awards a certain amount of money, the platform-provider then hosts a design contest and charges a fee of up to fifty per cent of the money is paid by the client, several dozen designers hand in finished designs, after one or two weeks, the client decides who won and will get paid, or if unsatisfied, get the money back and nobody gets paid. If someone wins, which is usually the case, the copyright and the image files move from the designer to the client. Many of the logo platforms are outright clones of each other. Nevertheless they were frequently awarded locally for their innovative business model.[16]

The largest and best known of these platforms today is 99designs, founded by the serial entrepreneurs Mark Harbottle and Matt Mickiewicz in Melbourne. Mickiewicz, who is originally from Poland did not go to college and was just 25 when he founded 99designs. It was already his third successful company, and as of 2017 he has an estimated net worth of US $ 100 million. 99designs was a spin-off of his previous company SitePoint, which offers tutorials for web developers. Mickiewicz explained in an interview that 'the design contests idea was born out of the SitePoint forums – designers basically started to create logos and other designs for people in exchange for the chance to win a certain amount of money, and that happened quite organically.'[17] Since 2008, 99designs received US $ 45 million in venture capital and in July 2016 it announced that it had paid out a total of US $ 150 million to the designers working on its platform.

On its landing page 99designs describes itself as 'the world's largest online graphic design marketplace', as of early 2017 boasting over 1.3 million registered designers. Its biggest competitor, DesignCrowd, was founded by Alec Lynch and Adam Arbolino in Sydney (2008); it describes itself as 'the world's #1 custom design marketplace' and has over 550,000 registered designers (as of early 2017). Third in line is crowdSPRING, launched by Ross Kimbarovsky and Michael Samson in Chicago (2008), which also claims to be 'the world's #1 marketplace for logos, graphic design and naming', with over 195,000 registered designers and writers in 2017. German logo platforms are designenlassen.de, founded by Michael Kubens in Nuremberg (2008), with 26,000 registered designers as of 2017; and 12designer, founded by Eva Missling in Berlin (2009) and acquired by 99designs in 2012 – at the time it had 30,000 registered designers. In addition, there is also jovoto, founded by

---

16 To give just one example, the German logo platform designenlassen.de, one of the clones (or parallel inventions) of 99designs, was launched in November 2008 and was awarded for its innovative business model by the German Ministry for Economic Affairs and by the Chamber of Commerce, in 2009 and 2011.
17 Interview with Matt Mickiewicz, *entrepreneurs journey* (2010) min 18:00.

Bastian Unterberg in Berlin in 2008, which has a different, more complex contest model (see on p. 196 ff.).

From 2009 onwards, these platforms entered into a phase of rapid growth and competition, the larger ones with access to venture capital swallowed some of their countless smaller regional competitors and clones that had emerged in the meantime, thus localising their reach and offering their service in more and more languages. As of 2017 after this phase of market consolidation, 99designs has come out on top of the competition. Based on the number of registered users, the other logo platforms now grow substantially slower or not at all anymore. That said, these figures publicised by the platforms are unreliable because they typically represent the number of all users who have at some point in the past registered with a platform. Many creative crowdworkers register in multiple platforms to have a look or give it a try, but never come back. The number of active workers is much smaller.

This phenomenon became particularly evident between August and September 2014, when the number of designers supposedly working on 99designs jumped from about 300,000 to 850,000, without any acquisition having taken place at the time. The company had just decided to 'count differently', in reaction to seemingly being overtaken by DesignCrowd. Eva Missling, at the time General Manager for Europe of 99designs, told me in an interview that the company used to count only the designers who had at least once uploaded a logo to the platform. But 99designs then decided that this number would misrepresent the size of the company in comparison with it competitors – since then they count everyone who has ever registered.[18]

As with all online platforms, network effects play an important role in this area and make it seem beneficial, or at least promising for clients to frequent a large crowdsourcing marketplace to find a designer. For the platforms it therefore makes sense to convey the impression that they have a 'standing army' of hundreds of thousands of creatives eager to work for the client. From the perspective of the designers, however, it is questionable whether they improve their chance to win by joining such a large crowd of competitors. However, because large platforms attract many clients, the participating designers at least have a much greater variety of specialised design tasks to choose from, even though it is not easy to stand out in such a large crowd of creatives.

Several factors fostered the sudden rise of contest-based platforms for logo design in 2008. The dissemination of cheap laptops and fast internet connections also in less developed countries; easy access to professional creative tools and tutorials; the success of *user-generated content* platforms in the so-called 'Web 2.0'.

18 I met Eva Missling for the first in 2009 in Berlin, briefly after she had started her own platform12designers. In August of 2012, her platform was acquired by 99designs for an undisclosed sum; until 2014, the two platforms continued to run in parallel, but 12designers is now discontinued. In January 2015, I met Missling again for an interview in Berlin, that time in her ro.e as General Manager Europe for 99designs.

More importantly, the high popularity of working in the creative industry enabled the platforms for creative crowdwork to tap into three vast and overlapping new groups of creatives willing to work for payments far below the industry standards in developed countries: professional designers in the Global South, amateurs designing in their spare-time, and young designers at the beginning of their career – three groups marginalised by the established design industry in the Global North, for whom it was hitherto hard to win the trust of a client and develop their skills on real projects. Furthermore many people in the south of Europe and especially across the US were struggling after having lost their job in the wake of the financial crisis of 2008, which lead to a steep increase in freelancers and people looking for work online.

As Jeff Howe put it in 2009: 'Aided by a new generation of sophisticated start-ups, ever cheaper creative tools and – most of all – a recession that is forcing cost-saving measures on businesses, crowdsourcing is rapidly migrating from the fringe to the mainstream.'[19] In 2006, in the article in which he had coined the term 'crowdsourcing', he had shown how iStockphoto.com, a crowdsourcing website for stock photography had 'disrupted' the stock photo industry by reducing the worth of an image by 99%. It is a prime example for platform capitalism at work: Shutterstock, which sells crowdsourced stock photography, charges up to 85% of the revenues per image for its service of providing the virtual marketplace for photographers.[20] In 2008, Howe posed the question, whether stock photography was only an isolated case in the creative industry or the canary in the coalmine. In 2009, he announced that 'the canary is prone, lying motionless on a bed of its own droppings. It looks like it's time to find another mine.'[21]

At an early stage Howe pointed to the downsides of disruption through crowdsourcing, especially with regard to the devaluation of creative labour. But to investors in the platform economy, disruption has mostly positive connotations as it promises huge profits from dismantling existing industries that are not quick enough to digitise and 'uberize' their business model. Disruption has become the contemporary shorthand for Schumpeter's notion of creative destruction: 'The opening up of new markets [...] illustrate the same process of industrial mutation [...] that incessantly revolutionizes the economic structure from within, incessantly destroying the old one, incessantly creating a new one. This process of Creative Destruction is the essential fact about capitalism.'[22] The promise is that while this process undoubtedly causes hardship in the short run, the benefits of getting rid of out-dated ossified structures will prevail in the end (until the next disruption strikes).

19 Howe, 'Is Crowdsourcing Evil? The Design Community Weighs In', *Wired* (2009).
20 'What Does iStock Pay? We pay contributors a base royalty rate of 15% for each file downloaded with [iStock] credits. Exclusive contributors can earn up to 45%.' (istockphoto.com/sell-stock-photos) accessed 5 January 2017.
21 *Ibid.*
22 Schumpeter, *Capitalism, Socialism, and Democracy* (1994): p. 83.

Unsurprisingly, the appetite for disruption is also what drove the pioneers of the crowdsourcing industry to creative tasks. As Alex Lynch, founder of Design-Crowd explained: 'I could see the global design industry was large – at least $ 44B – and ripe for disruption.'[23] In 2013 he estimated that the crowdsourcing industry had managed to get a 0.1% share of that industry, $ 44 million at the time.[24] Not a big proportion, but one that was quickly growing. The share of the design industry that the platforms were able to claim was won by establishing the lowest end of the market, populated by myriads of freelance graphic designers working with nothing more than a laptop, even cheaper, while for the time being leaving the large agencies unaffected.

Large design projects typically demand well structured teams and hierarchies to orchestrate the division of labour, take the responsibility for its completion, function as a reliable partner for the client over longer stretches of time, and maintain a level of confidentiality regarding the strategic decisions and internal processes of the client. All this is hard, if not impossible to achieve via crowdsourcing. In 2008 Alec Lynch, founder of DesignCrowd, started a blog post to promote his fledgling company by sneering at the £ 400,000 that branding agency Wolff Olins was paid for the corporate identity of the London 2012 Olympics. 'I looked at that logo and thought "I know 10 people that could do better than that" – but they were never given the opportunity.'[25] Lynch went on to announce that his company aspired to shake the graphic design business by making it more accessible and doing away with conventional reputation. 'We are not exclusive, we are an open meritocracy.'[26]

What is often overlooked by those who claim that 'everybody could have done this or that design', is that a corporate identity is much more than just a logo. The visual identity of the Olympics is quite a good example of this.[27] Questions of taste aside, it is a complex visual system of colours, shapes, and custom-made fonts that has to function across the world in a wide range of contexts and formats, culturally and technologically, from small printed documents to facades of large venues. Outsourcing the responsibility of developing the corporate identity for an international event on the scale of the Olympics to a crowd would be reckless: it demands a reliable team of well trained, experienced professionals properly paid over long stretches of time to develop and apply the design concept for the various scenarios in which it has to function. Still, many people seem to think that the design process starts and ends with the logo and that the rest is just mumbo-jumbo – a scam by the design profession.

23 Simon, 'Crowdsourcing Design: An Interview with DesignCrowd Founder Alec Lynch', *Huffington Post* (2013).
24 *Ibid.*
25 Lynch, 'Fire Up and Disrupt the Market', DesignCrowd Blog (2008). At that point, the platform was still called 'DesignBay.'
26 *Ibid.*
27 Kushins, 'The Surprisingly Smart Strategy Behind London's Infamous Olympic Branding', *Fast Company* (2012). See also: Hurst, 'FAIL! Why Olympic Designers Got It So Wrong (and Occasionally Right), *Wired* (2012).

Then again, not every small shop or website needs a full-blown corporate iden-tity, but they all do need a logo, and the platforms for creative crowdwork cater to ex-actly those clients who just want a quick and cheap solution. For the level of com-plexity needed in those cases, it is indeed questionable if the designer needs to have studied for several years at an art school. One could also argue that the start-up cul-ture on the internet, with its uncountable new small business, websites, blogs, pod-casts, apps etc., as well as the imperative for every 'brick-and-mortar business' to also have an online presence, has created an unprecedented demand for logos, to which the logo mills have provided the appropriate answer. In the US in 2012 there were 28 million small businesses with less than 500 employees. 22.5 million of these were 'nonemployer' firms (no staff) and 52% of the small businesses were home-based. Every month more than half a million new businesses were launched in the US alone (though only half of them survived the first five years); the most common new busi-nesses were auto-repair shops, beauty salons, and dry cleaners.[28] These numbers are only approximations, but they give a glimpse of the dimension of the global demand for new logos, websites, and stationary by businesses with a very small budget.

In reaction to the emergence of the logo platforms, there was also the occa-sional schadenfreude and resentment against designers by parts of the business press. In a *Forbes* article from 2009 the author wrote that crowdSPRING had the goal to 'help thousands of struggling entrepreneurs'.[29] The subtitle of the article implied that the graphic designers got what they deserved: 'CrowdSpring aims to slash the cost of graphic design work – and democratize a snooty business.'[30]

This kind of sentiment against designers, especially in combination with the questionable use of the term 'democratisation', was common among those promot-ing the crowdsourcing of design at the time, although it is never quite clear what is meant by democratisation. Does it mean that design, as a profession, should be-come more accessible to young designers without a degree? That it should be more affordable to clients? Or that design quality is something best to be decided by vote? In cases like the *Forbes* headline, the term democracy remains blurry and it is thus hard to argue against it – it is such an unequivocally positive term – never mind that is being instrumentalised to justify letting people work for free to help struggling entrepreneurs.

The Philadelphia-based platform MycroBurst.com, yet another of the logo mills that claimed to be 'world leading', wrote on its front page: 'Traditional mar-keting firms are professional and know how to manage a customer, but they will charge somewhere between $ 2,500 and $ 15,000 for a branding package. These packages often include superfluous services including "research" and lengthy

---

28 Nazar, '16 Surprising Statistics About Small Businesses', *Forbes* (2013).
29 Steiner, 'The Creativity of Crowds', *Forbes* (2009).
30 *Forbes* removed the subtitle from the online version of the article, but the many reactions to its original version can still be found online. See for example: Airey, 'Forbes Calls Designers Snooty', DavidAirey.com (2009).

presentations.'[31] The relatively small logo platform ZenLayout.com advertises its marketplace with the slogan: 'Cool designers working for you. Hire 700 designers. Pay one.' It is no wonder that established designers started to decry the devaluation of their profession.

One typical (knee-jerk) reaction of established designers to defend themselves against the creative work done on platforms is to dismiss all that is being produced there as substandard work of amateurs. And it is easy to get this impression confirmed by looking at the majority of contributions in any of the contests on a logo platform. The amount of technically and aesthetically substandard work is staggering. But on the other hand, the inconvenient truth (from the perspective of professional designers outside the platform) is that there is also almost always a handful of contributions that have a quality way above what passes as professional standard – truly creative designs, perfectly crafted. And from the client's perspective, a few of those are enough. Who cares if the rest is bad? But the amateur argument is also problematic for another reason: In a press kit of CrowdSpring, the founders assert that their platform makes geography as irrelevant as academic degrees, job titles, and experience. 'A creative could be a janitor by day and a designer by night, or a stay-at-home mom who doesn't have the time to run her own web studio.'[32] This shows that the platforms do address amateurs directly – amateurs in the sense of people having a day job, who design on the side. Professional designers, those who do design as a primary job and have to make a living from it, often use the term amateur as a strategy to belittle the participants on the crowd platforms. For them, amateurs are those without talent, skill, and education – good reasons, they insinuate, why clients should stay away from the platforms if they want good design. This perspective was perpetuated by Jeff Howe, who on different occasions described the situation of crowdsourcing in the creative industries with 'barbarians at the gate' of the professions – the old elites under a siege by an army of amateurs; a tone that is very much reminiscent of the nineteenth century crowd debates.[33]

Yet, Daren C. Brabham, assistant professor at the Annenberg School for Communication & Journalism at the University of Southern California and an expert on contest-based crowdwork has compellingly shown that 'the crowd of amateurs in crowdsourcing is a pervasive myth.'[34] I do agree with him on this point. Although there are many amateurs trying out platforms such as 99designs, those who are doing the majority of the work, who are winning the contests and are building up a portfolio over time are seriously trying to build a career in graphic design and see this as an entry point. As such, they are not appropriately described with the term amateur. As Brabham has pointed out, to do so justifies low compensation and in-

---

31 As of early 2015, MycroBurst was discontinued and merged with ZillionDesigns.com another 'logo mill', supposedly with 100,000 designers. The citation from the 2014 front page of MycroBurst.com can still be accessed via the WaybackMachine of the Internet Archive.
32 Kimbarovsky/Samson, 'crowdSPRING Press Kit' (undated, pre 2014).
33 Howe, 'Is Crowdsourcing Evil? The Design Community Weighs In', *Wired* (2009)
34 Brabham, 'The Myth of Amateur Crowds', *Information, Communication & Society*, 15 (2012): 394–410.

hibits self-organisation of the workers and a fight for fair labour standards. The 'myth of the amateur crowd' creates an atmosphere of democratisation and inclusion while perpetuating a fiercely capitalist logic:

Any individual in the crowd engaged in a for-profit crowdsourcing application, amateur or professional, accepts his or her position within a capitalist enterprise. That the crowd controls the products they produce or the means of production through their submissions to a crowdsourcing site is an illusion. They are laborers, not owners, and 'amateur' laborers accept an even lower status in that arrangement than 'professionals'. Yet, the label of amateur conjures a democratic, 'of the people' impression of what is really taking place on a crowdsourcing Web site.[35]

In this sense, the false classification of the members of the design crowd as amateurs is just another way for the platforms to eschew responsibility for them as employees or workers. Paradoxically, from time to time the platforms publish portraits of their most successful designers to demonstrate how professional they are and how well they are doing in their business. The platforms are sending mixed messages by addressing designers first as amateurs, with the offer to 'become a designer', while also presenting them as professionals. Behind this is of course the promise of a transformation from amateur to entrepreneur, as in the story of Nicolas Sheriff, a 'natural-born entrepreneur', or so the 99designs blog assures us, who grew on the platform and now has a job as a product manager at a San Francisco start-up via a client he met through crowdsourcing.[36] In that blog post, 99designs paints a picture of itself as a business school: 'Sheriff considers the 99designs model to be somewhere in between being a freelancer and running a business. The site teaches designers how to deal with a series of clients on a particular time schedule. It teaches time management in a semi-corporate business structure.'[37]

Fight Logos With Logos

The sudden rise of platforms for contest-based design work triggered a wave of indignation among designers accustomed to and insisting on getting paid for their work. The chorus of outrage was met by incomprehension on the side of the platform-providers as well as the clients of crowdsourced design, who were happy to get a bargain while at the same time thinking of themselves as offering emerging designers a great job opportunity.

35 Brabham (2012): p. 14.
36 Lekach, 'Nicholas Sheriff Grows from 99designer to Business Innovator', 99designs blog (2014).
37 *Ibid.*

20 Fighting logos with
logos – protest material
by the initiative Spec
Watch, 2009.

In the English-speaking graphic design community there had already been awareness and occasional debate about so-called 'speculative work' for decades.[38] On the internet, controversies had sporadically flared up when a designer reported in a forum that she or he had been asked by a client to design something for free, with the prospect of maybe getting a big contract later, if the client was satisfied with the result of the free labour. Whenever the issue came up in forums, designers closed ranks, dismissed such offers as 'spec work', and agreed that professional work ethics demanded that such offers to work for free should always be declined, since experience showed that they rarely evolved into a good designer client relationship.[39]

Needless to say, many designers did spec work anyway, but it was something that happened occasionally in specific situations. When the contest platforms arrived on the scene in 2008, the debate came to a head. Now that platforms started to build their entire business model on spec work, designers felt they had to fight back. They gathered under the banners of organisations such as the American professional association for design (AIGA),[40] and the Alliance of German Designers (AGD), as well as under those of in single purpose initiatives such as 'SpecWatch', 'No!Spec', and 'Anti-Spec'.[41] In Germany, the intellectual property lawyer Sabine Zentek fought for fair contests and offered legal advice in her association Fidius e.V..[42]

The core argument of all of these initiatives was that the systematic organisation of design work in a way where getting paid became a gamble would inevitably erode and eventually destroy the design profession – that the contest model was unethical and economically unsustainable. As a countermeasure these groups started campaigns to educate young designers and clients about the detrimental effects of this method. They tweeted about specific contests in which the client didn't pay anyone at all and about those in which the client ended up with a plagiarised logo. They

---

38 'Why We Don't Make Speculative Presentations', *Creative Business*, 2003. In an email, Cameron Foote, long time editor of the trade publication *Creative Business* told me that they had first written about 'Spec Work' in 1992, but that he believes that 'the term was in common use well before then.' Online, the debate became more frequent since 2005. See for example the thread on 'Spec Work!' on GraphicDesign-Forum.com (2005).
39 'AIGA Position on Spec Work', aiga.org (2009).
40 *Ibid*.
41 No!Spec (nospec.com); SpecWatch (specwatch.info); AntiSpec (antispec.com; offline).
42 Sabine Zentek was a speaker at the conference 'Volkssport Design' which I organised in 2009. Back then she was still very engaged fighting against unfair design competitions.

also started to attack the crowdsourcing platforms by spamming the forums with propaganda against spec work – essentially fighting logos with logos.

I write about these initiatives in the past tense because after a burst of activity, most of the initiatives gave up the fight – No!Spec, run by the graphic designer and writer David Airey from Northern Ireland is the only project I know of that is still active. In March 2015, I interviewed Airey via email and he rejected my impression that designers were fighting against spec work: 'I wouldn't call it a battle.' Airey explained: 'As designers, avoiding spec work is about having respect for ourselves, for our education, our time, and our experience. What impression do we give our clients (and future clients) if we value our work at nothing?'[43]

The anonymous Twitter account of SpecWatch petered out in 2010 and Sabine Zentek officially gave up her fight in August 2012.[44] In a final statement she explained, that in order to cope with the steep increase of legally questionable contests, she would have needed support from design schools and the government and also from designers willing to go to court, none of which occurred. From her point of view, the design contests were just the latest iteration in an on-going trend towards insufficient remuneration in the creative industries and she advised designers to refrain from taking part in order not to further undermine their right for fair payment.[45]

In 2012, tech-journalist Sarah Lacy wrote: 'Get over it haters, 99designs has tipped.'[46] She went on to explain that the designers had to accept that the internet had disrupted every other service industry and that design would not be an exception. She wrote that it is only 'the people in the middle who haven't yet made a name for themselves, but feel they are above designing logos and tshirts *[sic]* on spec who balk.' To Sarah Lacy's incomprehension, the designers 'balked' even though 99designs was 'sending out Tshirts *[sic]* and modest bonuses' and was 'also investing in some game mechanics to keep designers motivated: Things like ratings, leader boards and more contests and recognition for good work.' Lacy also praised the amounts of money that individual designers made on the platforms and concluded, that they had two chances: 'Get in the game or keep complaining on the sidelines.'[47]

While I think that it is inappropriate to reduce the critics of crowdsourcing to 'haters', one can't argue with the fact that the platforms had indeed reached a tipping point and are now widely adopted in the lower segment of the graphic design industry and are unlikely to disappear. However, to imply that there is easy money in creative crowdwork (for anyone else than the platform providers), is deceptive and statistically wrong. So how are the win/lose ratios? How much money is involved and how do those using the platforms deal with the difficult situation?

43 Interview via email on 5 March 2015.
44 AGD, 'Zu viele Beschwerden, zu wenig Klagen – Der Fidius e.V. beendet die Arbeit', *AGD Magazin* (10 August 2012).
45 *Ibid.*
46 Lacy, 'Get Over It, Haters: 99designs Has Tipped', *PandoDaily* (2012).
47 *Ibid.*

WHAT ARE THE ODDS?

Most platforms for contest-based creative crowdwork prominently display a selection of constantly updated key figures on their front page: the number of currently open contests, the sum of all contests done so far, the amount of money paid out per month as well as in total. After a rebrand of 99designs.com, the financial figures are less 'in your face' than they had been for many years, as the company tries to rid itself of its discount image.

As mentioned above, the total number of registered designers is notoriously unreliable, so the total number of money paid out is much more meaningful, especially if put in relation to the total number of hosted contests. A comparison of these numbers leaves no doubt that the platforms are doing well, with 99designs now being the undisputed market leader. In the first three years of its business, the platform paid out US$ 19 million in total. In June 2013 the company had paid out US$ 54 million to the crowd who had in turn uploaded a total of 23 million designs at that point.[48] In summer 2014, the company had so far hosted a total of over 300,000 contests and paid out a total of over US$ 80 million. In February 2015 the total payout was US$ 95 million – spread over 377,000 contests. Up to this point, the average reward for a contest winner was 252 dollars. Based on calculations that I made in 2012 and 2013, when 99designs still published the total number of designs handed in, a contest on average had 116 contributions.[49] That means the average remuneration per uploaded design was about US$ 2.30.[50]

In March 2016, 99designs announced in a press release that the company was now paying out $ 3.5 million per month to its designers. 'In its eighth consecutive year of double-digit growth, 99designs achieved revenue approaching $ 60 million. The 99designs platform facilitates over 10,000 design contests every month, and in total, customers have launched over 500,000 design contests over the life of the company.'[51] This means that the average money paid out per contest has risen to $ 350, which has to do with the fact that 99designs is now holding more contests in design categories like web design and mobile app design, which are far more complex and time intensive than logo design and therefore have higher rewards.

Via 99designs, a variety of creative tasks can be outsourced – from web design, to book covers and illustrations – but the core of the business is the design of logos. This is why platforms like these are sometimes referred to as 'logo mills'. Until 2016

---

48 Wee, '99designs: "There's Raw Talent in Indonesia and Philippines"', *Tech in Asia* (2013).
49 In 2013, the platform had run about 2000,000 contest to which the crowd had contributed 23 million designs. The total number of entries and contest used to be displayed on the website; the average entries per contest stayed between 110 and 120.
50 In April 2011, based on $20 million paid out for 6.5 million logos, the price per logo was $3.
51 '99designs Enters Next Phase of Growth Amidst Record Breaking Year – Discloses Key Financial Metrics for First Time in Company History', press release, 8 March 2016.

2,902	377,597	$2,487,564	$94,869,730
Open contests	Contests to date	Payouts last month	Payouts to date

99designs also had an online-shop for readymade logos, selling at the price of $ 99, where only the client's company name had to be added after purchase. When 99designs sold one of these logos, the designer received 30 dollars; the rest was commission for the platform.[52] Other logo mills still offer this option, but it seems that 99design got rid of it as part of a relaunch of the brand that is trying to move the company away from its discount image.

The most typical scenario is that a new and small business is using the platform to let the crowd quickly and cheaply generate a custom-made new logo with the method of the design contest. 85% of 99designs revenue comes from hosting these competitions.[53] The process usually takes between one and two weeks. In order to initiate a design contest, the client has to first fill out a form and describe what the logo should be like, enter some information about his or her business, and link to a few examples for inspiration. Via a dashboard of sliders, the client is then asked to define 'what values the logo should communicate'.

After giving the information for the brief, the client has to choose how much she or he is willing to pay. 99designs offers different packages, from 'Bronze' to 'Platinum'. In the more expensive categories the platform offers a 'dedicated account manager' and makes a pre-selection of designers allowed to take part in the contest. By handpicking a smaller number of designers, the quality rises, and so does the chance for the individual to win.

Eva Missling indicated an interesting trade-off to me with regard to the question of fairness here: is it fairer to have smaller crowds and thus allow fewer people to work for free? Or is it fairer not to exclude anyone who also wants to participate and is willing to take the risk, lowering the statistical chance of winning for everybody else?[54] She also said that she was sometimes irritated by the herd instinct that occurs in contests where the task is relatively simple and the awarded money is higher than the average. This can lead to a surge of contributions, substantially lowering the chance for each participant to win. In contests, like those for web design, where the prize money and the chances of winning are much higher, fewer designers participate.

52 In April 2015, 99designs listed over 60,000 ready-made logos. Regarding the commission, 99designs wrote: 'Once your design is approved, it's time to kick back and wait for the sales to roll in. To start with, you'll get 30% of each sale. As you sell more logos, win more contests, and submit more designs to the 99designs Readymade Logo Store, your percentage of the sale will increase up to 50%!' The company eventually stopped the sale of ready-made logos to focus on contests.
53 99designs press release from March 2016; the remaining 15 per cent come from '1-to-1 projects' where the client hires a designer directly via the platform.
54 Personal interview with Eva Missling from 22 January 2015.

22 The four different packages 99designs has on offer for logo design; the information that the platform takes up to 50% of the money is neither disclosed to the client nor to the designers.

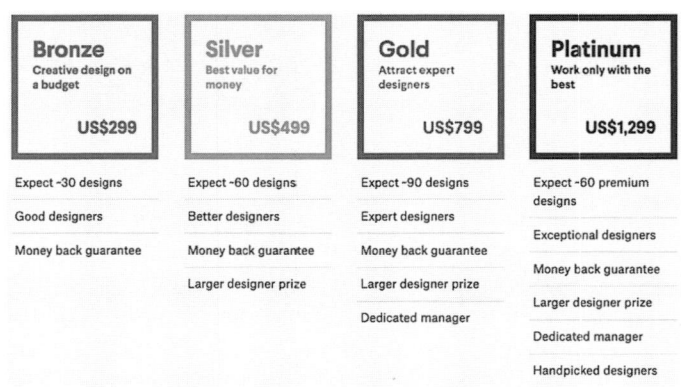

Bronze Creative design on a budget	**Silver** Best value for money	**Gold** Attract expert designers	**Platinum** Work only with the best
US$299	**US$499**	**US$799**	**US$1,299**
Expect ~30 designs	Expect ~60 designs	Expect ~90 designs	Expect ~60 premium designs
Good designers	Better designers	Expert designers	Exceptional designers
Money back guarantee	Money back guarantee	Money back guarantee	Money back guarantee
	Larger designer prize	Larger designer prize	Larger designer prize
		Dedicated manager	Dedicated manager
			Handpicked designers

It seems that more people are willing to take the higher risk of wasting a few hours of work on a task of low complexity than taking the lower risk of wasting more hours on a more complex task. Missling pointed out that this is also reflected in the popularity of contests in which the client wants the crowd to draw a mascot, a task that seems more intrinsically rewarding and fun than developing a website.

To show how the process works, here are two examples from the summer of 2014. The Berlin-based company Peak Ace needed a new logo and chose the Gold package for its contest. The brief read: 'We are looking for a smart design. Preferably with a subtle "aha" effect. A design that tells a little story about either what we do, or one that is connected to the name of the company.'[55] Unusually many designers participated, presumably because the awarded money was above average, the logo was supposed to be very simple, abstract, black & white, and the client communicated clearly with the designers. After the contest was finished 99designs announced: 'For just $ 799, they received 1,630 designs from 377 designers. From the perspective of the client, each of the 1,630 designs handed in came at the cost of just 0.49 dollars per design. In the end, it was 'Suhartinipaimin', a designer from Indonesia, who won $ 450 for his contribution, while 99designs made $ 349 – the other 376 designers, who each handed in between four and five logos, had worked completely for free.

The sportswear company Shūma from Atlanta in the US also needed a logo and was willing to pay $ 499 for it. In contests with less money involved, such as this, fewer participate. So, while the potential award is lower, the chances to win are higher. With a chance of 33 to 1 against, 'LeverageDesign' from India managed to earn $ 300, while 99designs earned $ 199 without even having to employ a 'dedicated account manager' as this was one of the cheaper contest where the platform doesn't get involved in the process at all. It just provided the platform for a 40% cut.

55 http://en.99designs.de/logo-design/contests/want-smartest-design-logo-395592/brief#contest-breadcrumbs.

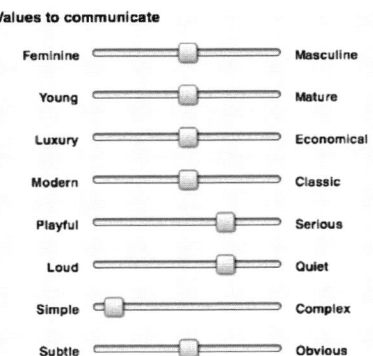

Values to communicate

Feminine ——■—— Masculine

Young ——■—— Mature

Luxury ——■—— Economical

Modern ——■—— Classic

Playful ———■— Serious

Loud ———■— Quiet

Simple ■——— Complex

Subtle ——■—— Obvious

23 A client on 99designs can use sliders to communicate to the designers what characteristics a new logo should have.

Even though 99designs' website and its press releases boast a lot of impressive numbers, one key economic figure is always missing: the fee that the platform charges for hosting the contests. The pricing scheme of 99designs is complicated and deliberately opaque in this regard. Clients and designers only see their own end of the deal and nowhere on the site, not even in its terms of service is it made explicit what the rake is, which has caused a lot of controversy among its users.[56] It is however easy to calculate the amount case by case for finished contests by looking up separately how much the client paid and how much the designer got. The percentage of commission varies for the different design categories and the different packages on offer. For logo design contests in 2014, the fee taken from the client's payment were as follows: Bronze: 33.5%; Silver: 40%; Gold: 43.8%; Platinum: 50%.

99designs has a user forum, where designers and clients can discuss issues, ask questions, and make suggestions to the company. In March 2012 a user named 'Vitcom' opened a thread in the forum, demanding the platform to lower the commission or at least make it transparent to the contest holders.[57] Even though it was one of the most actively debated topics in the forum, and many users agreed with Vitcom, 99designs ignored the thread for one and a half years before explaining that they needed the money for marketing and that they were supposedly explaining

---

56 In April 2014, I contacted 99designs several times in order to get accurate figures for the commission of each of the packages, but the company only gave evasive answers. The UK marketing manager of 99designs offered to give me the figures in exchange for a mentioning of 99design on the website of the RCA, which I declined. After that, he stopped replying to my requests. When I asked Eva Missling about the exact fees (in the interview from January 2015) she said they were not a trade secret and they would tell them if asked, but she still remained evasive and didn't give me a concrete answer.

57 https://99designs.uservoice.com/forums/198-01-general/suggestions/2714560-lower-the-commission-99designs-takes-from-designer [accessed 15 August 2014] – In February 2015, 99designs created a new user-forum, the old entries cannot be accessed anymore but I have text copies and screenshots of some of the debates.

24 Screenshot; 99designs announces the winner of a Gold contest, August 2014.

Peak Ace picked a winning design in their logo design contest

For just $799, they received 1,630 designs from 377 designers.

the pricing to the clients. Several comments by clients suggested otherwise. One design client posted anonymously on 17 May 2013:

Hi, I am a new contest holder on 99designs. I was shocked at how big a commission they take, 25% seems reasonable. 40% seems like robbery not to mention the fact they do not make this fact public to the contest holders. I only discovered it when publishing my contest to twitter it said the actual amount given to designers and then using a calculator I figured out their commission fee percentage. [...]

Another client wrote under the name Giorgi on 8 August 2013:

I just ran a design contest where I paid $799, and the winning designer only made $387! That's over $400 (about 52%) in commission. I wish I had at least been informed about how little the designer would've made before I ran the contest.

On 15 May 2014, a client wrote anonymously:

NOPE, the percentage is NOT stated as part of the contest agreement! I'm a customer, and I had to go sniffing around to find out how much of my prize was paid as overhead (the answer: 30%!) I was NOT told this up front, nor was it possible to search "HELP" to find out. I had to create a designer account and look at the contest as an outsider!

Finally, Ashish Desai (Head of Product, 99designs) closed the thread on 10 July 2014, declining the demand for a lower commission fee as well as for more transparency:

Hi All,
We have left this thread open for a long time because we like the open dialogue and honest feedback. However, at this point, we feel that we have answered the original question and have clearly articulated the value that we provide to the creative process. If you believe that our fees are not aligned with the value we provide, then we certainly encourage you to find an alternative that is more in line with your perceived value.

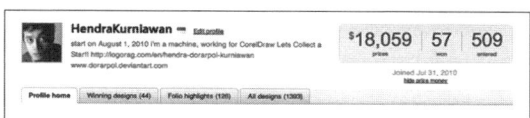

25 Screenshot; header of the profile page of 99designs user HendraKurniawan in 2011.

At this point, the thread was closed by 99designs; the demand was declined in spite of 1,598 votes in favour of it. I can only agree with the many users in the thread, who came to the conclusion that the company doesn't care about transparency at all when this interferes with its profit margin. Another user quickly opened a new thread on the same issue, but there is no reason to believe that this will make any difference, especially since new designers are not in short supply.

I asked Eva Missling about the reasoning behind this lack of transparency, also with regard to the fact that on her old platform, 12designer.com, clients and designers were told in a straightforward manner how the pricing structure came about, and with twelve per cent the fee was substantially lower than on 99designs. She answered that the fixed price packages on 99designs would be a service to the client, who doesn't want to get confused by a complicated pricing scheme.[58] She also argued, that even for taking only the twelve per cent on her old platform, she was heavily attacked by designers via email. She expressed that the designers generally don't seem to appreciate the high costs of running a platform and the service they get from it. Missling implied, that if the designers protest anyway, even with a very low fee, the platforms might as well take more.

What is more: since March 2015, the terms of use on 99designs demand that all following communication and future contracts between the designer and the client must go through the platform for the next two years, so that 99designs gets a percentage of every follow-up job. The only option for designers to get out of this contract is to pay 2,500 US dollars to the platform to buy themselves free.[59]

On 99designs, each designer has a portfolio page that shows a selection of contributions entered in previous contests as well as data on the performance of the designer. 99designs used to display the amount of money earned, the number of contests entered, and the number of competitions won for each designer. The header of a portfolio used to look like fig. 25, taken from the page of the Indonesian designer Hendra Kurniawan in 2011. At that point he had earned the impressive

---

58 Interview from 22 January 2015 in Berlin.
59 99design terms of user section 4: 'Exclusivity and Non-Circumvention: 'for 24 months from the time you meet any party through the Site (the "Exclusivity Period"), you must use the 99designs Services as your exclusive method to request, make, and receive all payments for work directly or indirectly with that party or arising out of your relationship with that party (the "99designs Relationship"). You may opt-out of this obligation only if Customer or prospective Customer pays 99designs an "Opt-Out Fee" computed to be the greater of the following amounts: (a) $ 2,500; or (b) 15% of the cost to the Customer of the services to be performed in the 99designs Relationship during the Exclusivity Period, as estimated in good faith by the prospective Customer. (99designs.com/legal/terms-of-use) update from March 2015.

sum of 18,000 US dollars, but this was for 509 designs he had submitted to contests. On average he therefore earned about 35 US dollar per contest he participated in. If one factors in the different version within a contest, he even uploaded a total of 1,393 designs. He managed to win at a ratio of one to ten. This performance is well above average.[60] Since early 2014, the profile pages show significantly less information. All that is shown is the number of contests won and the number of contests in which the designer was shortlisted. The ratio looks much better this way. It could be argued that the platform has done a service to the designers, because they now look more successful. But this new set of numbers obscures how low the chances of winning actually are.

In an extensive quantitative study of 99designs, Ricardo Matsumura Araujo, a Brazilian professor of Computer Science, analysed data from over 38,000 contests conducted on the platform between 2010 and 2012.[61] He wanted to find out whether there is a correlation between the number of designers per contest and the quality of the results, measured by the ratings clients gave to uploaded designs. His results showed that indeed, 'higher financial incentives lead to an increased number of designers submitting to contests and a higher financial incentive also has a positive impact in a contest's probability of success.'[62] But he was also able to show that it is only a very small number of designers who turn out to be successful at winning these contests, while the majority lose even more often than might be expected statistically.

From the 63,049 designers in the data set, 25,384 (40.2%) only participated in one contest. The most active designer participated in 1,071 contests and the mean is 7.8 contests per designer. The most successful designer won 150 contests (0.4% of the total number of finished contests). On the other hand, 84% of designers did not win a contest and 8% won a single contest. The distribution closely follows a power-law.[63]

Araujo found out that the most successful designers choose the contest they participate in carefully and then put a lot of effort in them, in the form of several revisions of a design, based on the client's wishes. The research confirmed that a larger crowd indeed increases the chance that the client is satisfied in the end, but not because of the total amount of good work. Instead, Araujo notes, 'having more designers is just a way to increase the odds of having those good designers, but it may not be the most effective way to do so. In the limit, if one knew beforehand who the best designers are, one could do better by approaching them directly.'[64]

60 Screenshots of the profile of Hendra Kurniawan. See also: Gremillion, 'An Interview with talented illustrator Hendra Kurniawan', 99designs blog (2011).
61 Araujo, '99designs: An Analysis of Creative Competition in Crowdsourced Design' (2013).
62 *Ibid*. p. 4.
63 *Ibid*. p. 6.
64 *Ibid*. p. 8.

26 Designer rankings based on 'projects won' on the platform designenlassen.de, January 2017.

	designers	won	participated	success rate	Ø evaluation	
#1	kraskosha Russia (Russian Fed.)	757 projects 42 1to1-projects	6014	13 %	★★★★★	1TO1-PROJECT
#2	twins2design Germany	360 projects 9 1to1-projects	3020	12 %	★★★★★	1TO1-PROJECT
#3	darkviruz Germany	310 projects 137 1to1-projects	2439	13 %	★★★★★	1TO1-PROJECT
#4	virtua73 Germany	230 projects 31 1to1-projects	1469	16 %	★★★★★	1TO1-PROJECT
#5	midesign Uruguay	224 projects 1 1to1-projects	1349	17 %	★★★★★	1TO1-PROJECT
#6	fimwasit Germany	190 projects 23 1to1-projects	1479	13 %	★★★★★	1TO1-PROJECT
#7	Yaleri Germany	179 projects 14 1to1-projects	492	36 %	★★★★★	1TO1-PROJECT
#8	zisdsg Germany	179 projects 10 1to1-projects	1381	13 %	★★★★★	1TO1-PROJECT
#9	armonioso Spain	173 projects 8 1to1-projects	2500	7 %	★★★★★	1TO1-PROJECT
#10	ZEL France	166 projects 34 1to1-projects	4270	4 %	★★★★★	1TO1-PROJECT

The German logo platform designenlassen.de allows more insights in this respect. Here, visitors can get the designers displayed in a 'top 100' list. Even among the 'top 10' who have won the most contest in absolute numbers, the success rate quickly drops to just 4%. The buttons on the right in the ranking give clients the possibility to start a '1to1-project' with a specific designer. This feature seems almost like a response to Ricardo Araujo's conclusion. It is more efficient to hire a good designer directly than to sift through the flood of mediocrity in a contest and give everybody in the crowd feedback. The problem for the client is usually to find or attract the good designer in the huge crowd. The ranking makes this easy. For the designers in the lower ranks, however, it is unlikely to get the attention of clients for a direct order. It is again a winner-takes-it-all game.

I have shown above that on average, the money paid out per design uploaded to a logo platform comes down to $ 2.30. Professional designers trying to gain an income in such a market only have two options: self-exploitation or plagiarism. Either, they think economically and spend only a few minutes on each design. They then upload generic or derivative logos of low quality and little inspiration, often slightly altered copies of free vector files, clip art, stock illustrations – literally clichés.[65] The contests on 99designs are abundant with examples of this type of logo-trash and, as and the anti-spec movement was able to show on many occasions, people actually win contests by just uploading clip art.[66]

Participating designers who aim for quality and honesty need a lot of time to study the brief, research the client's business environment, and sift through the design of the client's competitors. Communication with the client, reacting to feedback that the client gives to other contributions in the same contest, providing redesigns, and finally producing a polished version of a design also all take time.

65 Clichés were used in printmaking in the 19th century, metal *stereotype* blocks to include images into moveable type.
66 Douglas, 'An Anti-Spec Work Parable – the Jon Engle vs. Stockart.com Story', The Logo Factor Design Blog (2009).

If all this is taken seriously it is almost impossible not to fall into the trap of self-exploitation. As someone with a background in graphic design who also participated in contests on 99designs and similar platforms as part of my research, I can tell from experience that it is hard to resist the temptation of putting far more hours into a design than would be economically reasonable under these conditions. In a professional relationship with a client, it makes sense to always produce the best possible results. It is an investment into future business. On crowd design platforms this is not necessarily the case, because the designers are, from the client's perspective, interchangeable.

There are different factors at play: a professional work ethic makes it difficult to stop working on a design that can still be improved; a sense of competitiveness to create the best suited, most beautiful solution for the brief, a design that stands out from the crowd – put simply, a winning design. Ideally, the design conveys the core characteristics of the client's business, makes the designer proud, leaves one's peers impressed and, most importantly, convinces the client to decide the contest in one's favour.

It is this mixture of professional work ethic, ambition, vanity, and thrill of gambling, which drives many designers to put in the extra hours, and this is significantly enhanced by the existence of the portfolio page on the platform and by the mind-set of working for one's portfolio outside the platform. In the graphic design world outside of crowdsourcing, designers also often take on badly paid jobs, pro-bono work, and unpaid internships, especially early on in their career, in order to have presentable real world examples of their skills, and to have something impressive to show to potential clients or employers. In the case of the 'logo mills', the portfolio is even more important, because it is permanently public and there is no personal contact with the clients. The quality of the designer is judged (by peers and clients) primarily based on the quality of the portfolio.

Speaking from my own experience, but also from knowing many other designers, a design that is publicly accessible, attached to the name of the designer, feels to some extent like an externalised piece of one's personality; at the very least it is a calling card, promoting the designer's skill. Each design has to stand for itself, nobody who looks at it later cares about whether there was no time to do it properly or only a small chance of eventually getting paid. It has to look professional and original. Because the platforms organise public contests with public portfolios and constantly foster the hope of finding new clients through the exposure of work, they entice designers to act in a way that is economically unreasonable.

This is an inversion of the problematic in microtasking crowdwork. In this instance the situation is difficult for the workers because they are anonymous, invisible, dehumanised, and alienated from their work. Designers on logo platforms fall into the trap of self-exploitation because their work and their professional persona as a creative is so exposed. Designers have to constantly come across as friendly, cheerful, innovative, diligent, and industrious. All theirs designs – and comments –

are being recorded on the public platform. The result is a cheery Panopticon of a workplace, one that never forgets but constantly gives gamification points (see chapter three) for favourable behaviour. The portfolio entices designers to work harder, and the gambling aspect that comes with the contests significantly enhances this tendency. The dangerous delusion is that it is worth putting in just a few hours more in order to win, to be the best – against all odds.

For those who try not to fall into the trap of self-exploitation, there is still the other option – cheating – trying to game the system by uploading plagiarised designs. As much as it is against the ethos of originality usually held in high esteem in the design community, and despite the fact that designers are legally responsible for such copyright infringements, this strategy is common in contest-based creative crowdwork. Many creative crowdworkers seem to underestimate the risk of uploading stolen graphic content – if a client buys such a design, uses it, and then gets sued for copyright infringement or has already printed for example an edition of books with plagiarised covers it is of course the designer who is liable for damages, not the platform. For the small chance of winning a few hundred dollars by taking an illegal shortcut in a contest, one can easily face costs many times higher than the awarded money.

In a contest on 99designs in which I myself participated in 2012, a community college from the US wanted the crowd to design a logo based on their mascot animal, a sculpture of a lion. As usual, dozens of designs were submitted, among them, also the lion on the left in fig. 27. It wasn't before long that another competitor in the contest pointed out to the client:

google head or lion head tattoo, you can find so many lion head that really similar with the designs that submitted here. for example: design #97 is an istock image, you can find it here: [htttp:/...] or a little bit customized from lion head tattoo, design #38 #39 from tattoo design here: [http://waktattoos.com...] you can see the hair pattern is so similar. just fyi :) [67]

And indeed, the the pattern of the mane is a slightly modified copy of the vector file found under the given address, while the face of the lion handed in to 99designs seems to be pasted in from another source.

This is a very common situation on logo platforms. In addition to the design work, the crowd also takes on the job of reporting infringements of others in the crowd to the platform or the client. One can't expect solidarity among competitors in cases of fraud within a competition, but what becomes evident once again is that the individuals in the crowd are pitted against each other in an economical race towards the bottom. The clients are not able to tell which designs are rip-offs because

---

67 https://99designs.de/other-art-illustration/contests/help-pierpont-community-technical-college-art-illustration-204333/messages [accessed 10 January 2017].

27 On the left, an example of a plagiarised logo posted in a contest on 99designs, based on a tattoo clip-art from the website 'Waktattoos.com – A Resource of Your Masterpiece', depicted on the right (2012).

they lack the expertise and typically don't stumble on potential sources of 'inspiration' as the designers in a contest do. Despite the high commission fee, the platform providers don't engage in this kind of policing. They let the crowd do it and only then take action after a copyright breach has been reported. When this happens after the design was sold, the client gets his or her money back from the platform.

99designs describes itself as a 'community'. And many of the designers who work on the platform accept that terminology. However, it is questionable as to what the communality or the shared interest of this particular crowd is, since its interactions constantly revolve around winner-takes-it-all contests. It is an environment in which everybody fights for themselves. On top of the already problematic situation of having to win a contest against all other 'community members', the two approaches of trying to make ends meet in this environment – self-exploitation or plagiarism – at times create a poisonous working environment in which community members have a strong incentive to report each other's misconduct to the contest platform and the client. Understandably, those who invest many hours into an elaborate original design can't risk being outmanoeuvred by fraudulent competitors with a copy and paste attitude.

GLOBAL CROWD, LOCAL COMMUNITY

Some crowd-workers have a very low cost of living and no other option to find clients nearby because they often live in remote areas or regions with a struggling economy. This is why globalisation is the most relevant economic driving force behind the rise of the crowd platforms for design. To describe the outsourcing workforce in developing countries sweepingly as amateurs is a blatant misrepresentation.

The role of globalisation in shaping the way the crowdsourcing of design has developed can hardly be overestimated. As Thomas L. Friedman has described vividly in his seminal book on outsourcing, 'the world has become flat'.[68] For jobs that can be done by an individual on a laptop – a significant portion of design work – the internet has created an increasingly level playing field. The main prerequisites are that both parties in an outsourcing operation speak the same language, have access to a fast internet connection, and that the product or service can be digitised. Within professions where that is given, everybody stands or will stand in competition with everybody else who is offering the same service over the internet. In this respect, crowdsourcing is really just an intensification of a much larger economic development that has been going on since at least the 1990s. Now, though the partners on both sides of the outsourcing process are potentially individuals, not necessarily companies. This is unlike Apple outsourcing to Foxconn. With crowdsourcing, the competition happens on the individual level on both sides and without anyone being employed. With the click of the mouse you can either hire or join a crowd no matter where you are.

According to an interview that 99designs CEO Patrick Llewellyn gave in 2013, about half of the money that the platform pays out to designers goes to Asia – to the Philippines and India in particular – while about 70% of the clients come from the US and 15% from Europe.[69] Unsurprisingly, the outbreak of indignation regarding the business model of 99designs happened primarily in wealthy western nations, while designers from poorer regions in the world are more likely to identify with doing spec-work for a living. This becomes clear when looking at the size of the self-organised local MeetUp groups of 99designs workers, which in 2014 could be found in more than 200 cities worldwide. To join such a group and go to the regular meetings shows a level of identification and dedication that is geographically very unevenly distributed. While in 2014, the groups in London and Berlin only had eight members each, the ten largest groups were in:

---

68 Friedman, *The World Is Flat* (2007).
69 Ho, 'Design Competition Model is Working for 99designs, especially in Asia', *TechCrunch* (2013).
    See also: Wee, '99designs: "There's Raw Talent in Indonesia and Philippines"', *Tech in Asia* (2013).

28 The distribution of 208 self-organised Meet-up-groups of the 99designs workforce across the globe.[70]

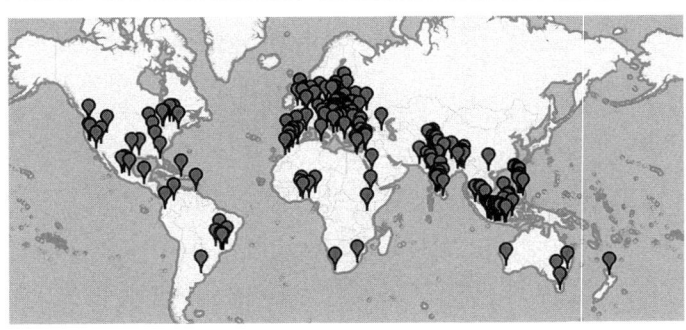

1. Yogyakarta (Indonesia) 164 designers
2. Belgrade (Serbia): 130 designers
3. Novi Sad (Serbia): 124 designers
4. Davao (Philippines): 78 designers
5. Bucharest (Romania): 74
6. Bandung (Indonesia): 70
7. Manila (Philippines): 70
8. Jakarta (Indonesia): 60
9. Karachi (Pakistan): 57
10. Dhaka (Bangladesh): 56

The local 99designs community of Yogyakarta in not only the largest one, but as it seems to be also the most dedicated. At a meeting in 2012, depicted on the photo on the right, the group composed a creed that is a remarkable expression of their identification with and their loyalty to the platform:

We who are present at the 99designs Meetup in Yogyakarta-Indonesia are proud of our identities as Indonesians and as designers, and we are committed to representing our community with integrity and professionalism. Sadly, there are some negative perceptions of our community that have taken root because of the unsavory actions of a small minority of players. We are here to take a stand against those perceptions by establishing and maintaining a high set of behavioral standards.

Resolutions:
– We strive to cultivate an informed and respectful community of designers who are well educated in international copyright law and the 99designs Code of Conduct and help share that knowledge with others.

70 '99designs Meetups Everywhere', Meetup http://www.meetup.com/99designs/ [accessed 16 August 2014], the group does not exist anymore, but the data can still be accessed via the Internet Archive.

29 The 99designs crowd of Yogyakarta,
Indonesia, 2012, in front of a collectively
made 99designs-mural.[71]

- We will carefully review any copyright infringements and accurately report violations of the 99designs Code of Conduct to the site administrators.
- We will help minimize negative and inappropriate comments targeting designers and clients by setting a positive example and cultivating a community of professionalism and respect.
- We support the crowdsourcing platform as an outlet for creative and professional services. We invite all fellow designers to join us and help uphold its rules and regulations.

We hope that with the creation of this resolution of graphic designers in the Meetup Yogyakarta-Indonesia, creatives and designers from all countries will understand the true and honest spirit of the Indonesian graphic design community. We are members of 99designs and we will always strive to do clean and honest work while maintaining a purity of creativity in accordance with the rules of the site.[72]

This creed is remarkable on several levels. First of all it shows how differently 99designs is perceived in a developing country like Indonesia. It is a highly visible and symbolic expression of a crowd that has transformed into a local community, by meeting in a physical place and by setting themselves rules to which they pledge to abide. What they did could be regarded as the epitome of professionalism. Almost like a guild, they guarantee to ensure quality to the outside world by applying social self-control with regard to the ethics and standards of their craft. They also directly address one of 99designs' biggest problems with quality, namely plagiarism and neglect of copyright issues. They seem to have had the feeling that they as Indonesian designers of 99designs had to defend themselves against such accusations and they

71 Ellison, 'An Epic 99designs Meetup in Yogyakarta, Indonesia', 99designs blog (2012).
72 *Ibid*.

decided to do this by building a local community that is proud of its identity, first of all as Indonesians and then as designers.

To fully understand the power of crowdwork, it is crucial to acknowledge the opportunities it offers for people who were previously excluded from participating in Western creative industries, not because they were amateurs or 'barbarians at the gate', held at bay by a 'snooty elite' of professional designers, but because of much larger inequalities and injustices of the capitalist world order. Designers in the rich half of the world must be very careful not to attack the injustices of crowdsourcing by dismissing their colleagues in the other half of the world as amateurs. What is needed instead is solidarity between the designers and a critique of the platforms on the level of the asymmetrical power structure they systemically establish.

In March 2011, Grace Oris, a designer from the Philippines published a remarkable and much read post on her blog about quitting her 'Spec Addiction'.[73] Her voice is important because it comes from a country where the salary per day, according to Oris, can be as low as $4. She described her experience with the logo platforms as a trap that novice designers can easily fall into:

It may start with 'Wow, that's easy! I can do a much better design than that.' So you sign up and if you are any good, you might get 4 or 5 stars and feedback that goes something like: 'I really, really love your design! Could you please make the following changes ...?' Anticipating a win, you happily make the changes, create as many variations as possible and go so far as to show your design in context. Unfortunately, you lose. You wonder what you did wrong, was definitely sure you were going to win, and overall feel pretty rotten. But you move on to the next contest. [...] It's a pathetic cycle of excitement-discouragement-delight-dejection ...

Grace Oris is an engineer by training, writes fluently in English and is very outspoken. In her blog post against the 'spec addiction', she referred to numerous articles from professional bodies of the western design industry, especially from the anti-spec movement.

I stumbled into design through this (crowdsourcing) design backdoor while looking for online work. Although I am grateful that these contest sites introduced me to a passion I wasn't previously aware of, I am certainly not proud of it. After reading countless anti-spec articles (you can start by reading David Airey and No!Spec), I was convinced spec work was unethical. You can sum up all the arguments in a simple analogy like, would you order various dishes at a restaurant and pay only for the one you like best? It is embarrassing that I used to value myself so poorly as to be counted among seemingly dispensable designers who get no compensation for hours of work.

---

73 Oris, 'How I Quit Working for 99Designs, Crowdspring and Mycroburst', blog post, graceoris.com (2011).

Her post shows that it is a prejudice to see outsourcing as being limited to unskilled, uncreative labour, performed by people otherwise disconnected from the labour marked or the design discourse in the Global North. Western design activists such as David Airey are read at the other end of the world, too. He in turn also took notice of Oris's article and responded in the comments section – together with many long statements by designers from developing countries, either strongly agreeing with Oris criticism or defending creative crowdwork as a boon. The entire thread is 17,000 words long. The world of digital creative labour has truly become flat, with a shared language, the same access to resources like tutorials and image databases, the same digital tools, and shared concerns exchanged in trans-national debates via social media. Grace Oris is also an example that the professionalisation promise of 99designs can to some extent become true, as she describes that only through the platform had she discovered her passion and talent for graphic design, which she went on to do full time – though not by participating in contests anymore. She looks back at the platforms with disgust – because they provide an 'atmosphere' as she puts it, 'that could eat you.' She clearly states that even if one can manage to generate a living wage this way because of low cost of living, what remains is a sense of indignation, of having to gamble for fair payment. Which is why she argues that people from developing countries have to come to recognise their true value in a globalised economy. The Philippines is a country with a large number of adults working abroad, for example as sailors or nannies, often having to leave their children behind. For people like Oris, the internet is the great opportunity to put an end to that, yet she came to regard crowdsourcing as a trap undermining the ambition to become a self-determined and proud professional.

DESIGNING A FAIRER CROWD DESIGN PLATFORM

The previous sections showed that contest-based creative crowdwork in the manner of 99designs and other logo mills is a race to the bottom, a winner-takes-it-all system in which getting paid is a gamble for the creative workers – though not for the platform. There is fierce competition based primarily on price not on quality, resulting in self-exploitation and plagiarism and a working environment in which designers are pitted against each other also with regard to the self-policing of copyright infringements. All legal and economic parameters are geared decidedly against the participating designers and the platform has successfully outsourced all risks to the crowd while deliberately obfuscating its pricing structure and the win/lose ratios. The following questions arise from this: are these negative conditions inherent to contest-based creative crowdwork? Or is it possible to create a system with a better balance between the interests of the three main stakeholders, the clients, the designers, and the platform providers? Can creative crowdwork be organised in a way that is fair and economically sustainable for all stakeholders?

The Berlin-based crowd-platform jovoto aspires to do just that, and has been doing so since its public launch in October 2008. The company was created in 2007 at the University of the Arts in Berlin and was financed by individual investors, so called 'business angels'.[74] Its founder and CEO, Bastian Unterberg, has studied computer science as well as design. His art-school background and that of the platform might be the reason why jovoto is more sympathetic to the position of the creatives. In many interviews and presentations Unterberg explicitly distanced jovoto from platforms like 99designs and emphasised the importance of fairness for running a crowdsourcing platform for design.[75] He describes jovoto as an 'evolved form of crowdsourcing' with the goal of being 'as sustainable as possible for the community.'[76] Unterberg claims that his platform deals with the 'future of creative work', which he envisions as transparent, collaborative, and interdisciplinary, with open processes and flat hierarchies.[77] Unterberg states that the launch of the company was a response to the question 'How do we want to work? In what kind of structures?' In an interview in 2013, he said that his key motivation for founding jovoto was the observation that 'too much exploitation of creative talent happens in the

---

74 One of them is Prof. Dr. Thomas Schildhauer, who is also the head of the Institute of Electronic Business, associated with the Universität der Künste Berlin; Jovoto originated from this institute.

75 I met Unterberg personally in 2009 and 2010 at the conferences Volkssport Design and Typo Passion, both held in Berlin, were I invited him in my role as conference organiser to speak about his business model. I met him again for an in-depth interview in October 2014. The following synopsis is partly derived from these encounters. Schmidt/Grüner, *Volkssport Design* (2010). 'Quo Vadis Design Profession', Typo Berlin (2010).

76 Räth, 'Bastian Unterberg (jovoto) im Interview', *Gründerszene* (2011).

77 *Ibid.*

ideas industries. No matter if you look at fashion, design, architecture, or advertising most of these industries are not doing a good job at nurturing talent.'[78] According to Unterberg, the entry barriers for new designers to get into the creative industries are far too high and the goal of jovoto is to change this by connecting big brands with a large pool of young creatives. For obvious reasons, interviews with CEOs tend to contain a good deal of self-promotion and thus have to be assessed in that light, but Unterberg claims that he approaches the crowdsourcing of creative work from the perspective of the creatives and thinks that the controversial method could also be instrumental against exploitation, instead of fostering it. For Unterberg, crowdsourcing, as a concept, is first of all a neutral form of organising work that can be structured in a way that is fair and sustainable for the participating designers. So how exactly does jovoto operate and can it live up to its ambitious goals of being fair and economically sustainable?

Jovoto is significantly smaller than 99designs with regard to the size of its crowd, the number of contests held, and subsequently also its turnover. As mentioned above, 99designs is now running up to 10,000 contests a month, while as of early 2015 jovoto had run not more than a total of about 250 contests. Jovoto has twenty employees in Berlin, a core group of 2,500 very active crowdworkers who are on the platform almost every day, and a total of about 62,000 registered designers, the vast majority of whom only contribute occasionally. In comparison, as of April 2015, 99designs had almost a million registered designers. If we assume that the proportion of really active users is of a similar size, about five per cent, 99designs would have had a core group of 50,000 productive designers at the time – a workforce twenty times that of jovoto. Both platforms were launched around the same time in early 2008, but the model of 99designs became mainstream and spawned many epigones, while jovoto exists in a small niche without any direct competitors; there are other platforms that compete for a similar crowd, but not for the same clients and not with the same platform architecture. In 2010, jovoto unsuccessfully tried to expand into the US market and opened an office in New York. But the company has downsized itself again to its Berlin office plus one representative for American clients, who is based in Silicon Valley. The company has been profitable since late 2013. In Unterberg's view, 'jovoto started too early, the market wasn't ready in 2009 and the company almost went bankrupt in 2011 because it was doing too many things at once.'[79]

In comparison to the 'logo mills', the structure of jovoto is significantly more elaborate in almost every aspect – with regard to the variety and complexity of the tasks, the way contests are organised and moderated, and also the structure of its community. The term community, as mentioned earlier, is always a bit problematic in the context of crowdwork platforms, but the crowd on jovoto is certainly more

---

78 Sonne, 'Interview with jovoto's founder Bastian in Colombia's newspaper El Tiempo' (2013).
79 Unterberg: 'in late 2013 the company reached break even, but wasn't making huge profits yet'. (From my interview with U. in October 2014.)

community-like than on the 'logo-mills' because the platform tries to encourage collaboration in addition to competition.

Jovoto's clients are not small new businesses in search of cheap logos but well-established multi-national brands such as Starbucks, Coca Cola, and Unilever, but also NGOs like Greenpeace and the World Wildlife Fund, and even political parties such as the Sozialdemokratische Partei Deutschlands (German Social Democratic Party) and Die Grünen (Green Party) in Germany. In general, it can be said that the projects on jovoto are more about 'ideation' than about finished design products; consequently, jovoto markets itself as platform for Open Innovation, seeing itself not primarily as a solution for corporate clients to outsource labour, but as a way for them to harvest fresh ideas from the creative crowd.

In the field of ideation it is much harder to estimate the value that is created by the crowd, because the quality of ideas doesn't directly correlate with the invested working hours. Coming up with new ideas can feel less like work and more like play, and good ideas potentially generate much more value than the cost of labour. It is important not to confuse play, the free experimentation without strict rules, with gamification, the rule-based, quantified reward system installed on top of play and work. Jovoto is a creative playground as well as a workplace that uses gamification to reward certain behaviour. If we compare the repetitive, unskilled labour of microtasking crowdwork, the discount production of finished designs on the 'logo mills', and the development of ideas for marketing and product design as on jovoto, the work process becomes increasingly playful and harder to measure and evaluate, and the same is true for the results. A brilliant and a lousy idea can take equal amounts of time to generate, so a piece rate or an hourly rate as a basis for remuneration doesn't work well in an open crowd in which contributors potentially try to scam the platform or the client by just uploading anything.

Jovoto's contests cover a wide spectrum of creative disciplines. The platform categorises its tasks into four categories of work: Design & Branding (50% of the contests; mainly graphic design); Innovation (32% of the contests; mainly ideation for product design); Communication (11% of the contests; mainly marketing and advertising), and Architecture (8% of the contests; mainly interior design).[80] Designers who have at some point participated on jovoto came from 190 different countries; the active members come from 83 countries.[81] 24% of the members come from Germany, Austria, or Switzerland, 44% in total from Europe (including the German-speaking nations), 19% from the Americas, and 11% from Asia, mainly from China and India.[82]

---

80 Data from an info-graphic jovoto released in December 2013. The data is not online anymore, but I have a copy.

81 'About / jovoto' http://www.jovoto.com/about [accessed 22 August 2014]; the number of countries the active users come from is from the interview in the next footnote; the total number of countries ever registered is 190, according to jovoto.com.

82 The numbers date from April 2014 and were published on Slideshare: jovoto GmbH, 'Jovoto Company Presentation', 2014 http://de.slideshare.net/jovoto/jovoto-unternehmensprasentation-23404102 [accessed 27 August 2014]. Now marked by jovoto as 'private', but I hold a copy.

The strong German-speaking member base in combination with a high percentage of clients from Germany sometimes lets the conversations on the platform slip into German, but jovoto encourages its members to converse in English.

The prize money that is awarded per contest on jovoto is much higher than that on the logo platforms. Common sums paid to winners in the crowd are between 2,500 and 5,000 euros; occasionally the prize money passes the mark of 10,000 euros per contest. The Swiss army-knife brand Victorinox, one of jovoto's best and returning clients, awarded a prize pool of 24,500 euros in December 2013,[83] and in January 2011, the founder of the company LifeEdited, Graham Hill, paid the crowd on jovoto the record sum of 70,000 dollars for architectural design ideas for an ecologically sustainable flat in New York.[84]

Equally relevant to the higher sums per contest is the fact that jovoto is not based on a winner-takes-it-all system. There is always a second and third prize, usually up to ten participants win money, sometimes even more. Winners in the higher ranks usually receive rewards of about a thousand euros; those on the lower ranks earn about 250 euros per win. Most importantly, it is the community, not the client, who decides about the ranking through voting.

Such a spread of the prize money across several competitors is a demand that between 2012 and 2015 more than 3,000 designers had called for in the user forum of 99designs – though unsuccessfully: 'Designers spend their lives to create for 99designs, so they deserve to be awarded for 2nd and 3rd places. All contests should be guaranteed [...] no work without payment, designers are not a "crowd" or "herd," we are humans and deserve payment for our hard work.'[85] Obviously, the total sum of money that is being awarded per contest must be relatively high in order to allow for a reasonable distribution to a number of winners. Since this is not compatible with 99designs' discount approach, this demand of the crowd, like the one for transparency, will most likely remain unheard.

Even though also on jovoto most designers work without payment – it is a contest platform after all – all contests are guaranteed, in the sense that in any case a number of designers will win some money. In every contest, a large part of the money is distributed based on the votes of the crowd; jovoto calls this the 'Community Prize'. In addition, a 'Client's Choice' award is given to a designer if the client wants to actually use a particular outcome of the contest – this award is then coupled with an additional licensing fee for the transfer of the copyright. Until then all copyright remains with the participating designers, although for six months they are not allowed to sell their idea to a third party, in case the client decides that he or she wants to buy the idea after the contest is over. A third type of award, the 'Jury Prize', is sometimes awarded by a designated group of experts, typically in the more

83 https://victorinox2014.jovoto.com/briefing [accessed 25 January 2017].
84 https://lifeedited.jovoto.com/briefing [accessed 11 January 2017].
85 https://99designs.uservoice.com/forums/198-01-general/suggestions/2649337-award-2nd-and-3rd-places-all-contests-should-be-g [accessed 22 August 2014]. Only accessible via the Internet Archive.

prestigious, large, and public contests (this then resembles the architectural competitions discussed at the beginning of this chapter).

The client has to decide before initiating a contest on which level of the platform it should take place. There are three layers: 'jovoto.public', 'jovoto.private', and 'jovoto.invited'. In public contests, everybody can participate, no matter what their qualification is and the entire design process and its results can be seen by anyone. This can be attractive for clients who want to generate publicity for a product or a brand via various social networking platforms (and who use the crowdsourcing process as marketing tool). Private contests are limited to designers who have reached a certain level of seniority on the platform or have applied with a portfolio to prove their professional skills. These contests are smaller, more focused on quality than on quantity and often confidential. This means that the designers have to sign a non-disclosure agreement (NDA), which protects information that the client wants to share with the crowd but not with the public (e.g. concepts for a new product-line still in development). In the third layer, jovoto only works with a small number of designers, handpicked for that particular project. This third layer used to be called 'jovoto.labs' and guaranteed payment for every contributor. Not organised as a contest, it functioned more like outsourcing work to a (tightly monitored) community of freelancers.

In a 2014, business-to-business presentation by jovoto, the company explained its pricing structure in a model calculation.[86] For public contests, jovoto charges two to three times more than for private contests – the company explains this with the fact that the community management is more expensive for a large crowd with unrestricted access and also more prize money is needed to motivate a large crowd. With five to seven weeks, the contests run much longer than on platforms like 99designs and are more labour intensive for the crowd and for jovoto's staff. Jovoto separates its billable positions into five categories:

1) Access to the community and infrastructure
2) Strategy, project management, and community management
3) Award money for the community
4) Evaluation
5) Documentation and analysis

The cheapest package in this model calculation from 2014, for a private contest without any extras, was billed with 25,500 euros (with 6,500 euros going to the crowd); the most expensive one, for a public contest with extras, was billed with 82,600 euros (with 15,600 euros going to the crowd). Optional positions are the

---

86 Jovoto GmbH, 'Jovoto Company Presentation', 2014 http://de.slideshare.net/jovoto/jovoto-unternehmensprasentation-23404102 [accessed 27 August 2014] now marked by jovoto as 'private', but I hold a copy.

inclusion of external juries, a 'Facebook Voting App', and an analysis as well as presentation of the results for the client by jovoto staff. Fifty-five per cent of all projects on jovoto were public at the time; the others were private.[87] In comparison with 99designs, the crowd on jovoto gets much more money but a substantially smaller share of what the client pays: 75 per cent or more of the fee goes to the platform. However, the crucial difference is that jovoto is much more involved in guiding the design process and consulting the client, from developing the brief to guiding the designers, with a lot of design expertise, giving the client productive professional feedback based on a brief developed in collaboration with the client. The company also helps the client with the evaluation of the outcome, presenting the results in a meaningful way. 99designs typically only provides the client access to the platform and is doing the billing, while staying out of the production process, jovoto operates like a design agency with an army of mostly unpaid interns. Jovoto is not an automated, scalable software platform, and only functions with a lot of involvement of its staff, but the company is built on free labour of the crowd nonetheless. Jovoto's employees substantially contribute to the successful outcome of the design process, in close collaboration with the community, which is why the platform is usually not confronted with accusations of being exploitative by asking for spec work (though it certainly does). And yet, the gap between the market value of the aggregated labour of the huge expert crowd and the market value of jovoto's skills and infrastructure to guide the crowd is remarkable, as shown in the fact that at least 75 per cent of the client's money stays with the platform.

Gamification (see on p. 130 ff.) plays an important role for managing the behaviour of the crowd on jovoto and for transforming it into a community. The virtual gamification currency that is applied by jovoto to reward desired behaviour is called 'Karma'. The concept of 'Karma Points' to incentivise good behaviour in online communities was first introduced in the late 1990s by the news site Slashdot in order to coordinate its system of distributed content moderation. Today it is commonly used on large websites such as Reddit. As jovoto explains on its support site: 'Karma shows us how active a person is and what quality the community member's activity has. High Karma is always a good thing!'[88] Community members get Karma points for contributing ideas and for rating and commenting the designs of others. The rating of ideas is very important because it not only serves as a feedback loop to guide the design process, but is also part of the voting mechanism by which it is decided who will get one of the Community Prizes in a contest.

Since the voting behaviour of the crowd has direct financial consequences for the individuals within it, some users try to turn the odds in their favour and game the gamification system. One such strategy that has caused disputes among

87 The proportions are from the info-graphic released by jovoto in December 2013 (see above) – for some reason, they had not factored in the percentage of jovoto.invited projects.
88 http://www.jovoto.com/support/profile#5.

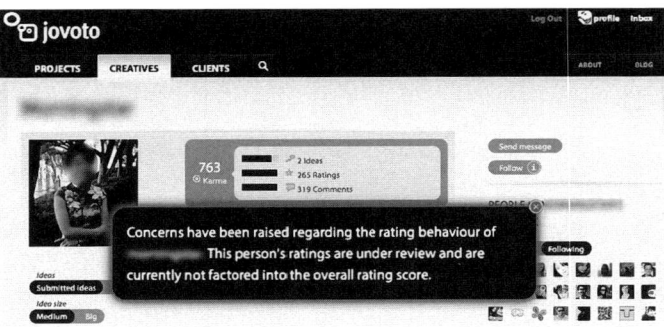

30 A profile page of a jovoto user (with 763 Karma points) who was flagged because of her rating behaviour.

community members in the past was to get friends that were previously not on jovoto to open accounts just to vote in one's favour. Now, members have to first gather 150 Karma points before their ratings are counted. By doing so, jovoto has stopped this form of manipulation or at least made it much harder. Another strategy employed by contributors to manipulate the outcome is the systematic negative rating, or 'bashing', of the contributions of competitors, regardless of their actual quality. Alliances between members that always rate each other's contributions positively are a known problem. Such strategies are harder to track and counter, but jovoto is monitoring the voting behaviour algorithmically, as well as through its community managers to discover such irregularities.

The Karma point system provides designers on jovoto with a strong incentive to interact with each other, as well as to rate and comment on the ideas of others. Through this, the creative crowdworkers get to know and help each other and together evolve from an anonymous crowd into a community with a shared history and a shared goal – to be as creative as possible for the international brands, for whom they are proud to get the chance to work. Because it is the community that decides by vote about the distribution of the money (at least to some extent), the designers have much more creative freedom. They can allow themselves to take the client's brief as just a loose starting point and 'think out of the box' to develop something that might not be marketable but still wins them a prize when the community recognises its originality and quality. In that sense, the designers on jovoto have much more creative license than their colleagues working for a particular client or agencies outside of a platform. Tasks can be approached like in art school. But in order to be awarded money, they have to rank high in the popularity contest on the platform. While the system seems to work quite well, in the sense that the highest ranked designs on jovoto, in contrast to the winners on 99designs, who tend to also be the most elaborate and creative ones, it can become a problem that the ranking is not exclusively decided on the basis of the quality of the designs, but also on the popularity of the respective designer on the platform. Voting and commenting is a reciprocal activity and community members who are very engaged in this exchange increase their chance of being awarded a community prize. An effect of this is that the feedback that designers give each other on jovoto is plentiful, concise, and overwhelmingly positive. The typical tone is that of excited cheering, maybe motivating for some but in its essence empty. Constructive criticism occurs rarely, and if it does, it is often interpreted as bashing and frowned upon.

I confronted Unterberg with my observation that the communication between the designers on the platform, although marketed to the clients as a surplus insight, tends to degenerate into a form of meaningless white noise. Unterberg admitted that he is not happy about the 'lack of criticality among community members.'[89] He told me that he had sometimes even intervened personally with critical feedback to specific designs, but that this had already led to an active community member leaving the platform for good. He explained: 'I was personally frustrated about the cheesy comments that praise mediocre ideas. And so I posted what I really thought of an idea, and I asked why it was praised to such an extent and why nobody was telling the author constructively that this could have been done better.' In order to address the problem of the hyper-friendly critically lax response, jovoto experimented with adjustments of the incentive and gamification system. Unterberg explained in 2014 that a special 'Best Feedback Award' would be introduced (which happened in May 2015) as an incentive for those crowdworkers who give meaningful, critical comments – the money for that would be deducted from the budget of the Community Award.[90] In other words, the platform was about to introduce a new lever to steer behaviour through tracking and positive reinforcement in the form of financial rewards.

Like designenlassen.de, jovoto also has a feature to rank all the designers on the platform according to the number of contributed ideas, as well as according to their Karma points. In 2015 Xavier Iturralde, a designer from Equador had more Karma points than anyone else. In early 2015 his counter read 64,026, about four thousand Karma points more than the runner-up on the leaderboard. Xavier joined the platform in September 2010 and until early 2015 rated 10,911 ideas, commented 10,354 ideas, and submitted 314 ideas of his own to 123 different projects. 73 of his ideas won a prize, in many cases one of the lower community prizes worth 250 euros, but occasionally he won more than a thousand euros for an idea. In his four years on jovoto he has earned a total of 34,577 euros, which on average earned him 110 euros per idea or 720 euros per month.[91] Xavier is one of the members in the crowd for whom it is beneficial to invest not only in the quality of his designs, but also in the affective labour of positively commenting on thousands of other ideas.

---

89 Interview I conducted with Bastian Unterberg on 8th October 2014 in Berlin.
90 *Ibid.*
91 The monthly minimum wage in Ecuador at the time was US$318 US dollars. With 745 euros or US$ 980 per month, Xavier earned three times as much through his work on jovoto.

As of 2015, his most successful contest to-date was a poster campaign for Cisco Systems from 2011, advertising a specific network router.[92] Xavier won a total of 6,000 euros in that contest. He had submitted five different design concepts, one poster series was awarded the second place of the community prize, worth 3,500 euros. Another idea, based directly on the image 'Brain/Cloud (With Seascape and Palm Tree)' by artist John Baldessari, was awarded ninth place in the competition and the community prize of 500 euros; the idea was then additionally licensed by Cisco for 2,000 euros (which of course raises the question if he and jovoto even had the copyright to sell Baldessari's image to Cisco.)

In an interview that I conducted with Xavier Iturralde in September 2014, he was very enthusiastic about every aspect of contest-based creative crowdwork.[93] Iturralde had studied design, advertising, and communication at the Universidad Casa Grande in Guayaquil, was 33 years old at the time and had 13 years of work experience as a designer in an agency. Between 2010 and 2013 he worked on jovoto as a side job in the evenings. 'Jovoto has been always my side work, the last 7 years I was a prisoner at a local agency working as Head Creative Director and Designer, but finally I claimed my independence day in August 2013 to build my dreamed design studio and private crowdsourcing platform.'[94] Before joining jovoto, he had also contributed to Threadless, a highly successful platform for the contest-based crowdsourcing of T-Shirt designs. Via a cooperation between Threadless, Starbucks, and jovoto, Xavier discovered the platform in 2010 and stuck with it. His original motivation was to see if his designs could live up to the standards of international clients and competitions. He saw the opportunity to work for globally known brands as a reward in itself, even without winning anything. He reported that he had tried out various other platforms but came to the conclusion that for him 'jovoto is the best of all by far according to: prizes, community members, type of projects, team members, interaction, brands, professionalism, fairness [...] and community sense [...].'[95] Xavier reported that he was even able to build up an on-going client relationship with a German company through jovoto. Furthermore, he pointed out that jovoto had continuously improved the platform, under involvement of the community, with the goal of making the contests as fair as possible. This is certainly very different from how 99designs deals with its crowd, where, as I have shown above, the

---

92 Cisco systems is a multi national corporation based in Silicon Valley, selling hardware for networked computing. In 2013 the company had annual revenue of US$ 48 billion.

93 In 2014, he had just launched Pictosis.com, his very own crowdsourcing platform for design, inspired by jovoto. In February 2015 it had run two contests, one for a company from Berlin that sells travel bags and awarded 5,000 dollars to the participating designers, the other one for Ecuavisa, a television network from Ecuador that awarded 4,500 dollars prize money; like on jovoto, the money was split between twenty winners, who produced exceptionally elaborate illustrations. As of 2017 it seems that this project was discontinued.

94 From the interview I conducted with Xavier Iturralde in September 2014 via email.

95 *Ibid.*

demands of thousands of designers in the support forum were ignored for more than a year and the discussion then shut down without any concessions.

To return to my initial question: Can contest-based creative crowdwork be organised in a way that is fair and economically sustainable for all stakeholders? The way jovoto has designed and developed its platform over the recent years shows that the company is sincere about creating a fair system. When it comes to platforms for contest-based creative crowdwork, jovoto is definitely fairer than comparable platforms. However, given that even Xavier Iturralde, one of the most successful designers on the platform was on average earning only 110 euros per fairly elaborate design concept that he was doing for big brands on jovoto, this is still a badly paid and precarious job by Western standards of design professionals.

It seems that Iturralde is providing more value than he is getting paid for, thus, one can argue, that he is getting exploited by the system; especially when the enormous amount of additional affective and cognitive labour is taken into account that he has to invest in form of rating and commenting the ideas of others in order to get a high Karma level, be friends with everybody and through that increase his chances of winning a community prize. If this additional amount of networking is perceived as labour is of course a question of personality: one has to be extremely passionate about designing for big brands and enjoy spending so much time in an online community – as is obviously the case for Iturralde. If all the extra communication on top of the actual design work is perceived as fun, and if all the design work is perceived primarily as a learning process and not as work, it is hard to argue from the outside that this is exploitation; especially in cases like Iturralde's, who obviously knows exactly what he is doing and is quite successful at it.

But because only tiny minority can get as much out of the platform as Iturralde and because of the imbalance between the amounts of unpaid labour and the money paid out to the crowd in total, this is a system that takes more from its contributors than it can reimburse them for. Jovoto is a substantially fairer system than 99designs, probably as fair as it gets. But it is still exploitative and, because of the use of gamification as a method of crowd control, also manipulative.

What can be said with certainty is that jovoto does not provide a sustainable workplace for those in the crowd. Unterberg admits that 'it is evident, that only a fraction are earning real money on the platform – under five per cent – our job as platform providers is it to think about the next steps towards how to further develop the system in a way that those who understand it as a workspace also get some security.' He is very aware that the fundamental problem is the contest model itself, that this cannot be sustainable for the majority of the participants. Unterberg acknowledges that 'a contest-based model of course benefits first of all the client with regard to price and not the workers.' But he continues to explain that jovoto wants to use the contest approach only for certain jobs and wants to handpick the best designers from the crowd and pay them in full for more advanced jobs. He says that his goal is to identify those community members who perceive jovoto primarily as a workplace and is thinking about how to 'improve their income perspectives sustainably and generate more security for them. We have to offer more security to the people – and get out of the contest model, in this segment.'

Furthermore, Unterberg revealed that in order to keep the company afloat, it relies on the large percentage of the community who regard their labour on the platform not as a job, but as a creative leisure time or as professional training. 'We need the contest model, and it makes sense when many people work together, learn from each other, have fun, and also generate solutions; some earn money, others generate new skills or a network, then that is okay for everybody, and at the end of the day there are solutions for clients who pay for it. We need the large talent pool in order to extract the best from it.' Unterberg's vision for the future of creative crowdwork, the way he imagines it to be in 2030 is as follows:

I see a creative playground for a quarter million people who get the possibility to test out their abilities, get access to tasks … and that has something of an internship … from among those are five thousand people (2%) who went through an assessment centre within the system in order to then work in a space that offers them all the securities that an employment would, but with the advantage that they can choose with whom they want to work, when they want to work, on which topics they want to work. We will even create safety measures such as labour union engagement, lobbying for the creatives, [...] and think about different insurance policy products, so that people can work securely also in these environments [...] that is the great goal that we are aiming for with jovoto.

No matter how fair jovoto designs its contests, it can't do without them and it is thus best described as a very lean design agency that manages to run its business with ninety-five per cent of its staff being 'unpaid externs'. Like with internships, this can make sense for young designers as a career stage to pass through, but it is certainly not a sustainable source of income in the long run. The biggest problem with jovoto as a model, is that it makes it feasible for big clients to take advantage of the crowd and use it to develop much more complex and valuable projects than it is possible on more primitive, scalable platforms like 99designs. The logo platforms exert pressure on the income of individual freelance designers outside the platform. Jovoto has constructed a more elaborate system by which it can use the freelance designers to exert pressure on other design agencies and compete for their much larger budgets. By doing so, jovoto is encroaching on a higher segment of the design industry. This seems to be working to some extent, but the comparatively slow growth of jovoto and the fact that there are no competitors using this advanced model of contest-based creative work shows that this market segment cannot get as easily disrupted as the low budget logo market. The logo platforms have established themselves as an industry, while jovoto has created a niche as a laboratory for a potential future of work.

To conclude this chapter on the crowdsourcing of design, it is insightful to have a very brief look at Quirky, another such laboratory for contest-based creative crowd-work with a fairer distribution model. Founded by the young entrepreneur Ben Kaufman in 2009 in New York, Quirky applied the method of crowdsourcing to the field of product design, and for a few years it seemed to be quite successful at that and Kaufman became something of a celebrity with his own reality TV show about Quirky. Between 2009 and 2013 Quirky raised US$ 169.5 million in venture capital from big investment firms but also from General Electric (GE Ventures). In November 2013, it was still described as 'New York's most underrated start-up' by the tech press.[96] But in September 2015 the company had to file for bankruptcy and the remaining parts of Quirky and its spin-off Wink were sold off for just 4.7 and 15 million US dollars respectively.[97] What did Quirky do differently and why did it fail?

Ben Kaufman's goal was to democratise innovation, invention, and design by letting the crowd vote at almost every step of the development process and that way ensure that the company would only create products that the masses wanted and would buy in large quantities.[98] Quirky appealed to inventor types who had an idea for a new product, ideally a small, plastic-based household appliance with a clever twist. The inventor would then present the idea to the crowd, who in turn would make suggestions regarding specific features as well as the overall design, the colour scheme, and the product name. It was a cycle with several iterations in which Quirky's team of about a hundred employees, many of whom are product design experts, produced prototypes, staged, and broadcasted public voting sessions on new products and eventually coordinated the mass manufacturing of the products bringing them to the shelves of massive retail stores such as Target in the US.

Quirky's most original and promising approach was that the platform tracked all the little micro-contributions by every crowd member and later distributed part of the retail revenue accordingly (10 to 30%). Basically, the crowd designers earned royalties when the products they had worked on made it to the shelves. Printed on the packaging was a long list of hundreds of co-designers from the crowd and a figure with the 0.X per cent each had contributed to the final result. This form of crowd-royalties can only work for products that are sold in discrete units because it must be possible to directly measure the revenue of what the crowd-designers have created. It would not be possible to apply this method to the types of design – branding, marketing, web-design – that 99designs and jovoto are offering. Who could say what exactly a new logo contributed to an increase in revenue by a company? For a while it looked like Quirky had found a way to at least make crowdsourced product design fairer – not a winner-takes all game. But the economics of physical retail products that this solution was based on also played an important role in Quirky's

96   Griffith, 'With $79 million Series D round, Quirky is New York's most underrated (yet well-funded) startup' *PandoDaily* (2013).
97   Gleason/Mann, 'Invention Startup Quirky Files for Bankruptcy', *Wall Street Journal* (2016).
98   Schmidt, 'Hive: From the Production for the Masses to Design by the Masses', *Bauhaus Magazine* (2012).

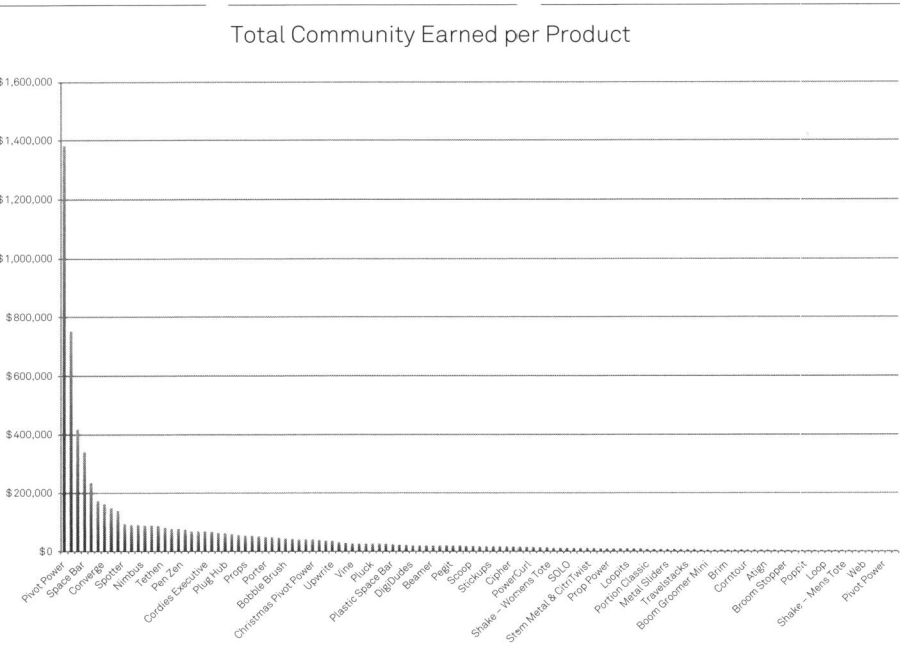

Total Community Earned per Product

31 Revenue paid out to the crowd on Quirky for each product, calculation by Miles Grimshaw, 2014.

downfall. In order to be able to bring the products to the shelves of large US retail chains, Quirky had to produce in advance quantities of tens of thousands of units; also the in-house team of design experts and the machinery for physical prototyping was expensive. All this brought with it a lot of risk and it turned out that Quirky's core idea, to let the crowd vote at every stage to make sure that only products that the masses really wanted make it into mass production didn't work. Most of its products were silly gadgets nobody needed or bought. In 2014, the data analyst Miles Grimshaw revealed that Quirky's assumed success was based on a typical power law distribution: essentially the company had one and a half big hits and a long tail of duds.[99] The hit was 'Pivot Power' a bendable multiple socket strip.

In the later phase of Quirky, Ben Kaufman made a series of other strategic mistakes by expanding the business to produce more complex, expansive, risky, and silly 'Internet of Things' appliances. The most infamous one is probably 'Egg Minder', a 'smart' egg tray (produced together with General Electric) that is connected to the internet so that one can see on the smartphone how many eggs are currently in the fridge.

99 Grimshaw, 'Analysis of Quirky: Do Consumers Know What They Want?' (2014).

Without going into the details of how exactly Quirky failed, the case still offers a few important insights on platform-based crowd creativity: first of all, a truly open creative crowd that demands no professional qualification as an entry barrier inevitably produces a lot of bad ideas. As long as this is only happening in the digital domain, where the only production cost is the labour provided by the crowd, and this labour is not properly paid for because of the contest model, the marginal costs for the platform provider is almost zero. If in addition, the client makes the choice and bares the cost for what will eventually be produced, the platform has outsourced practically all risks of business to the other two parties in the platform triangle. But in the case of jovoto and Quirky, a lot of work is done by an in-house team of professional designers, which already means that the marginal costs for the development of each project increase, even if it stays digital, so that the platform cannot scale indefinitely without friction, that is to say without hiring more and more expensive employees. In the case of Quirky, due to the high costs of producing and distributing physical products, the financial risks that the platform has to bare are far greater, even if all the ideas and a lot of the design labour is almost free or only has to be paid for when the product becomes a success. Quirky believed that it could circumvent the risk of investing in the wrong products by letting the crowd filter out the potential hits through voting. Maybe if this filtering process had worked, all the bad design ideas wouldn't have mattered, because they wouldn't have been turned into physical objects. In hindsight, it is now clear that this failed miserably. Which of its own ideas the crowd on the platform liked turned out to be a very bad indicator for what people would actually buy. Groupthink set in, the most uncreative and stupid form of crowd behaviour, and people voted in favour of one silly product after another. Whether that was the case because Quirky didn't stick to what Francis Galton and James Surowiecki had found out about the importance of having the individuals in the crowd make their decisions in isolation in order to get wise results (see on p. 038 ff.)), or because the crowd had a vested interest in getting its products into the stores because it was the only way it could make money is hard to say. The sad moral of the Quirky story is, and Ben Kaufman said so himself in an incredibly candid interview about the failure of his company,[100] that in the platform economy, it is unwise for a platform provider to put its own capital on the line, when you can be so much more successful by outsourcing all the risks to the other players in the field. Event though it is the more complex, multi-layered models for the distribution of revenues to the crowd that at least hold the potential to be fairer for the creative workers investing their time, it is the more primitive, ruthless, automatable, and scalable models with very low overhead, like that of 99designs, that are inevitably more compatible in an unregulated market.

---

100 'Quirky CEO Ben Kaufman at Fortune's Brainstorm Tech 2015', *Fortune Magazine*, interview available on YouTube.

Conclusion: Towards an Ethics of Creative Crowdwork

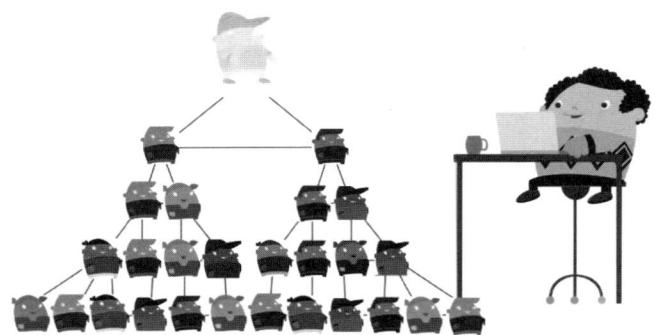

32 Juxtaposition of two illustrations showing computer-enabled pyramid structures: at the top, a critique of such a structure from 1964, below an advertisement of such structure from 2011.[1]

1   Above: Illustration from the W.E.B. Du Bois Newsletter, 1964. Below: illustration from a promotional video: 'MycroBurst Video – How It Works' (2011), available on YouTube.

TWO PYRAMIDS

The similarities between the 1964 caricature against a dehumanising computerisation of the university and the 2011 advertising for creative crowdwork are remarkable, even though they come from different contexts, or at least different phases of computing history. Both deal with the relationships between different groups of stakeholders, enabled through the introduction of an automated system. Both show a computer-enabled, hierarchical power structure, with masses of interchangeable sub-humans at the bottom and people with more human features residing over them. Taken out of context, the image from 2011 could easily serve as a critique of the structure it is advertising, a Darwinian survival of the fittest. It all depends on whose perspective we take. The upper image is designed to inspire indignation and protest among the students depicted as punch cards. The image below is designed to attract paying clients wanting to orchestrate the work of the minions. The new aspect about the contemporary pyramid structure is that everybody with a few hundred dollars to spend can temporarily be in charge and give orders to the crowd. It offers exploitation-as-a-service. The new system is open in this regard. In principle, the roles are flexible, everybody can choose whether to 'make money' or 'get work done', become a boss or a subordinate. But the system is based on economic inequality – it is built on the premise that the time of one person is much more valuable than the time of an entire crowd.

In comparison with the depiction of the more rigid, institutionalised power structure from 1964, it becomes clear that the contemporary illustration is incomplete, because it only shows two sides of the platform triangle. The true power, however, lies not with the client who can be king for a day, but with the platform providers who own the structure, make the rules, externalise all risks to the depicted stakeholders, and take a high percentage of all transaction that occur within the system. They are the ones who commissioned this drawing but preferred to stay out of the picture. In a more complete depiction, they would be positioned in an extra layer, above the client and the crowd. Above them there would be yet another layer, the equivalent to the men with the top hats on the left: the venture capitalists, who through their risky investments make the aggressive growth of these platforms possible in the first place, but who also expect a hefty return on their investment. This makes it difficult to change the existing platforms. The planning of new and fairer platforms has to factor in the larger market forces at play, as well as the inherent logic and limitations of virtual crowds.

The question of how to best design a platform for the outsourcing of digital labour that is fair and economically sustainable for all its stakeholders perfectly fits the definition of what German design theorist Horst Rittel calls a 'wicked problem'.[2]

---

2   Rittel/Webber, 'Dilemmas in a General Theory of Planning' (1972).

These problems occur when planners want to intervene in 'open societal systems', in order to solve 'distributional problems' from a position that is not primarily concerned with technical and financial efficiency but with equality and fairness.[3] Similar to Herbert Simon's definition of design as devising 'courses of action aimed at changing existing situations into preferred ones', Rittel writes that:

Problems can be described as discrepancies between the state of affairs as it is and the state as it ought to be. The process of resolving the problem starts with the search for causal explanation of the discrepancy. Removal of that cause poses another problem of which the original problem is a 'symptom'. In turn, it can be considered the symptom of still another, 'higher level' problem.

The wickedness of changing complex societal systems emerges partly because the question of the desired outcomes, the 'state as it ought to be' can never be answered in an objective, neutral, scientific, and definitive way. The answer is dependent on one's values, and these of course vary greatly across society and one's role in the system. It is not a scientific but a political problem, and as a designer or planner one can therefore not stay neutral in these interventions. Already the definition of the wicked problem means taking a political stance and the resolution of it derives directly from it. To be clear: I think that the wicked problem of crowdwork is exploitation. Thus, the formulation of the goal must be to change the system in a way that prevents or at least alleviates exploitation.

But people with varying sets of values also have different definitions of what exploitation is, some deny that this is happening in crowdwork. People with a neoliberal, free-market worldview argue that nothing should be done about the various types of digital labour platforms at all, that the invisible hand would arrange the playing field towards the best possible outcome. They argue that a politically motivated intervention in the form of political regulation would only hinder economic growth and entrepreneurial ingenuity. Some might even say that the power law probability distribution in contest-based creative crowdwork is a fair outcome, merely a reflection of how talented and hard working people are, that the losers have simply not tried hard enough, and that people must have the freedom to work for as little as they like.

In a *New York Times* article from 2013, Nancy Folbre, economics professor at the University of Massachusetts, discussed the question of whether crowdworkers should be entitled to minimum wage.[4] Her text concluded that in order for crowdsourcing to become a sustainable workplace it will 'require forms of collective gov-

---

3   Rittel uses the phrase 'concerns with equity', but because in today's common parlance, especially in the language of tech start-up, the term 'equity' is used in the sense of capital flow, I use the terms equality and fairness here instead to prevent confusions. The context in Rittel's paper leaves no doubt that this is what he meant.

4   Folbre, 'The Unregulated Work of Mechanical Turk', *New York Times* (2013).

ernance that mitigate the effects of market competition on those treated as mere links in a chain of algorithmic logic [...] it will require some assurance of human rights.'[5] The economist Tim Worstall, fellow of the Adam Smith Institute, a London-based think-tank committed to 'promote libertarian and free market ideas' attacked the 'stupidity' of the *NYT* in a rebuttal in *Forbes* magazine. His position is common among defenders of unregulated crowdwork, but it is rarely expressed so bluntly:

Apparently half a million people find work [on MTurk] at pay rates they're entirely happy with but pay rates that are below minimum wage. Even if we restrict ourselves only to those US based workers there are a quarter of a million people who are unemployed at minimum wage but who are entirely happy, eager even, to work for less than minimum wage. We must assume that they are unemployed at minimum wage otherwise they wouldn't be working for these sums. And we must also assume that they're happy working for these wages because they are in fact doing so. It is all voluntary, after all.[6]

Worstall grants Folbre that she has the correct facts 'lined up' but claims that she is 'stupid' because she allegedly jumps to false conclusions. From my perspective, this is exactly the problem with Worstall's statement. He acknowledges that people are only prepared to suffer this type of labour out of desperation, because they would otherwise be unemployed, but he then jumps to the conclusion that people are unemployed *because* of minimum wage regulations and, much more problematic even, that the workers must be 'happy, eager even', to work under these conditions. From my perspective, this displays not only a crooked logic but also a total lack of empathy and a remarkable degree of cynicism. With an argument like this, one can justify the most appalling forms of inequality and exploitation. And yet, both positions cannot be proven right or wrong objectively because of the 'wickedness' of the problem.

Most people have an intuitive grasp of what 'exploitation' means, but it is tricky to pin it down precisely. The *OED* defines exploitation as: 'the action or fact of treating someone unfairly in order to benefit from their work'; 'the action of making use of and benefiting from resources'. 'the fact of making use of a situation to gain unfair advantage for oneself'.[7] The term has a spectrum of meanings, reaching from merely 'utilising' a natural resource and 'putting it to good use', to 'taking advantage', 'manipulation', and 'victimisation' of 'the poor by the wealthy' – all synonyms offered by the *OED*. In the *OED* thesaurus one finds an array of alternative terms that graphically capture the common sense of what exploitation is: 'fleecing', 'milking', 'bleeding dry', 'sucking dry', 'squeezing', and 'wringing' – all these terms indicate the extraction of value, sometimes from a living source, sometimes with force.[8] This

5   *Ibid.*
6   Worstall, 'On the New York Times Stupidity Over Amazon's Mechanical Turk', *Forbes* (2013).
7   Oxford Dictionaries. Oxford University Press, n.d. Web.
8   *Ibid.*

leads to the question of sustainability: how much can one squeeze out of a natural resource without depleting it? How much does one have to feed back to those sources creating the value, in order for them to be able to regenerate? In my view, exploitation is best defined as extracting more over time than is needed for reproduction – a definition that works for natural resources as well as for human labour.

In digital labour the potentially exploited workers click on the 'agree' button from the safety of their home, without being physically coerced, which is why people like Tim Worstall argue that exploitation via the internet is not even possible. However, in 'What's Wrong With Exploitation' the philosopher and political theorist Robert Mayer, professor at the Loyola University in Chicago, explains why people can be exploited without the threat of physical force.[9] He writes that exploiters 'do harm to their victims, even when their interactions are mutually advantageous, by failing to benefit the disadvantaged party as fairness requires.'[10] Mayer clarifies that even if the workers are, in absolute terms, a little bit better off – e.g. by earning \$ 1.20 per hour for transcribing business cards instead of earning nothing – they are exploited when they do not get a fair share of the value they create. Coercion, according to Mayer, is a separate wrong and not a necessary precondition. It therefore doesn't have to be forced labour to justify the use of the term exploitation.

Treating people unfairly in an economic relationship based on an asymmetric power structure is enough, and what can be considered as fair must be negotiated. This in turn requires transparency with regard to the conditions of the deal and the possibility for the parties involved to negotiate their position. Mayer also points to the thorny problem of legal measures. An abolishment of exploitative working conditions can easily take away the little income that people make from getting exploited and therefore, in the short-term, can even worsen their situation. Crowdworkers frequently bring forward this concern, whenever legal measures to regulate digital labour platforms or a minimum wage are discussed. But without regulation, we would probably still have Manchester-style capitalism with child labour in hazardous factories. To achieve a long-term improvement of the situation for the majority of the workers, we will need some form of regulation.

One helpful way to look at the problem of how to design a fair system is a concept introduced by the political philosopher John Rawls, who argues that a social system can be fair if it is designed from behind a 'veil of ignorance'.[11] What he means is that those who design the system should not know beforehand what role they will eventually play in the system – in our case whether they will be winners or losers, platform capitalists, clients or crowdworkers. When we look at the pyramid illustration from 2011 or the information asymmetry in the architecture of any commercial platform with Rawls' concept in mind, the problem becomes immediately

9   Mayer, 'What's Wrong with Exploitation?', *Journal of Applied Philosophy*, 24 (2007): 137–50.
10   *Ibid*. p. 137.
11   Rawls, *A Theory of Justice* (1971), revised edition from1999: p. 118.

visible. It doesn't come as a surprise that it is those with privileged positions who design the playing field and prevent the disadvantaged from having a say in the structure or the making of the rules.

I have clarified why I regard exploitation as the root problem of the digital labour platforms and why I think some form of redesign of the system is necessary. But because this is a wicked problem, such an intervention in these complex sociotopes, which consist of many smaller interconnected systems and are imbedded in larger interconnected systems, it is not possible to test a solution beforehand under laboratory conditions or exhaustively describe its potential outcomes. What is even more wicked, is to define on what level of abstraction, of zooming in or out of the nested systems one should tackle the problem. Rittel writes that every wicked problem can be considered to be a symptom of another problem:

The level at which a problem is settled depends upon the self-confidence of the analyst and cannot be decided on logical grounds. [...] Of course, the higher the level of a problem's formulation, the broader and more general it becomes: and the more difficult it becomes to do something about it. On the other hand, one should not try to cure symptoms: and therefore one should try to settle the problem on as high a level as possible.[12]

Before I conclude with a number of vectors showing how to tackle the wicked problem of exploitation on digital labour platforms in general and of those for creative crowdwork in particular, I would like to briefly summarise the different levels of the problem, starting at the top and zooming further in.

Forces at Play

The phenomena that I have analysed in this book are part of a bigger picture. They are imbedded in, and the consequence of, a number of interconnected major developments transforming how work is organised in the early twenty-first century. Put in a simplified catchy form, the forces at play are: globalisation under a neo-liberal paradigm, rapidly increasing automation, flexibilisation and precarisation of work, and last but not least cloud-based virtualisation and platformisation as a means to orchestrate the distribution of labour, goods, and capital. Widespread digitisation of production and communication is a prerequisite for these developments and is already far advanced, now that the masses in the Global North have been online for years and two thirds of the population in developed nations and one third in developing nations have access to the internet. The number of self-employed people is rising and according to an annual survey by Upwork and the Freelancers

12 Rittel/Webber, p. 165.

Union (admittedly not an impartial source), there were supposedly two million people more doing freelance work in the US in 2016 than just two years earlier – all together about 35 per cent of the US workforce, or 55 million people.[13] In Europe, the percentage of freelancers in lower, but flexible, temporary and precarious forms of work are on the rise, too. Of course not all freelancers work under precarious conditions, and the times where traditional employment provided a secure career path seem to be over for an ever greater number of people. Working for a large corporation has become less attractive for lifestyle reasons, with many people longing for more independence. One consequence of digitisation is a virtualisation of infrastructure, labour, and services. Someone who wants to get work done can outsource the labour to 'the cloud' and doesn't really need to care about whether it is people, an algorithm, or a combination of both that is getting the job done, as long as the results are cheap and of good quality.

Offshoring and outsourcing are not just happening with manufacturing jobs anymore but with all kinds of services that are not bound to a specific location (see difference between cloudwork, crowdwork, and gigwork on p. 130 ff.), and not just on the level of companies, but also between individuals, outsourcing from one home office to another. If a job can be done from a laptop, it can also be done from anywhere in the world. The limiting factors are not technical but have to do with language skills and trust. For the offshoring of service jobs, countries like the Philippines are on the rise, because as a former US colony its citizens not only have good English skills, but also an understanding of American culture. It is likely that this development will occur more slowly in countries like Germany, where the language and cultural barriers to developing countries are higher.

Digital platforms play a pivotal role in this emerging global labour market for services provided by individuals – not only to organise the division of labour. Equally important is that they establish a level of trust between strangers doing business, through methods like ranking, rating, and tracking of the workers and their performance. Understandably, employers are much more willing to outsource work to strangers abroad when this occurs via an intermediary that keeps track of the independent contractors and can reward or penalise them for their behaviour.

Through the interplay of network effects, economies of scale, and venture capital there are strong monopolistic tendencies in the platform economy. The large platforms for digital labour have millions of users, those for social networking even billions. In this order of magnitude, as much communication between platform provider and users has to be automated, and the terms of use are not subject to deliberation but are decided upon in a strictly top-down undemocratic manner. So far, almost all globally operating platform monopolies are based in the US, most of them in the Silicon Valley, and as supra-national entities they manage not only to

---

13 Upwork, in cooperation with the Freelancers Union, 'Freelancing in America', annual study 2014, 2015, 2016 (upwork.com/i/freelancing-in-america/2016).

disrupt local industries, but also to circumvent, route around, override regulation and taxation that is happening on the national level – wherever possible, they favour a one-size-fits-all approach for the entire globe. In the case of gigwork platforms such as Uber, where the labour has to be done locally and therefore the client and the worker fall under the same jurisdiction, government regulations have already made great progress in recent years, making sure that laws that protect workers and clients are not completely undermined. But with regard to cloudwork that can be done from anywhere in the world, it is much harder to decide which rules and standards should apply, for example with regard to minimum wage, if workers, clients and platform-provider are based on different continents.

In the Global North and even more so in many developing nations, we are looking back at decades of deregulation. But the very least since the financial crash of 2008 and the subsequent 'rescue' of the banks that were 'too big to fail', with billions of tax money, it has become widely evident that neo-liberalism itself is a bankrupt ideology. If the citizens have to foot the bill anyway, and the state has to intervene in the market after the damage has been done, then it is clearly the better strategy to actively shape and regulate the markets and platforms to ensure they benefit the majority of the people in the long run. If platform providers take on the role previously held by employers, they also have to be held accountable by the same standards with regard to worker protection and government regulation. They are not just software companies or neutral infrastructure providers anymore. It is also important, not to fall into the trap of digital dualism here. There is no reason why the laws that have once been introduced to protect workers in the physical world against exploitation should not apply anymore, only because the work is now mediated through a platform, or done by someone across the border. We will need international standards to ensure decent working conditions.

From Tool View to Platform Politics

The counterculture figures around Stewart Brand and their various publications from the Whole Earth Catalog via the WELL to *Wired* advocated a 'tool view of the world'. They aligned their ideals with those of the early hackers with regard to their mistrust of authority and especially of large scale centralised institutions. Their analysis of the problem was right. Yet, their solution to oppressive structures was to drop out of them and create autonomous communities seemingly outside the system, independent because of their powerful tools. To change the rules change the tools was their motto. But history has shown that in a globalised, interconnected world, there is no outside anymore. To replace politics with better tools failed already in the 1960s and is much less of a viable option today. I argue that it is exactly the other way around, to change the tools and platforms, which have become increasingly complex, powerful, and oppressive, we have to change the rules on the policy level. The example of the WELL shows that as soon as the tools become multi stakeholder platforms, they are inherently political – the different users and groups on a platform have to find a decision-making process to define what interactions should be allowed in the shared infrastructure, what behaviour should be incentivised or punished, based at least on a rudimentary shared value system. So far, the dominant model is as undemocratic as it is efficient: the platform providers simply decide as (hopefully benevolent) dictators about the rules on the platform, and users who don't like the results are free to choose another platform or another market. This is not only very efficient but also convenient for all stakeholders most of the time. As long as there is truly diverse competition, this can work reasonably well.

However, the problem we are facing now arises from the fact that the wish for efficiency and convenience has led to a rise of monopolies of unprecedented scale. Some of them now reign over more users and cash reserves than nation states, but the masses of user, who are the origin of this great power, don't have a say in the definition of the rules.[14] Depending on the context and their functionality we can compare the massive platforms with states or factories. Either way, society is loosing hard won standards with regard to citizen and worker rights in these undemocratic, unregulated, and unaccountable systems. The model of coordinating social relationships via platforms is now affecting all areas of our digitally mediated life: from learning and research, to social networking and dating, to shopping and entertainment, to lodging and transportation, to, last but not least, work. The rise of the platform monopolies and their reach across all areas of life is not something a user can simply drop out of any longer without paying a high price, socially and economically. On the platforms, users can only click agree and submit to the terms of use. It's like voting in a one-party state. I argue that we must disagree and have a wide public debate about what the *terms of the users* should be and install new standards of codetermination (Mitbestimmung) and democratic representation of the masses on the platforms. We need participation, deliberation, transparency, accountability, and democratic oversight.

The platforms that we have today are not the result of technological determinism but of design decisions of the people who have developed them, and of what their users are willing to accept. Even though they can of course be redesigned, it would be naïve to regard this as a problem of design alone because the larger economic forces at play limit what is possible in this design space. An unfair, exploitative digital platform will always have an economic advantage over those who pay their workers decently. Without backing by governments, solutions designed in a way that is fairer will be eroded by market forces.

---

14 In January 2017 the news broke that Denmark will appoint an ambassador to negotiate with Google, Apple, Facebook and other tech giants: 'They are companies that influence Denmark as much as other nations do. It's a new reality. [...]They have become a new kind of nation, and we need to address that' Denmarks foreign minister Anders Samuelsen told the press. Copenhagen Post, 27 January 2017.

The Crowd Remains a Problem

Against the backdrop of these major developments, the strange reinvention of 'the crowd' in the first decade of the twenty-first century is only a symptom of subordinate relevance. As of 2017, the crowdsourcing hype is starting to wane and be replaced by the 'sharing economy' and other deceptive new buzzwords. What remains from the newly gained popularity of the term 'crowd' are at least two things: the reinvention of the crowd marks the historic shift of perspective from producing tools for individual users to producing platforms to get something from them. More importantly, in the more specific applications of the term – in crowdfunding and in crowdwork – the concept of the crowd will continue to define a platform architecture based on the principle of many-to-one. The working crowd has become an important subcategory of digital labour platforms, defined by the very specific characteristics of what constitutes a crowd. This has far-reaching explanatory power for the strengths and especially the weaknesses of this particular form of outsourcing in the wider platform economy. As such, the crowd is not an exchangeable or short-lived buzzword but continues to be an important concept for the analysis of digital labour.

As I have shown, the historic physical crowd was characterised by its hard-to-control power: Because it spontaneously gained strength in numbers it was potentially destructive and erratic. In paid crowdwork, the opposite is the case: the members of the crowd are competitors for the same sparse resources, everybody is fighting alone, and there is always someone somewhere willing to do the job for less. The potential strength in numbers is transformed into weakness. The mechanisms to control crowd behaviour through automatic tracking, five-star-ratings, and gamification are so advanced that the workforce can be kept productive, docile, and cheap. The individuals become mass-hermits in front of their screen and many choose crowdwork particularly *because* they don't want to be part of a group thing. Paradoxically, they join a crowd to be left alone. Yet it seems unlikely that their situation can be improved without some form of self-organisation.

From a conceptual point of view, any attempts to organise a crowd indeed run against the grain of what a crowd is. Prototypical crowds, online as well as offline, have no entry barriers, no boundaries, and no internal structure. There are no obligations, no hierarchies, no roles, no rules, and no binding relationships (it is what differentiates it from a community). In a true crowd, nobody has to know the other. It is a loose group of individuals, summoned by the open call, but without having to share the same values or interests. As soon as an internal structure for collective decision-making and coordinated collective action emerges, as soon as there is a division of responsibilities and roles, and as soon as the crowd gets or develops entry barriers, it stops being a real crowd. This must be understood as an opportunity. In order to gain strength in numbers, the workers have to stop being an open crowd and become an organised workforce – or subdivide into small local communities based on trust, as we have seen with the Indonesian creative crowd-workers.

The open call is a core characteristic of crowdwork, but it is also the root of its problem because of the ratio of pay per person and because of a high percentage of low quality results. By definition, the open call allows a crowd of virtually unlimited size and completely unknown level of skill to participate. This sounds inclusive and indeed offers an important entry point for marginalised people to enter a workforce. But as a result, a group of unlimited size has to compete for rewards that are inevitably always limited. For paid crowdwork with an open call, there are essentially only two methods of reimbursement: either everybody who does the job gets a tiny amount of money per task (as in microtasking) or only a tiny percentage of the very best workers 'win' a comparatively large amount of money (as in contest-based crowdwork). A third option would be to abandon the open call and preselect workers from the crowd based on their qualifications. This would reintroduce entry barriers and additional costs for 'human resources' management. Again the method would stop being 'proper' crowdwork.[15]

The employer of an open crowd has to factor in that without asking for qualifications or credentials beforehand, a large percentage of the results will be of inferior quality. This is why the platforms typically guarantee the clients that they don't have to pay anything if they are unhappy with the results. For the crowdworkers, no matter how good they actually are, this inevitably creates great uncertainty as to whether they will get paid in the end for work done in advance or on 'spec'. By joining a crowd with an unlimited number of potentially incompetent or fraudulent colleagues, the good crowdworkers devalue their own work because its worth has to be averaged with the many bad results.

Prototypical crowdwork is characterised by a mutual lack of responsibility in the sense that workers and clients *don't have to answer to each other*. They enter into a very temporary and indirect relationship, by knowing very little or nothing about each other and by not being responsible for each other. This gives both sides an unprecedented degree of flexibility and freedom. This is the crucial trade-off inherent to crowdwork as seen from the perspective of the workers: an unprecedented degree of freedom is paid for by an unprecedented lack of security.

Quality control that was once done by gatekeepers at the entry to the workplace inevitably shifts to the process and or the results. The clients can't know beforehand which of the workers will do a good job. Since crowdworkers don't have a boss, they are instead subjected either to an evaluation by other crowdworkers or to new forms of algorithmic management and surveillance. Their every mouse-click and keyboard stroke can be tracked, quantified, compared, and rated. As I have shown, some freelance marketplaces go so far as to take screenshots of the work-

15 One commercial advantage of the combination of crowdwork is that automation is that it makes jobs in middle management redundant. See: Reinhardt, 'Replacing Middle Management with APIs' (2015).

er's computer screen or even of the workers themselves via the their web-cam. The *constant real-time quantification* of their performance in comparison with other workers exerts a new level of pressure.

In principle, crowdworkers have the freedom to quit working in the middle of a task, without having to answer to anyone for their decisions or their results. In turn, the clients are not responsible to answer questions from the workers or to guarantee payment for work that is done under these conditions. The lack of responsibility on the client's side is often criticised, but when advocating for example minimum wages for crowdworkers, one has to take into consideration that both sides have very few obligations. If regulations forced clients to pay minimum amounts of money – either for the time workers invest or per task – they would indirectly be forced to control more strictly who is allowed to work on a task in the first place. The clients would have to demand previous qualifications and monitor the work process and the results more strictly, to ensure that they actually get what they are paying for. Regulations aiming for a minimum wage would therefore very likely force the crowdwork platforms to become more like freelance marketplaces. If labour unions or the government want to improve working conditions, while maintaining this high degree of freedom, as well as the low entry barriers, they will have to decide what is the lesser evil: uncertain and low pay (as on MTurk) or total surveillance of the work process (as in Upwork's Work Diary).

The economic and technical feasibility of crowdwork depends on the workers not being handpicked and individually controlled. If the clients were legally obliged to pay for each and every result produced under these conditions – as fairness towards honest workers would demand – fraudsters and dabblers would take advantage of this and inevitably force the clients into stricter pre-selection, more surveillance and human quality control of the end-results. Maybe, for regulatory purposes, this is the right way to go, but it would no longer be proper crowdwork if the workers were individually selected in advance. If a channel of communication for disputing rejected tasks was mandatory, the work would become so expensive that the process would only be feasible for bigger, more valuable tasks.

Microtasking Versus Contests

The type of labour that is outsourced to the crowd defines the method used to organise and incentivise the workforce, as well as the means for quality control. To understand the restraints for a redesign of digital labour platforms, it is insightful to compare microtasking and contests as the two core types of crowdwork. Their structure perpetuates patterns, processes, and inequalities from their offline equivalents and predecessors. Microtasking has distinctive 'blue collar' working class characteristics: it is essentially Taylorism on steroids. The contests in turn have a distinctive 'no-collar' creative class quality: it is a gamified version of unpaid extern-ships. Both systems are exploitative, but in different ways.

As unskilled labour, microtasking occurs in huge quantities of simple and re-petitive tasks. Large amounts of raw data have to be refined through human labour as one step in a much larger industrial production chain. Like at an assembly line, the workers do fractions of much larger tasks (which often remain unknown to them). The workers neither need to communicate or collaborate with each other to complete the work. Their social skills are as irrelevant for the employer as is their emotional state, as long as quality and speed remain within certain thresholds. The client knows beforehand what the result is supposed to look like – the more homog-enous the better. Originality, creativity, and personality are completely out of place. For all these reasons the work is alienating and not intrinsically rewarding. Which is also why people primarily do this work for money – not for fun, fame, or a career. Because it is unskilled labour and on top of that crowdwork the individual workers are by definition exchangeable. As a consequence, the employer invests little or nothing into the education, personal development, or health of the workforce. No formal education or training is needed to get the job, but people also leave the job without any meaningful credentials. Doing microtasking for a living is socially not held in high esteem and it doesn't offer a career. Piecemeal workers do of course get much better and more efficient over time, which is reflected in their approval rate and allows them to raise their income with seniority, but they can't climb the career ladder to a place that would provide more security and less alienating work.

The quality of the results is quantifiable and can be determined automatically. If results are substandard, the workers face algorithmically triggered sanctions in the form of a decreasing approval rates and exclusion from better paying jobs. This is control through negative reinforcement. Because quality and speed of the work are quantifiable, it is at least possible to consider either higher piece rates or even a minimum wage in this area. The psychologically most problematic aspect of this work is that it is perceived as dehumanising because the workers are treated as cogs in the machine. Yet from the clients' perspective, the invisibility and the dehuman-isation of the workers in microtasking is not a bug but a feature. This cannot be al-tered without a significant loss in efficiency and it is an important difference from the freelance marketplaces, where the clients handpick the workers and then want to virtually look over their shoulders. In microtasking, the units of work and the re-imbursements are so small that it would neither be practical nor economically fea-sible to deal with contractors on an individual level.

Contest-based creative crowdwork, on the contrary, is skilled labour. It is more intrinsically rewarding than microtasking and provides work experience that can be applied in other contexts or even serve as a starting point for a career. The design of a logo is among the smallest units possible in contest-based creative work. It would not be feasible to further subdivide this into smaller microtasks, so there is more sense of achievement from creating a complete product. Every new task is different from the last one and those who participate are free in their creative decisions. They are not meant to provide only innovative ideas but create things that are appealing, fashionable, and clever. The creative crowdworkers therefore have to invest more of their personality and empathy to produce a good result, and they have to communicate much more with each other and with the client. In other words, they have to invest a lot of affective labour, in addition to the actual task, but in turn the work is also far less alienating than piecework.

Although often badly paid, creative labour is generally held in high esteem. Many people want to work in the creative industries and creative crowdwork promises an entry into this line of work. Because of the perceived qualities of creative work, amateurism plays an important role in this type of work. Amateurs use the platforms to improve their skills, build a portfolio, and become professionals. But professionals also use the platforms to win new clients for their own business. The platform providers essentially promote creative crowdwork as an unpaid internship that will supposedly eventually transform into a career. Even though there are statistically only few winners, the opportunities to eventually apply the experience gained on the platform for a self-determined job outside of it are substantially higher than in microtasking. The skills are demonstrable through the portfolio, and all this leads to an interesting inversion with regard to the question of visibility: while people in microtasking suffer from a lack of visibility, the creative crowdworkers fall into the trap of self-exploitation through their search of exposure for their work and their professional identities. Those designers who work on the platforms to build a portfolio are always willing to put substantially more time into a design than the small chance of remuneration would allow for if seen in isolation. The high visibility of this so-called hope labour makes the people work harder. The crowdsourcer can thus harvest much more labour than he or she has to pay for.

The solutions in creative crowdwork are expected to be innovative and thus unknown to the client at the beginning of the process. That sought after solution can only be recognised in comparison with all the other solutions. This is probably the most important reason why from the client's perspective, contest-based creative crowdwork is so attractive: the client doesn't want to get stuck with just one solution or even a small set of solutions that an individual contractor (freelancer or agency) would be able to provide. The results of creative work can't be evaluated algorithmically and even humans can't evaluate them based on objective, quantifiable criteria alone. In the more primitive forms of contest-based creative crowdwork it is the client alone who decides what solution is the best and which ones will be discarded. On more elaborate platforms like jovoto, the evaluation is done by several stages of ranking, rating, commenting, and filtering, which adds another layer of unpaid labour.

While microtaskers can only stand out from the crowd by producing work faster and with fewer errors than their colleagues, creative crowdworkers are in constant competition with each other to be the most creative, most skilled, and most popular designer on the platform. The platform providers foster this behaviour through various gamification mechanisms like virtual bonus point, badges, awards, achievements, and leaderboards that reward certain behaviour through positive reinforcement in a constant feedback loop. If microtasking evokes the Taylorist techniques of Scientific Management, creative crowdwork evokes the behaviourist techniques of B.F. Skinner.

In a book on creative crowdwork, co-authored by jovoto founder Bastian Unterberg, the TV show American Idol is mentioned several times as an example for how good the contest model works in bringing forth the best performers.[16] The problem with stardom is of course that it must follow a power law distribution. It is lonely at the top and it takes a lot of losers to make one winner. This is hardly a sustainable model to organise the future of work. It's what labour scholar Andrew Ross calls a jackpot economy.[17] This pattern is not a problem of creative crowdwork alone. It is more visible there but can be found across many creative professions, in media jobs, in the arts but also in academia. Many years of free labour are expected and people take the risk not because of the economic prospects, but in spite of them. They put in the extra hours and endure self-exploitation and precariousness, out of passion and for the slight hope of being one of the few who hit the jackpot. Typically, it is an individual who wins the award, who gets the solo-show, and the tenured teaching position. Exceptions do exist but they are rare. Under the current economic paradigm of neo-liberalism, society is geared towards individualism and stardom and whoever fails has to blame him or herself alone.

Let's Redesign It

At the media festival transmediale in Berlin in 2015, Peter Sunde, co-founder of the Pirate Bay delivered a remarkable but depressing speech. He criticised the centralisation of power on the internet and argued that we have become isolated worker drones:

We all praised the internet for the liberty it brings but it has become the essence of what is wrong [...] We talk about robots and technology taking our jobs, as if jobs had a higher goal in themselves besides what needs to be done. [...] We don't see that we are becoming robots that work all the time [...] We talk about start-ups and entrepreneurship as the future [...] but we outmanoeuvred ourselves into believing that alone means strong.[18]

16 Abrahamson/Ryder/Unterberg, *Crowdstorm* (2013).
17 Ross, *Nice Work if You Can Get it* (2009).
18 Sunde, 'Peter Sunde at transmediale 2015 Opening Ceremony' (2015), available on YouTube.

At the same conference media scholar McKenzie Wark touched on a number of similar points, but ended on a lighter note. 'The whole planet has become a badly designed computer game; it is not working anymore. Let's redesign it – could be fun!'

In that spirit, I want to conclude with a look at the options for a redesigning of the digital labour landscape. The platforms market themselves as the future of work, and if these claims are to be taken seriously, we have to think about measures that alleviate their exploitative and manipulative effects. As I have shown, a part of these tendencies is inherent to crowdwork and can therefore not be solved within the crowd paradigm. The best advice for most people is therefore to stay clear of crowdwork entirely if they have better options. But it is important to keep in mind that for marginalised groups across the globe, in rural areas, in developing countries, in regions hit by recession, for people who can't get a better form of employment because they are bound to their home, because of health issues or because they take care of relatives, this method of work can offer an opportunity (as in creative crowdwork) or has become a necessity to make ends meet (as in microtasking crowdwork). The advice to simply stay away from the platforms doesn't solve the problem these people are faced with on a systemic level. I see essentially four different angles to address the problem of power asymmetry and exploitation in crowdwork and the wider platform economy: education, regulation, unionisation, and cooperativism.

Education of Crowdworkers and Clients

This first step is the easiest of the different approaches because it works without directly intervening in the structures, is not necessarily bound to national laws and can be achieved with comparatively low levels of engagement of the different stakeholders. The primary goal here is to create more transparency and knowledge regarding the processes and working conditions on the platforms, the terms of service agreements, the mediation fees incurred, average hourly wages, the win-lose-ratios, and the liability rules.

The watchdog project FairCrowdWork.org organised by Germany's largest labour union, IG Metall, is a step in this direction. On this website, legal experts of the union offer assessments and warnings regarding the terms of service agreements of numerous digital labour platforms and crowdworkers can report on their experience and grievances with particular platforms. Because of the many different digital labour platforms, with constantly changing terms of service agreements, and jurisdictions spread across the world, it is not possible to keep up with the workload of the legal evaluation in real time. The evaluation of working conditions is a bit easier, at least in principle, because the workers themselves can do this – in other words, it can be crowdsourced. This feature of FairCrowdWork.org is inspired by

Turkopticon, which as a tailor-made external add-on for Mechanical Turk counters the information asymmetry, enables mutual aid between workers, gives them more agency, and makes one particular platform a bit fairer. For a meta-evaluation website such as FairCrowdWork.org, the challenge is to find enough workers from across many different platforms to obtain meaningful and reliable assessments.

The goal must be to ensure that all stakeholders can evaluate their respective platform objectively and make informed decisions on whether they should get involved, based on economic, legal, and ethical considerations. This also means the education of crowdsourcing clients, teaching them that they potentially contribute to, or take advantage of, exploitative working conditions. And that this might not be in accordance with their corporate social responsibility programmes and could reflect negatively on their reputation (as with fashion companies producing clothes in Bangladesh under terrible conditions). As I have shown, clients on 99designs often don't even know how little of their money is eventually paid out to the designers.

One can also imagine measures like positive certificates awarded by independent, trustworthy labour organisations or consumer advocate institutions (like Stiftung Warentest in Germany), to test and evaluate working conditions on the various platforms. This could be an equivalent to *Organic* and *Fair Trade* labels that honour and reward those labour platforms with good working conditions and provide support to workers as well as to clients concerned with ethical work standards. In the same vein, efforts at self-regulation by the platforms should be supported. In 2015, the German crowdwork platform Testbirds published a 'Code of Conduct – a guideline for a prosperous and fair cooperation between companies, clients and crowdworkers'. The document, also signed by the management of the platforms Clickworker and Streetspotr, addresses a lot of the grievances brought forward by crowdworkers. It calls for fair payment and open and transparent communication between the different stakeholders. If nothing else, the document proves that there is a willingness on the side of some platform owners to counter the negative image of the industry and to improve conditions. Such advances can have an important signalling effect, at least for certain market segments, to reverse the downward spiral in terms of decent work conditions, quality, and price.

Further steps towards more transparency, which demand political backing, could be negative warnings issued by the government, like on tobacco, alcohol, and gambling products (the gambling parallel is of course particularly fitting for contest-based crowdwork). The platforms should also be obliged to present their terms of service agreements in a form that allows users to make informed decisions about the conditions under which they want to work. The platform companies have outstanding capabilities in the field of user-friendly interface design. They should use these skills to create navigable surfaces for the terms of service agreements, with more options than just an all-encompassing 'agree' button.

It also needs more robust data on the use of the platforms, which so far is often treated as a trade secret by the providers. It is still unclear, for example, which platforms are already profitable and which ones so far only burn the venture capital of their investors. Reliable data is also important to differentiate active workers from those who have only registered once and have never put in any hours, to calculate average hourly wages and to find out how many people have turned cloudwork or gigwork into a full-time job (according to all estimates, only a small minority of the general workforce).

Organisation and Unionisation of Crowdworkers

If we look at the history of labour struggles, this is the most promising approach in the long run. Yet many crowdworkers, even if they are dissatisfied with the working conditions or the remuneration on a specific platform, seem to have little interest in either self-organisation or representation of their interests by labour unions. Although network technology should make self-organisation much easier today, and there are various platform-specific worker forums, they usually revolve around how to individually get the best out of the difficult working conditions: They are less about workers' participation, collective bargaining, solidarity, and improvement of the digital labour model in general.

Organisation across different platforms and national borders turns out to be particularly difficult. The workers see themselves as individualist, competitors, not as members of a new digital working class. For the majority of the crowd, work on the platforms is temporary and sporadic anyway, a small side-job, not worth fighting for. For them it is much easier and more promising to simply search for a new platform with better working conditions. To improve their negotiating position, the workers will have to overcome the non-binding nature of a crowd and organise themselves to formulate and fight for shared goals. Crowdworkers could self-organise into nested groups, based on their platform, their country of origin, their language, the type of work they participate in, the industries that they work for, etc., and enter into collective bargaining for fair crowdwork standards. Because the crowdworkforce is atomised across the globe (to an historically unprecedented degree), an international umbrella organisation it probably needed, or at least a name, a recognisable banner, a list of members, and a crowdsourced manifesto or code of ethics. An international form of organisation and solidarity is also necessary to prevent the interests of crowdworkers from different regions of the world pitting themselves against each other. Existing labour unions will need to change their current policies regarding membership to take vulnerable crowdworkers into their fold. The greatest challenge for an organisation of the crowdworkers is that any such organisation would add an extra layer of free labour and of costs for the underpaid crowdworkers that would only be profitable over time and would therefore only make sense to people who are planning to be crowdworkers or platform workers in the future.

Regulation of the Platforms

If a business model is feasible only because it systemically underpays its workforce, which as a consequence has to fall back on social security measures eventually, the state must ensure that profits generated through underpaid crowdwork flow back to support these social security systems. Measures on the policy level could be the following: Application of national labour laws and minimum wage standards to digital labour platforms. Introduction of a special tax on profits generated through underpaid crowdwork. Such a tax could be levied on platform providers as well as on crowdsourcing clients. Platforms above a certain size that are based on the free or underpaid labour of their workforce should – because of their erosive effect on the welfare state – be subject to *more* control by the state than conventional companies, not less. They should be obliged to have democratic user council – representatives of the crowd who are able to influence the rules and regulations by which the users or workers are governed. If the platform providers don't grant their users the rights of employees, they must have the rights of democratic citizens. Plans for a potential regulation of digital labour platforms by the state are typically met with great scepticism by the crowdworkers. Professional full-time crowdworkers fear that regulation of the platforms would not improve their jobs, but destroy them. However, as soon as this reaches a certain scale, their willingness to accept exploitative working conditions also affects workers outside the platforms who have to compete with this – it is not just a private decision without consequences for others. It must be ensured that people are not involuntarily pushed into these precarious working conditions, because conventional companies that do pay for social security, safety, and training of their workers can no longer compete with the cheaper platform-based companies that have found a way to route around any social costs of labour.

Platforms for the outsourcing of location-based tasks (gigwork) have turned out to be particularly disruptive because they affect a larger percentage of the workforce and much more capital in the form of physical assets is involved. On these platforms the risk of work accidents and potential harm to people and property is far more pressing than on the web-based counterparts. As a consequence, the question of workers' compensation and liability insurance becomes important here. Furthermore, a great amount of sensitive personal data is collected by the location-based services, as the gigworkers (and, in the case of Uber, sometimes even the clients) are tracked via their smartphones. But since the gigwork platforms operate on the level of cities, they are far more visible and can be held accountable more easily than their web-based counterparts. The gigwork platforms clearly fall under the local legal framework; hence regulations are more easily accomplished and are already quite advanced in many jurisdictions. The self-organisation of independent contractors (who can meet in a physical space), as well as the development of more socially spirited non-profits and platform cooperatives seem to be more promising for location-based services. Legal claims for misclassification of employees as independent contractors are also particularly valid in this area of the platform economy. In addition, gigwork often disrupts service sectors that are already well organised when it comes to minimum wage and worker protection (in contrast to data processing and design jobs common in crowdwork).

The digital labour platforms for services that are not bound to a specific location (cloudwork), and of those especially the two forms of crowdwork (microtasking and contests), are particularly difficult to regulate because it is not always clear which national legal standards apply if all three groups of stakeholders reside in different countries. This is a tricky question, especially in relation to the minimum wage. As we have seen before in earlier phases of outsourcing and offshoring, certain jobs will inevitably be shifted to developing countries where there is still a low cost of living, but relatively high levels of education and a good knowledge of English. It is even questionable whether crowdwork in its core sense is at all structurally compatible with a minimum wage or if regulatory measures with that goal would inevitably cause crowdwork platforms to be transformed into freelance marketplaces, which would in turn be characterised by a much higher degree of worker surveillance. The organisation of labour as microtasking forms an interdependent relationship with automation. The workers are currently already training the very machines that are supposed to replace them. It is likely that a stricter regulation of microtasking platforms would accelerate the trend towards automation of these tasks.

Co-op Ownership and Design of Convivial Tools and Platforms

Over the past few years, a new movement has been taking shape under the name 'Platform Cooperativism'. It proponents are not trying to negotiate with platform owners but aspire to run their own platforms. Initiated and promoted by German-born digital labour scholar and activist Trebor Scholz, professor at the New School in New York, the movement advocates a new platform type based on cooperative ownership.[19] With the revival of this old approach and its application to new forms of labour, the workers can regain control over their working conditions. By building and owning the platforms themselves, they can redesign working conditions from the bottom up, which can be determined by workers' participation instead of investors' expectations of exponential growth and profit or economic-rent maximisation. It is highly questionable whether comparatively small and local coop-platforms can compete economically with exploitative competitors operating on a global scale. However, as with 'organic' and 'fair trade' labels, the activists could

---

19 Scholz, 'Platform Cooperativism – Challenging the Corporate Sharing Economy' (2016). Scholz, *Uberworked and Underpaid: How Workers Are Disrupting the Digital Economy* (2016).

foster a willingness in their clients to consciously pay a little more for a service that is guaranteed to have substantially better, more ethical working conditions. As of 2017, this movement is gaining a lot of traction, especially in the US and in the area of the location-based gigwork services in metropolitan areas where it is easier to organise. Platform co-ownership is an important step to counter the new challenges of platform capitalism, most importantly, because it enables the workers to take the intermediary platform provider, which usually reaps all the profits, out of the calculation. Even with a co-owned, democratically run platform, it is not easy to solve the inherent problem of creative crowdwork – the huge amount of redundant unpaid work entirely.

If one intends to maintain the crowd paradigm because of the flexibility and the low entry barriers it allows, one option would be the following: Instead of forming large, unionised super-crowds, crowdworkers could establish small, resilient units of trust. These could be 'tiny crowds' or crews, similar to guilds in online gaming, or local communities, as in the example of the 99designs group in Yogyakarta. This would mean the reintroduction of entry barriers, but on a small, personal scale. The size of a crew or community would depend on what its members would deem manageable. One entry barrier could be personal recommendations. Such a group would only take on members who are regarded as trustworthy and fit for the type of tasks in which the crew specialises. The reputation of the individuals would add up to the reputation of the crew. Risks, earnings, and information could be shared within the group and strengthen it in negotiations with potential clients. Such crews could ensure variety and quality without having to rely on academic degrees or self-policing by the larger crowd as measures for quality control. Like a guild, the group would enforce agreed standards within its own ranks and educate new members. Crews or communities of crowdworkers could form within existing crowdsourcing platforms and could gain in strength to an extent that the platform providers would have to take their views about the terms of use and working conditions into account. These crews could also form networks of small groups to gain more bargaining power. One can also imagine a network of crowdsourcing crews to build its own crowdsourcing platform based on open source software. Each crew could have its own, self-controlled, self-hosted website, but a standard protocol would unite them to form a large, decentralised crowdsourcing platform. They could become a recursive public, with full control over the infrastructure and the rules that would define their online work. Elected representatives of the crews could replace the platform providers in their current form. Or they could be reduced to the role of the neutral infrastructure providers – a role which they already claim for themselves anyway. The crews could choose their platform provider just as they would choose an internet service provider or web hosting service – a company that supplies an infrastructure for a fee (based on data processing volume rather than financial transaction volume) without interfering in the activities of its customers. In contest-based creative 'crewwork', groups could offer clients a variety of creative design solutions without having to do work entirely for free. The client would be able to choose from a dozen logos, instead of a hundred. The crew would ensure the overall quality of its contributions. The client could chose the number of desired solutions, but would have to pay a reasonably small fee for every single design. Paying, say, 600 euros for a dozen logos (50 for each) would be a similar cost to those who currently employ the crowds on 99designs, but nobody in the crew would work for free and the smaller number of results presented to the client would be compensated by a higher quality, ensured by the quality standards of the crew. More successful or famous crews could charge more. This way, the crucial connection between the total amount of work asked for and undertaken and the money paid for it would be re-established.

An unregulated, commercial contest-based crowdwork model can't be sustainable, but such a hybrid would offer the client most advantages from crowdwork without fostering exploitation. Such a system of networked communities or crews would inevitably demand extra effort from the workers as well as the clients. It would break with the crowdsourcing principle of non-binding reciprocal irresponsibility. The workers would be responsible for their crew and would have to answer to the client. The client would have to make the extra effort of finding a trustworthy and competent crew. But clients as well as workers would eventually benefit from cutting out the platform as the middleman.

Limits to Digital Labour Platforms

Over the past ten years, we have seen a rapid growth of platform-based precarious labour, but there is a lot of disagreement among experts about whether this development will continue to accelerate or reach a plateau. As with automation, the change is not yet happening across the board. Only some areas of work are suited for it. It is important to look closely at these emerging digital labour markets, from the perspective of both research and politics, to become familiar with their mechanics and develop ways to fix them. As of 2017, the new forms of digital labour only affect a small percentage of the labour market and only rarely take the function of a full-time job. Not every job can or will be outsourced to the crowd. But the basic principles of the platform economy do indeed have the potential to fundamentally disrupt the way work is distributed in society.

In the platform-mediated household services sector, one phenomenon is becoming particularly clear, which ultimately applies to all forms of digital labour: When the quality of the results and the trust between client and customer become more important than a low price, the platform model quickly reaches its limits. In those cases, it pays to invest in individual workers, train them, and bind them to the employer with fair working conditions and real career prospects. This also makes it highly unlikely that the entire labour market will eventually dissolve into gigwork and crowdwork. Nonetheless, ten years after the emergence of the first crowdwork platforms, it can be said with certainty that this is not just a temporary phenomenon any longer. A new low-wage sector for digitally mediated labour has been established and will continue to exist and grow. Disruption must not be an end in itself. The new structures must be measured against their social compatibility and, if necessary, regulated by law in order not to harm the public good.

THE AUTHOR

Florian Alexander Schmidt is a researcher, journalist, and designer from Berlin. Since 2015 he has been editor-in-chief of the German print magazine *agenda design*. From 2014 to 2016, he was guest professor for Design Theory at the University of Applied Sciences (HTW) in Dresden. He is the author of the book *Parallel Realitäten* (Niggli, 2006) on the design of virtual worlds; co-author of the book *Kritische Masse* (form + zweck 2010) on amateurism in design; as well as author of the policy paper *Digital Labour Markets in the Platform Economy* (FES, 2016). Schmidt holds a diploma in Communication Design from the Weißensee School of Art in Berlin and a PhD in Critical Writing from the Royal College of Art in London. His texts have won multiple awards for design criticism and have been published in various magazines, including *eye, form, design report,* and *t3n*.

ACKNOWLEDGEMENTS

I am very grateful to Professor David Crowley and Monika Parrinder, my supervisors at the RCA, who Socratically questioned my ideas without imposing solutions on me – they have been great teachers. A special thanks goes to my interviewees who gave of their valuable time to answer my questions. The book s also the result of countless conversations that I had with other researchers at various conferences, and with my dear friends. I am especially grateful to my brilliant wife Marie von Heyl, who patiently kept me on track with long discussions, long walks, and patient proof-reading sessions, who inadvertently had to become a expert on crowds, too, and without whom I would have likely neither started nor finished this endeavour. Finally, I would like to thank my parents, Alexander and Heidrun Schmidt, who have always been a great support to me.

BIBLIOGRAPHY

Abel, Bas van, *Open Design Now: Why Design Cannot Remain Exclusive*, BIS Publishers, 2011.

Abrahamson, Shaun, Ryder, Peter and Unterberg, Bastian, *Crowdstorm*, John Wiley & Sons, 2013.

Adamczyk, Georges, 'Architectural Competitions and New Reflexive Practices', presented at the ARCC-AEEA, Dublin (2004)

Adler, Paul S., *Market, Hierarchy, and Trust: The Knowledge Economy and the Future of Capitalism,* Social Science Research Network, Rochester, NY, 1999.

AGD, 'Zu viele Beschwerden, zu wenig Klagen – Der Fidius e. V. beendet die Arbeit', *AGD Magazin,* (10 August 2012).

von Ahn, Luis, 'Massive Scale Online Collaboration', Ted Talk (April 2011).

—'Human Computation', in *46th ACM/IEEE Design Automation Conference, 2009. DAC '09* (2009), 418–19.

— *Human Computation*, Ph. D. Thesis, Computer Science Department, Carnegie Mellon University, 2005.

von Ahn, Luis, and Dabbish, Laura, 'Designing Games with a Purpose', *Commun. ACM*, 51 (2008), 58–67.

von Ahn, Luis, Maurer, Benjamin, McMillen, Colin , Abraham, David and Blum, Manuel, 'reCAPTCHA: Human-Based Character Recognition via Web Security Measures', *Science*, 321 (2008), 1465–68.

Airey, David, 'Crowdsourced Design Is a Risky Business', *Wired UK*, (11 April 2012).

— 'Forbes Calls Designers Snooty', blog-post on davidairey.com, (3 February 2009).

Alexander, Christopher, *A Pattern Language: Towns, Buildings, Construction,* Oxford University Press, 1977.

Allan, Christopher, 'Tracing the Evolution of Social Software', blog-post on LifeWithAlacrity.com (13 October 2004).

Anbang Xu, and Bailey, Brian P., 'A Crowdsourcing Model for Receiving Design Critique', (2011).

Aneesh, Aneesh, 'Global Labor: Algocratic Modes of Organization', *Sociological Theory 27*, Nr. 4, (2009).

Anders, Günther, *Die Antiquiertheit des Menschen 1,* Munich: Beck, 2002.

— 'The World as Phantom and Matrix', *Dissent* 3:1 (1956), 14–24.

Anderson, 'Tim Berners-Lee on Web 2.0', blog-post, *Ars Technica* (1 September 2006).

Anderson, Chris, *Free: The Future of a Radical Price*, Hyperion, 2009.

—, *The Long Tail: Why the Future of Business Is Selling Less of More*, Hyperion, 2008.

Anderson, Chris, and Wolff, Michael, 'The Web Is Dead. Long Live the Internet', *Wired*, (17 August 2010).

Andersson, Jonas E, Bloxham, Gerd , Rönn, Magnus, *Architectural Competitions: Histories and Practice*, 2013.

Al-Ani, Ayad, Stumpp, Stefan and Schildhauer, Thomas, *Crowd-Studie 2014 – Die Crowd Als Partner Der Deutschen Wirtschaft (Crowd Study 2014 – The Crowd as a Partner of the German Economy)*, Social Science Research Network, 14 May 2014.

Antoine, Nadja Marlene, Ph. D. thesis 'Zwischen Kooperation und Wetteifer: Interaktionen Und Mediale Organisation von Kreativität Am Beispiel Des Koopetitiven Ideennetzwerks Jovoto', Goethe Universität Frankfurt (2014).

Araujo, Ricardo Matsumura, '99designs: An Analysis of Creative Competition in Crowdsourced Design', *First AAAI Conference on Human Computation and Crowdsourcing*, (2013).

Arneson, Richard J., 'What's Wrong with Exploitation?', *Ethics*, 91 (1981) 202–27.

Ashby, W. Ross, *An Introduction to Cybernetics,* Chapman & Hall, 1956.

Asher-Schapiro, Avi, 'Against Sharing', *Jacobin* (19 September 2014).

Askew, Kelly Michelle, and Wilk, Richard R., *The Anthropology of Media: A Reader,* Blackwell Publishers, 2002.

Autor, David H., Levy, Frank, and Murnane, Richard J., 'The Skill Content of Recent Technological Change: An Empirical Exploration', *The Quarterly Journal of Economics*, 118 (2003), 1279–1333.

Baldwin, Carliss Y., and von Hippel, Eric A., 'Modeling a Paradigm Shift: From Producer Innovation to User and Open Collaborative Innovation', *Social Science Research Network*, (2010).

Ball, Philip, *Critical Mass: How One Thing Leads to Another*, London: Arrow Books, 2005.

Banham, Reyner, 'The Great Gizmo', *Design by Choice: Ideas in Architecture*, Academy Editions (1981).

Bao, Jin, Sakamoto, Yasuaki and Nickerson, Jeffrey , *Evaluating Design Solutions Using Crowds,* Social Science Research Network, (16 January 2013).

Barab, Sasha A., Thomas, Michael K., Dodge, Tyler, Kurt, Squire, and Newell, Markeda ,'Critical Design Ethnography: Designing for Change', *Anthropology & Education Quarterly*, 35 (2004) 254–68.

Baran, Paul, *On Distributed Communications*, Santa Monica: RAND Corporation Memorandum, 1964.

Barbrook, Richard, *Imaginary Futures: From Thinking Machines to the Global Village*, London: Pluto, 2007.

— 'The Hi-Tech Gift Economy', *First Monday Special Issue #3: Internet Banking, E-Money, and Internet Gift Economies* (December 2005).

Barbrook, Richard, and Cameron, Andy ,'The Californian Ideology', *Mute* (1995).

Barbrook, Richard, and Schulz, Pit, 'The Digital Artisans Manifesto', *Imaginary Futures* (1997).

Barlow, John Perry, 'A Declaration of the Independence of Cyberspace' (1996).

— 'The Political Economy of Peer Production', *CTHEORY* 2005

Bayazit, Nigan, 'Investigating Design: A Review of Forty Years of Design Research', *MIT Press, Design Issues*, Vol. 20 (2004) 16–29.

Bayus, Barry L., 'Crowdsourcing New Product Ideas over Time: An Analysis of the Dell IdeaStorm Community', *Management Science*, 59 (2013) 226–44.

Benkler, Yochai, *The Penguin and the Leviathan: The Triumph of Cooperation over Self-Interest,* New York: Crown Business, 2011.

—, *The Wealth of Networks: How Social Production Transforms Markets and Freedom,* New Haven: Yale University Press, 2007.

—, 'Coase's Penguin, or Linux and the Nature of the Firm' (2001).

Benner, Christiane, ed., *Crowdwork - zurück in die Zukunft?: Perspektiven digitaler Arbeit,* Bund-Verlag, 2015.

Benner, Christiane, 'Online-Arbeit auf Abruf – Wer schützt die Clickworker?', *Frankfurter Allgemeine Zeitung* (19 March 2014).

Berardi, Franco, *The Soul at Work: From Alienation to Autonomy*, Semiotext(e), 2009.

Berg, Bruce L., *Qualitative Research Methods for the Social Sciences*, 7th ed., Allyn & Bacon, 2009.

Bernays, Edward L., and Miller, Mark Crispin, *Propaganda,* Brooklyn, Ig Pub., 2005.

Bernays, Edward – 'Soap and Art 1923', *The Museum of Public Relations*

Bernays, Edward – *Edward Bernays Speaks about His Work for Ivory Soap*, video by *The Museum of Public Relations*, available on YouTube.

Berners-Lee, Tim, 'Remarks by Tim Berners-Lee - The Evolution of the Internet: Emerging Challenges and Opportunities', talk at American Academy of Arts & Sciences (2012) video available on YouTube.

—IBM Developer Works Interviews, Tim Berners-Lee (28 July 2006).

—*Weaving the Web: The Original Design and Ultimate Destiny of the World Wide Web by Its Inventor*, 1st ed., San Francisco: Harper, 1999.

—'The World Wide Web: Past, Present and Future', w3.org, (1996).

Bernstein, Abraham, Klein, Mark, and Malone ,Thomas W., 'Programming the Global Brain', *Commun. ACM*, 55 (2012), 41–43.

Bernstein, Michael S. et al., 'Soylent: A Word Processor with a Crowd inside', *Proceedings of the 23nd Annual ACM Symposium on User Interface Software and Technology*, UIST '10, ACM (2010) 313–22.

Biewald, Lukas, Interview with CEO of CrowdFlower on TWiST #154 Bonus, June 2011, available on YouTube.

Biggs, John, 'Uber Opening Robotics Research Facility In Pittsburgh To Build Self-Driving Cars', *TechCrunch* (2 February 2015).

Bobrow, Daniel G., and Whalen, Jack, 'Community Knowledge Sharing in Practice: The Eureka Story', *Making Work Visible: Ethnographically Grounded Case Studies of Work Practice,* Cambridge University Press (2011), 257–84.

Boellstorff, Tom, *Coming of Age in Second Life: An Anthropologist Explores the Virtually Human,* Princeton: Princeton University Press, 2010.

—ed., *Ethnography and Virtual Worlds: A Handbook of Method,* Princeton: Princeton University Press, 2012.

Bogost, Ian, 'Gamification Is Bullshit', blog-post, bogost.com (8 August 2011).

—'Persuasive Games: Exploitationware', *Gamasutra* (3 May 2011).

Boltanski, Luc, and Chiapello, Eve, *The New Spirit of Capitalism,* Verso, 2007.

Le Bon, Gustave, *The Crowd: A Study of the Popular Mind,* Filiquarian Publishing, 2005.

Bonchek, Mark, and Choudary, Sangeet Paul, 'Three Elements of a Successful Platform Strategy', *Harvard Business Review* (31 January 2013).

Boradkar, Prasad, *Designing Things: A Critical Introduction to the Culture of Objects* 2010.

Borch, Christian, *The Politics of Crowds: An Alternative History of Sociology* 2013.

Botsman, Rachel, 'Welcome to the New Reputation Economy', *Wired UK*, (20 August 2012).

Brabham, Daren C., *Crowdsourcing*, The MIT Press Essential Knowledge Series, The MIT Press (2013).

—'The Myth of Amateur Crowds', *Information, Communication & Society*, 15, (2012), 394–410.

—'Crowdsourcing as a Model for Problem Solving An Introduction and Cases', *Convergence: The International Journal of Research into New Media Technologies*, 14 (2008), 75–90.

—'Moving the Crowd at iStockphoto: The Composition of the Crowd and Motivations for Participation in a Crowdsourcing Application', *First Monday*, 13 (2008).
Brand, Stewart, 'Hans Ulrich Obrist in conversation with Stewart Brand', *Electronic Beat* (2013).
—'Stewart Brand: Reviving Extinct Species - The Long Now', *The Long Now Foundation* (21 May 2013).
—Big Think Interview with Stewart Brand, 2009, video available on bigthink.com
—'We Owe It All to the Hippies', *Time* (1 March 1995).
—'Hackers' Conference 1984 – Keep Designing – How the Information Economy Is Being Created and Shaped by the Hacker Ethic', *Whole Earth Review* (May 1985), 44–59.
—'Spacewar: Fanatic Life and Symbolic Death Among the Computer Bums', *Rolling Stone Magazine* (7 December 1972).
—*Two Cybernetic Frontiers,* Random House, 1974.
—*Whole Earth Catalog - Access to Tools*, Whole Earth Catalog, 1, Portola Institute, 1968.
—Whole Earth Catalog, 2, Portola Institute (1969).
Bröckling, Ulrich, 'Selbstständigkeit: "Kreativ? Das Wort Ist Vergiftet"', *Die Zeit* (8 November 2010).
Brockman, John, 'Edge@DLD – An Edge Conversation in Munich', *TheEdge.org*, (2011).
—*Digerati: Encounters with the Cyber Elite*, Orion Business Books, 1997.
Brockman, John, and Shirky, Clay 'Gin, Television, and Cognitive Surplus', *TheEdge.org*, (2008).
Brundage, Miles, 'What Undercover Boss and The Jetsons Tell Us About the Future of Jobs', *Slate* (27 September 2013).
Bruns, Axel, *Blogs, Wikipedia, Second Life, and Beyond: From Production to Produsage*, Peter Lang, 2009.
—'FCJ-066 The Future Is User-Led: The Path towards Widespread Produsage' *The Fibreculture Journal*, 11 (2008).
—'Produsage : Towards a Broader Framework for User-Led Content Creation', *Creativity and Cognition: Proceedings of the 6th ACM SIGCHI Conference on Creativity & Cognition*, ACM (2007).
Budweg, Steffen et al. eds., 'Open Design Spaces Supporting User Innovation, *International Institute for Socio-Informatics*, 6 (2009).
Bührmann, Andrea D., 'The Emerging of the Entrepreneurial Self and Its Current Hegemony. Some Basic Reflections on How to Analyze the Formation and Transformation of Modern Forms of Subjectivity', *Forum Qualitative Sozialforschung,* 6 (2005).
Bunchball whitepaper, 'Gamification 101: An Introduction to the Use of Game Mechanics to Influence Behavior'(2010).
Burckhardt, Lucius, 'Design Is Invisible', first published in Gsöllpointner, Helmuth, Hareiter, Angela and Ortner, Laurids eds, Vienna (1981).
Burston, Jonathan, Dyer-Witheford, Nick, and Hearn, Alison 'Digital Labour: Workers, Authors, Citizens', *Ephemera: Theory & Politics in Organization*, 10 (2010) 214–21.
Burt, Tim, *Dark Art: The Changing Face of Public Relations*, Elliott & Thompson, 2012.
— Interview with Tim Burt, *Dark Art – The Changing Face of Public Relation*, London School of Economics (15. October 2013).
Bush, Vannevar, 'As We May Think', *The Atlantic* (July 1945).
Cabanieu, Jacques, 'Competitions and Architectural Excellence', *Places Journal*, (1994).
Cadwalladr, Carole, 'Stewart Brand and the Whole Earth Catalog, the Book That Changed the World', *The Guardian* (5 May 2013).
Canetti, Elias, *Crowds and* Power, Continuum, 1981.
Carey, John, *The Intellectuals and the Masses: Pride and Prejudice Among the Literary Intelligentsia, 1880–1939*, Faber and Faber, 1992.
Carman, Ashley, 'Google will tell you how crowded your favorite bar is in real time', *The Verge* (21 November 2016).
Carr, Nicholas, 'Sharecropping the Long Tail', blog-post, *Rough Type* (19 December 2006).
—'The Economics of Digital Sharecropping', blog-post, *Rough Type* (4 May 2012).
Castells, Manuel, *The Rise of the Network Society, The Information Age: Economy, Society, and Culture*, Wiley-Blackwell, 2010.
Castronova, Edward, *Synthetic Worlds: The Business and Culture of Online Games,* University of Chicago Press, 2005.
Catania/Harnad ed., *The Selection of Behavior: The Operant Behaviorism of B. F. Skinner* (1988).
Carpenter, Loren 'Experiment at SIGGRAPH '91', Curtis, Adam, *All Watched Over by Machines of Loving Grace*, BBC documentary (2011).

Carson, Biz, 'Uber is raising another $2 billion at a $62.5 billion valuation', *Business Inside* (3 December 2015).

Chaplin, Heather, 'I Don't Want To Be a Superhero', *Slate* (29 March 2011).

Chen, Adrian, 'The Laborers Who Keep Dick Pics and Beheadings Out of Your Facebook Feed', *Wired* (23 October 2014).

Cheung, Doris C., 'People's Computer Company/Homebrew Computer Club', *Digital Library Blog*, Stanford University Libraries (2014).

Cherry, Miriam, 'Beyond Misclassification: The Digital Transformation of Work', *Comparative Labor Law & Policy Journal* (2016).

—'A Minimum Wage for Crowdwork?', *Digital Labor Conference*, (2014).

—'Working the Crowd', *Concurring Opinions* (18 July 2012).

—*The Gamification of Work*, Social Science Research Network (2012).

Chesbrough, Henry, *Open Innovation: The New Imperative for Creating and Profiting from Technology*, Harvard Business School Press (2003).

—'The War for Talent and Open Innovation', *Forbes* (28 April 2011).

Chesbrough, Henry, Vanhaverbeke, Wim, and West, Joel, *Open Innovation: Researching a New Paradigm*, Oxford University Press, 2006.

Chiarella, Sharon, interviewed by Mark Pratt 'Amazon Mechanical Turk Crowdsourcing Marketplace for Work', The Cloud Show (2012), available on YouTube.

Chupin, Jean-Pierre, et al. eds., *Architecture Competitions and the Production of Culture, Quality and Knowledge: An International Inquiry,* Potential Architecture Books, 2015.

Clover, Joshua, 'Amanda Palmer's Accidental Experiment with Real Communism', *The New Yorker Blogs* (2 October 2012).

Coase, Ronald H., 'The Nature of the Firm', *Economica*, 4 (1937) 386–405.

Coffman, Keith, 'U.S. Company Puts Crowdsourcing to Work in Search for Malaysian Jet', *Reuters* (11 March).

Cohen, Nick, 'Money Talks Even in the Internship Slave Trade', *The Guardian* (16 October 2011).

Condon, Bernard, and Paul Wiseman, 'Recession, Tech Kill Middle-Class Jobs', *Associated Press: The Big Story* (23 January 2013).

Courtney, Tim, and Espersen, Peter, 'Shut Up and Take My Money: LEGO Does Crowdsourcing', *SXSW* (2013).

Cox, 'The Ruthless Overlords Of Silicon Valley', *Newsweek* (12 March 2012).

Cross, Nigel, *Designerly Ways of Knowing*, Basel: Birkhäuser, 2007.

— 'Can a Machine Design?', *Design Issues*, 17 (2001) 44–50.

— 'Designerly Ways of Knowing: Design Discipline Versus Design Science', *Design Issues*, 17 (2001) 49–55.

— *The Automated Architect*, Penguin, 1977.

Csíkszentmihályi, Mihály, *Flow: The Psychology of Optimal Experience*, Harper & Row, 1990.

Curtis, Adam, *All Watched Over By Machines of Loving Grace*, BBC documentary (2011).

Cushing, Ellen, 'Amazon Mechanical Turk: The Digital Sweatshop', *Utne Reader* (February 2013).

Däubler, Wolfgang, 'Crowdworker – Schutz auch außerhalb des Arbeitsrechts?',*Crowdwork – zurück in die Zukunft?,* Frankfurt am Main: Bund-Verlag (2015).

Danaher, John, 'The Threat of Algocracy', *Philosophy & Technology* (2016) 1–24

Davis, Rodrigo, 'Civic Crowdfunding from the Statue of Liberty to Now', *MIT Center for Civic Media*, (2013).

Dawson, Ross, and Bynghall, Steve, *Getting Results from Crowds*, Advanced Human Technologies, 2012.

Dean, Jodi, *Blog Theory: Feedback and Capture in the Circuits of Drive*, Polity, 2010.

Dean, Josh, 'Is This the World's Most Creative Manufacturer?', *Inc.com* (October 2013).

Denton, Jill, tran., *Lucius Burckhardt Writings Rethinking Manmade Environments. Politics, Landscapes & Design,* Springer Architecture, 2012.

Deterding, Sebastian, 'A Quick Buck by Copy and Paste', *Gamification Research Network* (15 September 2011).

Deterding, Sebastian et al. 'Gamification: Toward a Definition', presented in Vancouver at CHI (2011).

Dibbell, Julian, *Play Money, Or, How I Quit My Day Job and Made Millions Trading Virtual Loot*, Basic Books, 2007.

Diederichsen, Diedrich et al. *The Whole Earth: California and the disappearence of the* outside, exhibition: Haus der Kulturen der Welt, Berlin 2013, book: Sternberg-Press, 2013.

Douglas, Steve, 'An Anti-Spec Work Parable – the Jon Engle vs. Stockart.com Story', *The Logo Factor Design Blog* (14 April 2009).

Dow, Steven P., and Klemmer, Scott R., 'Shepherding the Crowd: An Approach to More Creative Crowd Work', *CHI EA* (2011).

DreamScaper, 'Turk Smarter Not Harder: Problem with Mechancial Turk Masters', blog-post, *SmartTurker* (11 July 2011).

Dubberly, Hugh, and Pangaro, Paul, 'Cybernetics and Service-Craft: Language for Behavior-Focused Design', *Kybernetes* (9 January 2007).

Dynamo, 'Guidelines for Academic Requesters', *We Are Dynamo Wiki* (2014).

Dyson, George, *Turing's Cathedral: The Origins of the Digital Universe*, Pantheon Books, 2012.

Dzieza, Josh, 'The rating game: how Uber and its peers turned us into horrible bosses', *The Verge* (28 October 2015).

Eagleton, Terry, *On Evil*, Yale University Press, 2010.

Ebner, Winfried, 'Community Building for Innovations - Der Ideenwettbewerb als Methode für die Entwicklung und Einführung einer virtuellen Innovations-Gemeinschaft', Fakultät für Wirtschaftswissenschaften TU Munich (2009).

Edwards, Paul N, *The Closed World Computers and the Politics of Discourse in Cold War America*, MIT Press, 1997.

Ekbia, Hamid, and Nardi, Bonnie, 'Heteromation and Its (dis)contents: The Invisible Division of Labor between Humans and Machines', *First Monday*, 19 (2014).

Ellis, Justin, 'It's People! Meet Soylent, the Crowdsourced Copy Editor', *Nieman Journalism Lab* (3 November 2010).

Ellison, Kaitlyn, 'An epic 99designs meetup in Yogyakarta, Indonesia', 99designs blog (2012).

Else, Jon, *The Day After Trinity: J. Robert Oppenheimer and the Atomic Bomb*, 1980.

Emerson, Robert M., *Writing Ethnographic Fieldnotes*, Chicago Guides to Writing, Editing, and Publishing, The University of Chicago Press, 2011

Empson, Rip, 'Everything You Wanted To Know About The Giant Elance, oDesk Merger & Ensuing Backlash (But Were Afraid To Ask)', *TechCrunch* (22 December 2013).

Endert, 'Von Der Sharing-Lüge Und Anderen Internet-Märchen', *JBlog* (2 September 2014).

Engelbart, Douglas, 'Authors@Google: Douglas Engelbart', 22 August 2007, available on YouTube.

— 'Toward Augmenting the Human Intellect and Boosting Our Collective IQ', *Commun. ACM*, 38 (1995), 30–32.

— 'Augmenting Human Intellect: A Conceptual Framework', Summary Report AFOSR-3233, Stanford Research Institute (1962).

Estellés-Arolas, Enrique, and González-Ladrón-de-Guevara, Fernando, 'Towards an Integrated Crowdsourcing Definition', *Journal of Information Science*, 38 (2012) 189–200.

Fabrice, Florin, *Hackers: Wizards of the Electronic Age,* TV documentary (1985), available on YouTube.

Fairclough, Norman, *Critical Discourse Analysis: The Critical Study of Language*, Longman, 2010.

Federici, Silvia, 'Wages Against Housework', 1975.

Fehr, Ernst, and Schmidt, Klaus M., *A Theory of Fairness, Competition and Cooperation*, Institute for Empirical Research in Economics, 1999.

Felsenstein, Lee, Felsenstein, Lee, Interview at *MakerFaire*, Hak5 (2013), available on YouTube.

— 'Social Media Technology', blog-post, leefelsenstein.com, no date of publication, (leefelsenstein.com/?page_id=125).

-— Convivial Cybernetic Devices', *The Analytical Engine*, Vol 3, 1, November 1995.

— 'Tom Swift Lives! & Convivial Design', *People's Computer Company*, (1975) 14–15.

Felstiner, Alek L., 'Working the Crowd: Employment and Labor Law in the Crowdsourcing Industry' *Berkeley Journal of Employment and Labor Law* Vol. 32 (2011).

Ferraira Paolo and Alves, Pedro, *Distributed Context-Aware Systems*, Springer Briefs, *Computer Science* (2014).

Feyerabend, Paul, *Against Method*, 3rd ed.,Verso, 1993.

Fezer, Jesko and Schmitz, Martin ed., *Lucius Burckhardt Writings. Rethinking Man-made Environments*, De Gruyter, 2012.

Fischer, Suzanne, 'Why the Landline Telephone Was the Perfect Tool', *The Atlantic* (16 April 2012).

Fish, Adam, et al. 'Birds of the Internet', *Journal of Cultural Economy*, 4 (2011), 157–87.

Fish, Adam, and Ramesh Srinivasan, 'Digital Labor Is the New Killer App', *New Media & Society*, 14 (2012), 137–52.

Folbre, Nancy, 'The Unregulated Work of Mechanical Turk', *New York Times* (18 March 2013).

Forty, Adrian *Objects of Desire: Design and Society from Wedgewood to IBM*, Pantheon Books, 1986.

Foucault, Michel, *The Birth of the Prison*, London: Penguin, 1991.

Frayling, Christopher, *Research in Art and Design*, London: Royal College of Art, 1993.

Freire, Karine, and Sangiorgi, Daniela , 'Service Design and Healthcare Innovation: From Consumption to Coproduction and Co-Creation', 2010.

Freud, Sigmund, *Group Psychology and the Analysis of the Ego*, The International Psycho-Analytical Library, 6, The International Psycho-Analytical Press, 1922.

—'My Contact with Josef Popper-Lynkeus' (1932), Freud, Sigmund, and Strachey, James, *New Introductory Lectures on Psycho-Analysis and Other Works; (1932–1936)*, Vintage, 2001.

Frey, Bruno S., and Jegen, Reto, 'Motivation Crowding Theory', *Journal of Economic Surveys*, 15 (2001), 589–611.

Frey, Carl Benedikt, and Osborne, Michael A., *The Future of Employment: How Suceptible Are Jobs to Computerisation*, Programme on the Impacts of Future Technology, Oxford: Oxford University Department of Engineering Sciences, 2013.

Friedman, Thomas L, *The World Is Flat: The Globalized World in the Twenty-First Century*, London: Penguin, 2007.

Fuchs, Christian, and Sevignani, Sebastian, 'What Is Digital Labour? What Is Digital Work? What's Their Difference? And Why Do These Questions Matter for Understanding Social Media?', *tripleC: Communication, Capitalism & Critique. Open Access Journal for a Global Sustainable Information Society*, 11 (2013) 237–93.

Fuchs, Mathias et al. *Rethinking Gamification*, Meson Press, Hybrid Publishing Lab, 2014.

Fuller, Matthew, and Goffey, Andrew, *Evil Media*, Cambridge, Massachusetts: MIT Press, 2012.

Gajardo, Marcelo, 'Ivan Illich', *Prospects: The Quarterly Review of Comparative Education*, UNESCO: International Bureau of Education, XXIII (1993) 711–20.

Galloway, Alexander, interviewed by Pau Alsina, 'We are the Goldfarmers', (12 September 2007).

Galton, Francis, 'Vox Populi', *Nature*, 75 (1907) 450–51.

Gates, Bill, 'An Open Letter to Hobbyists', *Computer Notes* (1976).

Geiger, David, et al. 'Managing the Crowd: Towards a Taxonomy of Crowdsourcing Processes', *AMCIS Proceedings* (2011).

Gelber, Steven M., 'A Job You Can't Lose: Work and Hobbies in the Great Depression', *Journal of Social History*, 24 (1991), 741–66.

— *Hobbies: Leisure and the Culture of Work in America*, Columbia University Press, 1999.

Giles, Jim, 'Getting the Job Done, with a Silicon Boss', *New Scientist*, 209 (2011) 20–21.

Gill, Rosalind, and Pratt, Andy, 'In the Social Factory? Immaterial Labour, Precariousness and Cultural Work', *Theory, Culture & Society*, 25 (2008).

Gleason, Stephanie, and Mann, Ted, 'Invention Startup Quirky Files for Bankruptcy', *Wall Street Journal* (22 September 2015).

Glynn, Carroll J., et al., *Public Opinion*, Third edition, Westview Press, 2016.

Gneezy, Uri, and List, John A., *The Why Axis: Hidden Motives and the Undiscovered Economics of Everyday Life*, Public Affairs, 2014.

Gneezy, Uri, and Rustichini, Aldo, 'A Fine Is a Price', *The Journal of Legal Studies*, 29 (2000) 1–17.

Goethe, Johann Wolfgang von, *The Collected Works 3, Essays on Art and Literature*, tran. by Ellen von Nardroff, Princeton Univ. Press, 1994.

Goethe, Johann Wolfgang von, and Schiller, Friedrich , *Briefwechsel Zwischen Schiller Und Goethe: 1794–1805, Band 3*.

Goldsmith, Kenneth, *Uncreative Writing: Managing Language in the Digital Age*, Columbia University Press, 2011.

Gorman, James, 'No Glass Ceiling for Worker Bees', *The New York Times* (8 September 2014).

Graeber, David, 'The Sadness of Post-Workerism', *The Commoner* (19 January 2008).

Gray, Mary L., 'Mary L. Gray on Digital Labor Economies & Demands for an Ambient Workforce', talk given at the The Berkman Klein Center for Internet & Society at Harvard University (2015), available on YouTube.

Green, Paul, and Wei-Haas, Lisa, *The Wizard of Oz: A Tool for Rapid Devlopment of User* Interfaces, University of Michigan, Transportation Research Institute, June 1985.

Greenbaum, David, 'Humans And Computers Will Come Together For Middle Work', *TechCrunch* (12 July 2014).

Grefe, Richard, 'What Is AIGA's Position on Spec Work? And How Are Ethical Standards Determined?', *AIGA, the Professional Association for Design* (27 May 2009).

Gremillion, Allison S., 'An Interview with talented illustrator Hendra Kurniawan (DorarpolHendra)', 99designs blog (2011).

Grennan, Kevin, *Authorship in the Hive – The Changing Nature of Authorship in Collaborative, Creative, Online Communities*, Master-Thesis Design Interactions, Royal College of Art, 2010.

Griffith, Erin, 'With $79 Million Series D Round, Quirky is New York's Most Underrated (yet Well-Funded) Startup', *PandoDaily* (13 November 2013).

Grimshaw, Miles, 'Analysis of Quirky: Do Consumers Know What They Want?', *CB insights* (29 September 2015); originally published on Grimshaw's private blog on 5 June 2014.

Groß, Martina, 'Hippies Und Cyberspace – "Wir sind wie Götter und wir können genauso gut werden"', Deutschlandfunk radio feature (2014).

Grossman, Lev, 'You – Yes, You – Are TIME's Person of the Year', *Time* (25 December 2006).

Grossman, Wendy M., 'Salon Sells The WELL to Its Members', *The Guardian* (27 September 2012).

Grudin, J., 'Computer-Supported Cooperative Work: History and Focus', *Computer*, 27 (1994) 19–26.

Guo, Bin, and Yu, Zhiwen Daqing Zhang, Xingshe Zhou, 'From participatory sensing to Mobile Crowd Sensing' (2014).

Hack, Günter, 'Internetkultur: Der Aufstieg Des Datenproletariats', *Die Zeit* (10 September 2014).

Hafner, Katie, and Lyon, Matthew, *When Wizards Stay up Late: The Origins of the Internet*, Touchstone, 1996.

Hagiu, Andrei, Wright, Julian 'Multi-Sided Platforms', *Harvard Business School Working Paper Series* (2015).

Han, Byung-Chul, 'Neoliberalismus: Verführt von systemerhaltender Macht', *Süddeutsche Zeitung* (2 September 2014).

Hancox, Simone, 'Art, Activism and the Geopolitical Imagination: Ai Weiwei's "Sunflower Seeds"', *Journal of Media Practice*, 12 (2012) 279–90.

Hardt, Michael, 'Affective Labor', *Boundary 2.*, 26 (1999) 77–88.

Hardy, Quentin, 'Big Brother in the Home Office', *New York Times Bits Blog* (5 December 2011).

Harris, Christopher G., 'Dirty Deeds Done Dirt Cheap: A Darker Side to Crowdsourcing', IEEE Third International Conference on Social Computing, Boston (2011).

Harvey, David, *The Enigma of Capital: And the Crises of Capitalism,* Profile Books, 2011.

Hatton, Celia, 'China 'social credit': Beijing sets up huge system', BBC News (26 October 2015).

Hauben, J., 'Norbert Wiener, J. C. R. Licklider and the Global Communications Network', *Columbia University* (1996).

Hayles, Katherine, *Writing Machines*, MIT Press, 2002.

Heeks, Richard, 'Current Analysis and Future Research Agenda on "Gold Farming"', *Development Informatics Group*, University of Manchester (2008).

Hermosillo, Carmen 'humdog', 'Pandora's Vox: On Community in Cyberspace', *The Alphaville Herald* (1994).

Herz, J. C., 'Harnessing the Hive: How Online Games Drive Networked Innovation', *Esther Dyson's Release 1.0* (18 October 2002).

Hesmondhalgh, David, 'User-Generated Content, Free Labour and the Cultural Industries', *Ephemera*, 10 (2010) 267–84.

Heylighen, Francis, 'Conceptions of a Global Brain: A Historical Review', in *From Big Bang to Global Civilization*, University of Cal. Press (2012).

Heylighen, Francis, and Bollen, Johan ,'The World-Wide Web as a Super-Brain: From Metaphor to Model', *Cybernetics and Systems '96*, Austrian Society For Cybernetics (1996) 917–22.

Heylighen, Francis, Joslyn, Cliff, and Turchin, Valentin, 'Principia Cybernetica Web', *Principia Cybernetica Web* (1993).

Higgins, Charlotte, 'People Power Comes to the Turbine Hall: Ai Weiwei's Sunflower Seeds', *The Guardian* (11 October 2010).

Hight, Christopher, and Perry, Chris, *Collective Intelligence in Design*, Wiley-Academy, 2006.

von Hippel, Eric, *Democratizing Innovation*, MIT Press, 2005.

— *The Sources of Innovation*, Oxford University Press, 1988.

— 'User Toolkits for Innovation', *Journal of Product Innovation Management* (2001).

Hippel, Von, Eric A, and Katz, Ralph, *Shifting Innovation to Users Via Toolkits*, Social Science Research Network, 1 April 2002.

Ho, Victoria, 'Design Competition Model Is Working For 99designs, Especially In Asia', *TechCrunch* (6 August 2013).

Hodson, Hal, 'Crowdsourcing Grows up as Online Workers Unite', *New Scientist* (February 2013).

Holt, Jim, 'Smarter, Happier, More Productive', *London Review of Books* (3 March 2011) 9–12.

Horn, Eva, 'Das Leben Ein Schwarm – Emergenz Und Evolution in Moderner Science Fiction', in *Schwärme – Kollektive ohne Zentrum,* Transcript (2009).

Horowitz, Sara, 'Hives: A Community for the New Workforce', *Freelancers Union* (2014).

Horst, Heather A., and Daniel Miller, eds., *Digital Anthropology*, Berg, 2012.

Howe, Jeff, 'Crowdsourcing – Now at a Store Near You', *Wired*, (16 April 2013).

— *Crowdsourcing: How the Power of the Crowd Is Driving the Future of Business*, Random House Business, 2009.

— 'Is Crowdsourcing Evil? The Design Community Weighs In', *Wired* (10 March 2009).

— 'Crowdsourcing: Mechanical Turk Targets Small Business', blog-post, *Crowdsourcing.com* (1 August 2008).

— 'Crowdsourcing: Taking Measure of Mechanical Turk', blog-post, *Crowdsourcing.com* (3 November 2006).

— 'Crowdsourcing: A Definition', blog-post, *Crowdsourcing.com*, crowdsourcing.typepad.com (2 June 2006).

— 'The Rise of Crowdsourcing', *Wired* (14 June 2006).

Hurst, Nathan, 'FAIL! Why Olympic Designers Got It So Wrong (and Occasionally Right)', *Wired* (7 August 2012).

Hustwit, Gary, *Urbanized*, PlexiFilm, 2011.

Huws Ursula, 'iCapitalism and the Cybertariat', *Monthly Review* 66, Nr. 8 (2015).

Illich, Ivan, *Deschooling Society: Social Questions,* Marion Boyars Publishers,1999.

— *Tools for Conviviality*, Open Forum, Calder and Boyars, 1973.

Ipeirotis, Panagiotis G., 'Analyzing the Amazon Mechanical Turk Marketplace', *XRDS*, 17 (2010), 16–21.

— *Demographics of Mechanical Turk, A Computer Scientist in a Business School*, 6 April 2015.

— 'Mechanical Turk Account Verification: Why Amazon Disables so Many Accounts', *A Computer Scientist in a Business School* (2013).

— 'Why People Participate on Mechanical Turk?', *A Computer Scientist in a Business School* (2008).

Irani, Lilly, C., 'Difference and Dependence among Digital Workers: The Case of Amazon Mechanical Turk', *South Atlantic Quarterly*, 114, (2015) 225–34.

— 'The Cultural Work of Microwork', *New Media & Society* (2013).

— 'Tweaking Technocapitalism', blog-post, Turkopticon.ucsd.edu (30 January 2009).

Irani, Lilly C., and Silberman, M. Six, 'Stories We Tell About Labor: Turkopticon and the Trouble with "Design"', Proceedings of Special Interst Group in Human Computer Interaction, University of San Diego (2016).

— 'From Critical Design to Critical Infrastructure: Lessons from Turkopticon', *Interactions*, 21 (2014) 32–35.

— 'Turkopticon: Interrupting Worker Invisibility in Amazon Mechanical Turk', in *Proceedings of the SIGCHI Conference on Human Factors in Computing Systems*, CHI '13, ACM (2013) 611–20.

Isaac, Mike, 'Why Designers Hate Crowdsourcing', *Forbes* (12 June 2010).

Jobs, Steve, commencement speech at Stanford University, 12 June 2005.

Johnson, Joel, '1 Million Workers. 90 Million iPhones. 17 Suicides. Who's to Blame?', *Wired* (28 February 2011).

Jones, J. Christopher, *Design Methods: Seeds of Human Futures*, J. Wiley, 1981.

Jong, Cees de, and Mattie, Erik , *Architectural competitions 1791–1949 & 1950 – today*, Taschen, 1994.

Jordan, Gregory, 'The 60's Had Free Love; The 90's Have Free Information', *The New York Times* (1 September 1996).

Joyce, Alexandre, 'User Generated Content in Researching for Design: How the Internet Supports Creativity', University of Montreal (2008).

Jung, E. Alex, 'Wages for Facebook', *Dissent*, (Spring 2014).

Jurgenson, Nathan, 'Digital Dualism and the Fallacy of Web Objectivity', *Cyborgology* (13 September 2011).

— 'Digital Dualism versus Augmented Reality', *Cyborgology* (24 February 2011).

Keen, Andrew, *The Cult of the Amateur: How Today's Internet Is Killing Our Culture*, Doubleday/Currency, 2007

Kelly, Kevin, *Cool Tools: A Catalog of Possibilities*, KK, an imprint of Cool Tools Lab, 2013.

— 'Futurist Stewart Brand Wants to Revive Extinct Species', *Wired* (17 August 2012).

— *What Technology Wants*, Viking, 2010

— 'The New Socialism: Global Collectivist Society Is Coming Online', *Wired* (22 May 2009).

— 'The Tools of Cool Tools', *Cool Tools* blog (2008).

— 'The Whole Earth Blogalog', *KK** blog (September 2008).

— *Out of Control: The New Biology of Machines, Social Systems, and the Economic World*, Addison-Wesley (1995).

Kelty, Christopher M., 'There Is No Free Software', *Journal of Peer Production* (2013).

— *Two Bits: The Cultural Significance of Free Software*, Duke University Press, 2008.

— 'Punt To Culture', *Anthropological Quarterly*, 77 (2004), 547–58.

Kennedy, Maev, 'Tate Buys Eight Million Ai Weiwei Sunflower Seeds', *The Guardian* (5 March 2012).

Kenney, Martin, 'Rethinking Labor (and Capital) in the Era of the Cloud', presented at the BRIE-ETLA Annual Meeting, Helsinki (2014).

Kessler, Sarah, 'Pixel And Dimed: On (Not) Getting By In The Gig Economy', *Fast Company* (18 March 2014).
— 'The Gig Economy Won't Last Because It's Being Sued To Death', *Fast Company*, (17 February 2015).
Kimbarovsky, Ross, 'The NO!SPEC Campaign vs. crowdSPRING', blog-post, *Basecamp* (22 September 2008).
— CrowdSpring Press Kit 2014 & 2016, <http://assets.crowdspring.com/docs/cS-Press-Kit.pdf> [accessed 10 January 2017].
Kingsley, Sara C., Gray, Mary L., and Suri, Siddharth, 'Monopsony and the Crowd: Labor for Lemons?', *Microsoft Research* (2014).
Kirk, Andrew, 'Appropriating Technology: The Whole Earth Catalog and Counterculture Environmental Politics', *Environmental History* (2001).
Kittur, Aniket, Nickerson, Jeffrey, Bernstein, Michael S. et al., 'The Future of Crowd Work', presented at the CSCW Conference on Computer Supported Cooperative Work and Social Computing (2013).
Klebe, Thomas, 'Crowdwork erfordert zusätzliche Regeln', *Frankfurter Rundschau* (19 Mai 2016).
Klug, Thomas, 'Nudging: Wie Frau Merkel uns hilft, die bessere Wahl zu treffen', *Deutschlandradio Kultur* (15.07.2015).
Knott, Stephen, 'Amateur Craft as a Differential Practice', Ph. D. thesis, Royal College of Art (2011).
Koblin, Aaron, 'The Sheep Market: Two Cents Worth' Master's Thesis in Design/Media Arts, UCLA (2006).
Koskela, Hille, '"Don't mess with Texas!" Texas Virtual Border Watch Program and the (botched) politics of responsibilization' Crime Media Culture, Sage, 7 (2011) 49–65.
Kosner, Anthony Wing, 'Google Cabs And Uber Bots Will Challenge Jobs "Below The API"', *Forbes* (4 January 2015).
Kracauer, Siegfried, *The Mass Ornament: Weimar Essays*, Harvard University Press, 1995.
Kreider, Tim, 'Slaves of the Internet, Unite!', *New York Times* (26 October 2013).
Kreiner, Kristian, 'Architectural Competitions - Empirical Observations and Strategic Implications for Architectural Firms', *Nordisk Arkitekturforskning*, 21 (2009).
Kücklich, Julian, 'Precarious Playbour: Modders and the Digital Games Industry', *The Fibreculture Journal*, FCJ-025 (2005).
Kushins, Jordan, 'The Surprisingly Smart Strategy Behind London's Infamous Olympic Branding', *FastCo.Design* (6 August 2014).
Lacy, Sarah, 'Get Over It, Haters: 99designs Has Tipped', *PandoDaily* (24 January 2012).
Lanier, Jaron, *Who Owns the Future*, Allen Lane, 2013.
— *You Are Not a Gadget : A Manifesto. Jaron Lanier*, Penguin, 2011.
— 'Beware the Online Collective', *The Edge* (27 December 2006).
— 'Digital Maoism: The Hazards of the New Online Collectivism', *Edge - Third Culture* (May 2006).
— 'One Half a Manifesto', *The Edge* (11 November 2000).
Lanxon, Nate, 'How the Oxford English Dictionary Started out like Wikipedia', *Wired UK* (13 January 2011).
Laurel, Brenda, ed., *Design Research: Methods and Perspectives*, MIT Press, 2003.
Laurier, Eric, 'Participant Observation', in *Research Methods in Human and Physical Geography*, Sage (2010).
Lazzarato, Maurizio, 'Construction of Cultural Labour Market', *European Institute for Progressive Cultural Policies* (November 2006).
—, 'Immaterial Labor', *Generation Online* (1997).
Leadbeater, Charles, *We-Think: Mass Innovation, Not Mass Production*, Profile Books, 2008.
Leadbeater, Charles, and Miller, Paul, *The pro-Am Revolution: How Enthusiasts Are Changing Our Society and Economy*, Demos, 2004.
Lee, Min Kyung et al. ,'Working with Machines: The Impact of Algorithmic and Data-Driven Management on Human Workers, Proceedings of the 33rd Annual ACM Conference, 1603–1612. CHI '15. New York (2015).
Lehrer, Jonah, 'Groupthink', *The New Yorker*, 30 January 2012.
Leimeister, Jan Marco et al., Crowd Work im Netz, Arbeitspapier der Hans-Böckler-Stiftung.
— et al., New Forms of Employment and IT – Crowdsourcing, in: 4th Conference for the Regulating for Decent Work Network (Geneva, 2016).
Lekach, Maya, 'Nicholas Sheriff Grows from 99designer to Business Innovator', 99designs blog (25 August 2014).
Lessig, Lawrence, *Code: Version 2.0*, Basic Books, 2006.
—'Do You Floss?', *London Review of Books* (18 August 2005) 24–25.
— *Free Culture: The Nature and Future of Creativity*, Penguin Books, 2005.
— *The Future of Ideas: The Fate of the Commons in a Connected World*, Random House 2002.
Levine, Rick, Weinberger, David , Locke, Christopher, and Searls, Doc ,'The Cluetrain Manifesto' (1999).

Lévy, Pierre, *Collective Intelligence: Mankind's Emerging World in Cyberspace*, Perseus Books, 1997.
— 'Pierre Lévy Talks about Collective Intelligence' at Senac, São Paulo (2014), available on YouTube.
Levy, Steven, *Hackers: Heroes of the Computer Revolution*, Penguin Books, 2001.
Lialina, Olia, 'One Terabyte of Kilobyte Age – Digging through the Geocities Torrent' (blog.geocities.institute).
— 'Turing Complete User', Contemporary Home Computing (2012).
Lialina, Olia, Espenschied, Dragan, and Buerger, Manuel, *Digital Folklore: to computer users, with love and respect*, Merz & Solitude, 2009.
Licklider, Joseph Carl Robnett, *In Memoriam: J. C. R. Licklider: 1915–1990*, Systems Research Center, Digital Equipment Corporation, 7 August 1990, 21–41.
— 'Memorandum For Members and Affiliates of the Intergalactic Computer Network', Advanced Projects Research Agency (1963).
— 'Man-Computer Symbiosis', *IRE Transactions on Human Factors in Electronics*, HFE-1 (1960) 4–11.
Licklider, Joseph Carl Robnett, and Robert Taylor, 'The Computer as a Communication Device', *Science and Technology: For the Technical Man in Management*, No 76 (1968) 21–31.
Lippmann, Walter, *Public Opinion*, 1921.
Llewelly, Patrick, '99designs Acquires 12designer, Launches European Headquarters in Berlin', 99designs company blog (2014).
Lobo, Sascha, 'Auf Dem Weg in Die Dumpinghölle: Sharing Economy Wie Bei Uber Ist Plattform-Kapitalismus', *Spiegel Online* (9 March 2014).
Loewy, Raymond, *Never Leave Well Enough Alone*, Johns Hopkins University Press, 2002.
Lovelock, J. E., 'Gaia as Seen through the Atmosphere', *Atmospheric Environment, 1967*, 6 (1972) 579–80.
Lovink, Geert, Trebor Scholz, and Tony Conrad, *The Art of Free Cooperation*, Autonomedia, 2007.
Lubar, Steven, '"Do Not Fold, Spindle or Mutilate": A Cultural History of the Punch Card', *Journal of American Culture*, 15 (1992) 43–55.
Lubar, Steven D., *InfoCulture: The Smithsonian Book of Information Age Inventions*, Houghton Mifflin, 1993.
Luk, Lorraine, 'Foxconn Plans to Make Its Own Industrial Robots', *Wall Street Journal* (11 July 2014).
Lunden, Ingrid, 'LinkedIn Gives Up The Ghost On CardMunch, Inks Deal With Evernote To Migrate Users', *TechCrunch* (7 May 2014).
Lynch, Alec, 'Fire Up and Disrupt the Market', DesignCrowd company blog (10 January 2008).
Machiavelli, Niccolò, *The Prince*, NuVision Publications, 2004.
Mackay, Charles, *Extraordinary Popular Delusions and the Madness of Crowds*, Wordsworth Reference, 1995.
Madrigal, Alexis C., 'The Hut Where the Internet Began', *The Atlantic* (7 Juli 2013).
Malone, Thomas, '*The Future of Work with MIT's Thomas Malone*', interview with *The Economist*, Human Potential Forum (2013), available on YouTube.
— Malone, Thomas W., *The Future of Work,* Harvard Business School Press, 2004.
Malone, Thomas W., Laubacher, Robert, and Chrysantho, Dellarocas s, 'The Collective Intelligence Genome', *MIT Sloan Management Review* (2010).
— *Harnessing Crowds: Mapping the Genome of Collective Intelligence*, Social Science Research Network, 3 February 2009.
Manovich, Lev, 'Models of Authorship in New Media', Lev Manovich's website (2002).
Margonelli, Lisa, 'Inside AOL's "Cyber-Sweatshop"', *Wired* (7 October 1999).
Markoff, John, *What the Dormouse Said How the Sixties Counterculture Shaped the Personal Computer Industry*, Penguin Books, 2006.
— 'Whole Earth State-of-Art Rapping', *The New York Times – Sausalito Journal* (15 August 1989).
Markowitz, Eric, 'Crowdsourcing: Still Trying to Live Up to the Hype', *Inc.com* (10 July 2013).
Marshall, Andrew Gavin, 'The Propaganda System That Has Helped Create a Permanent Overclass is Over a Century in the Making', *AlterNet* (12 April 2013).
Marshall, Jennifer Jane, 'Clean Cuts: Procter & Gamble's Depression-Era Soap-Carving Contests', *Winterthur Portfolio*, 42 (2008) 51–76.
Martin, David et al., 'Being a Turker', in *Proceedings of the 17th ACM Conference on Computer Supported Cooperative Work & Social Computing*, CSCW '14, ACM (2014) 224–35.
Marvit, Moshe Z., 'How Crowdworkers Became the Ghosts in the Digital Machine', *The Nation* (4 February 2014).
Marx, Karl, *Capital – a Critique of Political Economy*, 1867.
Maslow, Abraham H., 'A Theory of Human Motivation', *Psychological Review*, 50 (1943) 370–96.
Matthew, H. C. G., and B. Harrison, eds., *The Oxford Dictionary of National Biography*, Oxford University Press, 2004.

Mayer, Robert, 'What's Wrong with Exploitation?', *Journal of Applied Philosophy*, 24 (2007) 137–50.

Mayer-Schönberger, Viktor, *Big Data: A Revolution That Will Transform How We Live, Work, and Think*, Houghton Mifflin Harcourt, 2013.

McCarthy, John, 'The Home Information Terminal', in *Man and Computer. Proc. Int. Conf.* (1972) 48–57.

Mcdonald, Kevin, 'From Solidarity to Fluidarity: Social Movements beyond "Collective Identity"', *Social Movement Studies*, 1 (2002) 109–28.

McGonigal, Jane, *Engagement Economy: The Future of Massively Scaled Collaboration and Participation*, Institute for the Future, September 2008.

— *Gaming Can Make a Better World*, TED Talk, 2010.

— *Reality Is Broken: Why Games Make Us Better and How They Can Change the World*, Vintage, 2012.

— 'Why I Love Bees: A Case Study in Collective Intelligence Gaming', *The Ecology of Games: Connecting Youth, Games, and Learning.*, ed. by Katie Salen, MIT Press (2008) 199–227.

McPhail, Clark, *The Myth of the Madding Crowd*, Social Institutions and Social Change, A. de Gruyter, 1991.

Meerman, Marije, 'Cybertopia: Dreams of Silicon Valley', *Tegenlicht / Backlight* (2015).

Mickiewicz, Matt, interviewed by Yaro Starak, 'Matt Mickiewicz, Founder Of Sitepoint, Flippa & 99Designs, Tells His Story', *entrepreneurs journey*, (entrepreneurs-journey.com/2873/matt-mickiewicz), last accessed January 2017 .

— interview 'Master Webmaster And Co-founder Of Sitepoint, 99Designs, Flippa', 2010 (blog.jointbf.com/matt-mickiewicz-sitepoint-99designs-flippa), last accessed 6 August 2014, not online anymore.

Milland, Kristy, 'Spamgirl', 'A Mechanical Turk Worker's Perspective' *Journal of Media Ethics*, 31, 4 (2016) 263–264.

— 'Spamgirl Speaks!', *BrokenTurk* (17 November 2010).

Miller, Daniel, *Tales from Facebook*, Polity Press, 2011.

Miller, Daniel, and Slater, Don, *The Internet an Ethnographic Approach*, Berg, 2000.

Mollick, Ethan R., 'The Dynamics of Crowdfunding: An Exploratory Study', *Journal of Business Venturing*, 29 (2014) 1–16.

Morozov, Evgeny, 'The Folly of Technological Solutionism', event posting, London School of Economics (21 March 2013).

— 'The Meme Hustler: Tim O'Reilly's Crazy Talk', *The Baffler*, No.22 (2013).

— *To Save Everything, Click Here: Technology, Solutionism, and the Urge to Fix Problems That Don't Exist*, Allen Lane, 2013.

— *The Net Delusion the Dark Side of Internet Freedom*, PublicAffairs, 2011.

Motoyama, Marti et al. 'Dirty Jobs: The Role of Freelance Labor in Web Service Abuse', in *Proceedings of the 20th USENIX Conference on Security*, SEC'11, USENIX Association (2011).

Murty, Paul, Paulini, Mercedes, and Maher, Mary Lou ,'Collective Intelligence and Design Thinking' (2011).

Nazar, Jason, '16 Surprising Statistics About Small Businesses', *Forbes* (9 September 2013).

Nelson, Ted, 'Computer Lib/Dream Machines', self-published, 1974. Re-published by Tempus Books/Microsoft Press (1987).

Neubacher, Alexander, 'Alchemie Im Kanzleramt', *Der Spiegel* (1 September 2014).

Norman, Donald A, 'Rethinking Design Thinking', *Core77* (19 March 2013).

— *Living with Complexity*, MIT Press, 2011.

— *The Invisible Computer: Why Good Products Can Fail, the Personal Computer is so Complex, and Information Appliances Are the Solution*, MIT Press, 1999.

O'Reilly, Tim, 'The Architecture of Participation', *O'Reilly* (2004).

— 'What Is Web 2.0', *O'Reilly Media* company blog (30 September 2005).

Olma, Sebastian, 'Never Mind the Sharing Economy: Here's Platform Capitalism', *Institute of Network Cultures* (16 October 2014).

Oris, Grace, 'How I Quit Working for 99Designs, Crowdspring and Mycroburst', personal blog of Grace Oris (15 March 2011).

Ortega y Gasset, José, *The Revolt of the Masses*, W.W. Norton, 1993.

Owyang, Jeremiah, 'Designers: Why Spec Work Is Not Going Away – How You Should Respond', web-strategist.com (13 December 2008).

— *Sharing is the New Buying*, web-strategist.com, 3 March 2014.

Papsdorf, Christian, *Wie Surfen zu Arbeit wird: Crowdsourcing im Web 2.0*, Campus, 2009.

Pasquale, Frank, 'To Replace or Respect: Futurology as if People Mattered', *Boundary 2 – an International Journal of Literature and Culture* (2015).

Patterson, Thom, 'Welcome to the "Weisure" Lifestyle', *CNN.com* (11 May 2009).

Pick, Daniel, 'Thousands of Little White Blobs', *London Review of Books* (23 November 1989) 20–22.

Piketty, Thomas, *Capital in the Twenty-First Century*, Harvard University Press, 2014.

PlagDoc, and Martin Kotynek, 'Reflections on a Swarm', GuttenPlag.Wikia.com, 8 June 2012.

Pontin, Jason, 'Artificial Intelligence, With Help From the Humans', *The New York Times* (25 March 2007).

Poole, Steven, 'What Does the Oculus Rift Backlash Tell Us? Facebook Just Isn't Cool', *The Guardian* (27 March 2014).

Postigo, Hector, 'From Pong to Planet Quake: Post-Industrial Transitions from Leisure to Work', *Information, Communication & Society*, 6 (2003) 593–607.

Prucher, Jeff, ed., *Brave New Words: The Oxford Dictionary of Science Fiction,* Oxford University Press, 2007.

Ptak, Laurel, 'Wages For Facebook' (2013) wagesforfacebook.ccm.

Puah, C., A. Z. A. Bakar, and Ching, Chu Wei, 'Strategies for Community Based Crowdsourcing', *2011 International Conference on Research and Innovation in Information Systems* (2011)1 –4.

Racknitz, Joseph Friedrich Freiherr zu, *Ueber den Schachspieler des Herrn von Kempelen und dessen Nachbildung,* J. G. I. Breitkopf, 1789.

— *Schachtürke, Tafel 3*, 1789, Wissenschaftliche Sammlungen an der Humboldt-Universität zu Berlin.

Räth, Georg, 'Bastian Unterberg (Jovoto) im Interview', *Gründerszene* (12 August 2011).

Ramdan, Jonathan, '99designs Meetup, Yogyakarta – Indonesia' (12 February 2012), available on YouTube.

Ramírez, Juan Antonio, *The Beehive Metaphor: from Gaudí to Le Corbusier*, Reaktion, 2000.

Rand, Ayn, and Branden, Nathaniel, *The Virtue of Selfishness : A New Concept of Egoism*, New American Library, 1970.

Raymond, Eric S., 'A Brief History of Hackerdom' (2000).

— 'Goodbye, "Free Software"; Hello, "Open Source"', on Raymond's home page catb.org (8 February 1998).

— 'Homesteading the Noosphere', *First Monday*, 3 (1998).

— *The Cathedral & the Bazaar: Musings on Linux and Open Source by an Accidental Revolutionary*, O'Reilly, 1999

— 'The Cathedral and the Bazaar', on Raymond's home page catb.org (1997).

— 'The Revenge of the Hackers', *Open Sources: Voices from the Open Source Revolution*, O'Reilly (January 1999).

Rayward, W. Boyd, 'H. G. Wells's Idea of a World Brain: A Critical Reassessment', *Journal of the American Society for Information Science*, 50 (1999) 557–73.

Rawls, John, *A Theory of Justice*, Harvard University Press 1971, revised edition from 1999.

Reckwitz, Andreas, *Die Erfindung Der Kreativität: Zum Prozess Gesellschaftlicher Ästhetisierung*, Suhrkamp, 2012.

Reicher, Stephen, 'The Psychology of Crowd Dynamics', in *Blackwell Handbook of Social Psychology: Group Processes*, ed. by Michael A. Hogg and R. Scott Tindale, Blackwell Publishers (2001), 182–208.

Reicher, Stephen, and Clifford Stott, 'Mad Mobs and Englishmen? Myths and Realities of the 2011 Riots', *The Guardian* (18 November 2011).

Reinhardt, Peter, 'Replacing Middle Management with APIs', rein.pk (February 2015).

Reisinger, Don, 'The Terrifying 'Yelp for People' App Is Now Available', *Fortune* (7 March 2016).

Rey, P. J., 'Gamification, Playbor & Exploitation', PJ Rey's Sociology Blog Feed (27 December 2012).

Reynolds, Craig W., 'Flocks, Herds and Schools: A Distributed Behavioral Model', in *Proceedings of the 14th Annual Conference on Computer Graphics and Interactive Techniques*, SIGGRAPH '87, ACM (1987) 25–34.

Rheingold, Howard, 'Virtual Communities – Exchanging Ideas through Computer Bulletin Boards', *Journal For Virtual Worlds Research*, 1 (2008). First published in: *Whole Earth Review*, Winter 1987.

— *Smart Mobs: The next Social Revolution,* Perseus, 2003.

— *The Virtual Community: Finding Connection in a Computerized World*, Minerva, 1995.

Ridgway, Renée, 'Crowdfunding or Funding the Crowds: A New Model for the Distribution of Wealth?', APRAJA — *A Peer-Reviewed Journal about*, transmediale Berlin (January 2013).

Rijks, Marlise, 'Conceptualizing the Masses. Discipline Formation & Concepts of Modernity', Thesis RMA: Historical and Comparative Studies of the Sciences and Humanities, Utrecht University (2011).

Rittel, Horst, 'The Reasoning of Designers', *Institut Für Grundlagen der Gestaltung, Stuttgart*, Working Paper A-88-4 (1988).

Rittel, Horst, and Melvin Webber, 'Dilemmas in a General Theory of Planning', *Elsevier*, Policy Sciences 4 (1973) 155–69.

Rosoff, Matt, 'Airbnb is now worth $30 billion', *Business Insider* (6 August 2016).

Ross, Andrew, *Nice Work If You Can Get It: Life and Labor in Precarious Times*, New York University Press, 2009.

— *No-Collar: The Humane Workplace and Its Hidden Costs*, Temple University Press, 2004.

Rushkoff, Douglas, *Cyberia: Life in the Trenches of Hyperspace*, Flamingo, 1994.

Russell, Peter, *The Awakening Earth: The Global Brain*, Ark, 1984.

— 'The Global Brain - Peter Russell' (1983), available on YouTube.

Rutkin, Aviva, 'Off the Clock, on the Record: Wearable Tech Lets Boss Track Your Work, Rest and Play', *New Scientist* (20 October 2014).

Sack, Warren, et al. 'A Methodological Framework for Socio-Cognitive Analyses of Collaborative Design of Open Source Software', *Computer Supported Cooperative Work (CSCW), the Journal of Collaborative Computing*, 15 (2006) 229–50.

Sakamoto, Yasuaki, Tanaka, Yuko, Yu, Lixiu, and Nickerson, Jeffrey V., 'The Crowdsourcing Design Space', in *Foundations of Augmented Cognition. Directing the Future of Adaptive Systems*, Springer (2011) 346–55.

Salehi, Niloufar, Irani, Lilly C., Bernstein, Michael S., Ali Alkhatib, Ogbe, Eva, Milland, Kristy, and others, 'We Are Dynamo: Overcoming Stalling and Friction in Collective Action for Crowd Workers' presented at CHI 2015, Seoul, Association for Computing Machiner (2015).

Sanders, Elizabeth B.-N., 'Perspectives on Participation in Design', in *Wer gestaltet die Gestaltung?: Praxis, Theorie und Geschichte des partizipatorischen Designs,* Transcript (2012) 61–74.

Sanders, Elizabeth B.-N., and Stappers, Pieter Jan, 'Co-Creation and the New Landscapes of Design', *CoDesign*, 4 (2008) 5–18.

Sandvig, Christian, 'Wireless Play and Unexpected Innovation', *MacArthur Foundation Series on Digital Media and Learning* (2007) 77–97.

Schiffrin, Deborah, Tannen, Deborah ,and Ehernberger Hamilton, Heidi, *The Handbook of Discourse Analysis*, Blackwell, 2003.

Schmidt, Florian A., *Arbeitsmärkte in der Plattformökonomie – Zur Funktionsweise und den Herausforde-rungen von Crowdwork und Gigwork*, policy paper, Friedrich-Ebert-Stiftung 2016.

— 'The Good, The Bad and the Ugly: Why Crowdsourcing Needs Ethics', *2013 Third International Conference on Cloud and Green Computing* (2013) 531–35.

— 'Crowdsourcing Design: For a Fistful of Dollars', *Researching BWPWAP - Peer Reviewed Newspaper Digital Aesthetics Research Center, Aarhus University in Collaboration with reSource Transmedial Culture Berlin/transmediale* (January 2013).

— 'Die Revolution Wird Nicht 3D Gedruckt', conference paper, Deutsche Gesellschaft für Designtheorie und Forschung DGTF, Politik der Maker (2013).

— 'For a Few Dollars More: Class Action Against Crowdsourcing', *A Peer-Reviewed Journal About (APRJA)*, 2 (2013).

— 'Hive: From the Production for the Masses to Design by the Masses', *Bauhaus magazine #3: Dinge/Things* (2012).

— 'Volkdesign', *Kritische Masse: von Profis und Amateuren im Design*, form+zweck (2010).

— *Parallel Realitäten*, Wilhem Braun-Feldweg Förderpreis für designkritische Texte, Niggli, 2006.

— 'Volkssport Design – Live and Let Live?', *Eye Magazine* (2009).

Schmidt, Florian A. and Grüner, Herbert, *Volkssport Design: Symposium zur Lage der Designprofession – Nachspiel,* Kunsthochschule Berlin-Weißensee 2010.

Schmidt, Florian A., and Pannicke, Danny,'Gamers als Designer: Nutzergenerierte Inhalte in Computer-spielen', *Informatik-Spektrum*, 34 (2011) 598–606.

Scholz, Trebor, *Uberworked and Underpaid: How Workers Are Disrupting the Digital Economy,* John Wiley & Sons, 2016.

— 'Platform Cooperativism – Challenging the Corporate Sharing Economy' (2016).

— 'Crowdmilking' (2014) <http://collectivate.net/journalisms/2014/3/9/crowdmilking.html> the original link offline but available via the Internet Archive.

— 'The Politics of the Sharing Economy', *Public Seminar* (30 June 2014).

— 'Digital Labor: Sweatshops, Picket Lines, Barricades', conference at *The New School* (2014).

— *Digital Labor: The Internet as Playground and Factory*, Routledge, 2013.

— 'What the MySpace Generation Should Know about Working for Free' (2007) <http://collectivate.net/jour-nalisms/2007/4/3/what-the-myspace-generation-should-know-about-working-for-free.html> the original link offline but available via the Internet Archive.

— 'Market Ideology and the Myths of Web 2.0', *First Monday*, 13 (2008).

Schön, Donald A., *The Reflective Practitioner: How Professionals Think in Action*, Basic Books, 1983.

Schrape, Niklas, 'Gamification and Governmentality', in *Rethinking Gamification*, Meson Press, Hybrid Publishing Lab (2014) 21–45.

Schumpeter, Joseph Alois, *Capitalism, Socialism, and Democracy*, Routledge, 1994.

Seago, Alex, *Research Methods for MPhil & PhD Students in Art and Design: Contrasts and Conflicts*, Royal College of Art, 1995.

Segaller, Stephen, 'Nerds 2.0.1: A Brief History of the Internet', TV documentary PBS (1998).

Seiner, Joseph A., 'Tailoring Class Actions to the On-Demand Economy', *Ohio State Law Journal*, 77 (2017).

Semple, Janet, *Bentham's Prison: A Study of the Panopticon Penitentiary*, Oxford University Press, 1993.

Shapiro, Ian, *The Flight from Reality in the Human Sciences*, Princeton University Press, 2005.

Shet, Vinay, 'Street View and reCAPTCHA Technology Just Got Smarter', *Google Online Security Blog* (16 April 2014).

Shirky, Clay, *Cognitive Surplus: How Technology Makes Consumers into Collaborators*, Penguin Books, 2011.

— 'How Cognitive Surplus Will Change the World', TED talk (June 2010).

— *Here Comes Everybody: How Change Happens When People Come Together*, Penguin (2009).

— 'Shirky: A Group Is Its Own Worst Enemy', O'Reilly Emerging Technology (24 April 2003).

Silberman, M. Six, 'What Is Fair? – Rational Action and its Residuals in an Electronic Market' (2010).

Silberman, M. Six, Irani, Lilly, and Ross, Joel, 'Ethics and Tactics of Professional Crowdwork', *XRDS*, 17 (2010) 39–43.

Silverman, Jacob 'The Crowdsourcing Scam', *The Baffler*, No. 26 (2014).

Simon, Herbert A, *The Sciences of the Artificial*, MIT Press, 1996.

Simon, Phil, 'Crowdsourcing Design: An Interview with DesignCrowd Founder Alec Lynch', *Huffington Post* (30 October 2013).

Smith, Douglas K., and Alexander, Robert C., *Fumbling the Future: How Xerox Invented, Then Ignored, the First Personal Computer*, ToExcel, 1999.

Sonne, Nathalie, 'Interview with Jovoto's Founder Bastian Unterberg in Colombia's Newspaper "El Tiempo"' (4 June 2013).

Stalder, Felix, *Digital Solidarity*, Mute & Post-Media Lab Books, 2013.

Stallman, Richard M., 'Free Software Is Even More Important Now', gnu.org (2013).

— 'The GNU Manifesto', Free Software Foundation (1985).

Staun, Harald, 'Shareconomy – der Terror des Teilens', *Frankfurter Allgemeine Zeitung* (22 December 2013).

Sterling, Bruce, *The Epic Struggle of the Internet of Things*, Strelka Press, 2014.

— *The Hacker Crackdown: Law and Disorder on the Electronic Frontier*, Bantam, 1993.

Steyerl, Hito, 'Freedom from Everything: Freelancers and Mercenaries', *e-flux*, journal #41 (January 2013).

— 'Proxy Politics: Signal and Noise', *e-flux*, No. 60 (December 2014).

Stone, Brad, 'Amazon Erases Orwell Books From Kindle', *The New York Times* (18 July 2009).

— 'My Life as a TaskRabbit', *BusinessWeek,* 13 September 2012.

Strube, Sebastian, 'Crowdwork: Vom Entstehen Der Digitalen Arbeiterklasse', radio feature, *Zündfunk – Bayerischer Rundfunk* (2014).

— 'Vom Lynchmob zum Smartmob: Wer oder was ist die Masse Heute?', *Zündfunk – Bayerischer Rundfunk* (2014).

Suchman, Lucille Alice, *Human-Machine Reconfigurations: Plans and Situated Actions*, 2nd ed., Cambridge University Press, 2007.

Sunde, Peter, opening ceremony, *transmediale* (2015), available on YouTube.

Surowiecki, James, 'Face Time', *The New Yorker* (18 March 2013).

— 'The Science of Success', *The New Yorker* (9 July 2007).

— *The Wisdom of Crowds : Why the Many Are Smarter than the Few*, Abacus (2005).

Sutherland, Ivan E., 'Sketch Pad a Man-Machine Graphical Communication System', in *Proceedings of the SHARE Design Automation Workshop*, DAC '64, ACM (1964).

Sützl, Wolfgang, Felix Stalder, and Ronald Maier, eds., *Media, knowledge and education: cultures and ethics of sharing*, Innsbruck University Press, 2012.

Swarns, Rachel L., 'Freelancers in the "Gig Economy" Find a Mix of Freedom and Uncertainty', *The New York Times* (9 February 2014).

Swartz, Aaron, 'Guerilla Open Access Manifesto' (2008).

Tapscott Group, 'From Crowdsourcing to Kony 2012: Macrowikinomics: New Solutions for a Connected Planet', promotional video (2012), available on YouTube.

— *Macrowikinomics: Rebooting Business and the World*, Penguin, 2010.

Tapscott, Don, and Williams, Anthony D., *Wikinomics: How Mass Collaboration Changes Everything*, Atlantic, 2008.

Taylor, Astra, *The People's Platform: Taking Back Power and Culture in the Digital Age*, Fourth Estate, 2013.

Taylor, Charles, 'Modern Social Imaginaries', *Public Culture*, 14 (2002) 91–124.

Taylor, Frederick Winslow, *The Principles of Scientific Management*, Harper & Brothers, 1911.

Terranova, Tiziana, 'Free Labor: Producing Culture for the Digital Economy', *Electronic Book Review* (2003).

Thacker, C. P. et al., 'Alto: A Personal Computer', *Computer Structures: Principles and Examples, Second Edition*, McGraw-Hill (1979) 549–72.

Thaler, Richard H., and Sunstein, Cass R., *Nudge: Improving Decisions about Health, Wealth, and Happiness*, Yale University Press, 2008.

Taffel, Sy, 'The Use and Abuse of Cybernetic Concepts: Where Part Two of All Watched Over By Machines of Loving Grace Went Wrong', *Media Ecologies and Digital Activism* (1 June 2011).

Theodore, Roszak, *From Satori to Silicon Valley*, Stanford University Libraries, 1985.

Thompson, Hunter S, *Fear and Loathing in Las Vegas: A Savage Journey to the Heart of the American Dream*, Harper Perennial, 2005.

Tice, Carol, 'Crowdsourcing Is Great – Except When It Fails', *Entrepreneur* (20 December 2009).

Timberg, Scott, 'Jaron Lanier: The Internet Destroyed the Middle Class', *Salon* (12 May 2013).

Toffler, Alvin, *The Third Wave*, Bantam Books, 1980.

Tomlinson, Bill, and M. Six Silberman, 'The Cognitive Surplus is Made of Fossil Fuels', *First Monday*, 17 (5 November 2012).

Tortorici, Dayna, 'More Smiles? More Money', *n+1*, 2013.

Torvalds, Linus, 'LINUX's History by Linus Torvalds', *LINUX' History* (31 July 1992).

— *Linus Torvalds: Disagreement With Free Software Foundation*, 2011, interview available on YouTube.

Trotter, Wilfred, *Instincts of the Herd in Peace and War*, T. Fisher Unwin, 1924.

Turner, Fred, 'From Counter-Culture to Cyberculture', Keynote, HKW Anthropocene (2013) available on YouTube.

— 'Burning Man at Google: A Cultural Infrastructure for New Media Production', *New Media & Society*, 11 (2009) 73–94.

— 'Romantic Automatism: Art, Technology, and Collaborative Labor in Cold War America', *Journal of Visual Culture*, 7 (2008) 5–26.

— 'From Counterculture to Cyberculture: The Legacy of the Whole Earth Catalog', Panel discussion with Brand, Turner, Kelly and Rheingold at Stanford library (9 November 2006), available on YouTube.

— *From Counterculture to Cyberculture: Stewart Brand, the Whole Earth Network, and the Rise of Digital Utopianism*, University of Chicago Press, first published 2006, (2008).

Turner-Rahman, Gregory, 'Parallel Practices and the Dialectics of Open Creative Production', *Journal of Design History, Volume 21, Issue 4* (2008) 371–386.

Uddin, Zakia, 'The Dystopian Digital Sweatshop That Makes the Internet Run', *AlterNet* (11 September 2012).

Unterberg, Bastian, 'Crowdsourcing (Jeff Howe)', in *Social-Media-Handbuch Theorien, Methoden, Modelle und Praxis*, Nomos (2010) 121–35.

Voss, G. Günter, *Der arbeitende Kunde: Wenn Konsumenten zu unbezahlten Mitarbeitern werden*, Campus, 2005.

Wales, Jimmy, and Lee, Ellen, 'As Wikipedia Moves to S. F., Founder Discusses Planned Changes', *San Francisco Chronicle* (20 November 2007).

Walker, Leslie, 'Taking a Cue from Tom Sawyer', *Washington Post* (15 July 1999).

Wasson, Christina, 'Ethnography in the Field of Design', ed. by Society for Applied Anthropology, *Human Organization*, 59 (2000) 377.

Wee, Willis, '99designs: "There's Raw Talent in Indonesia and Philippines"', *Tech in Asia* (11 June 2013).

Weinberger, David, *Everything Is Miscellaneous: The Power of the New Digital Disorder*, Henry Holt and Company, 2007.

Well Group, The, 'Salon Media Group Sells The WELL to The Well Group: First Time Online Business Taken Private by Users of the Business Itself', press release (2012).

Wells, H. G., *A Modern Utopia*, The Pennsylvania State University 2004.

— *World Brain*, 1938

Wingfield, Nick, 'The Well, a Pioneering Online Community, is for Sale Again', *The New York Times Bits Blog* (29 June 2012).

Wintour, Patrick, '"Nudge Unit" to Become Profit-Making', *The Guardian* (1 May 2013).

Witten, Kim, 'The Digital Dualism Debate', *MePhiD* (2013).

Wodak, Ruth, and Michael Meyer, eds., *Methods of Critical Discourse Analysis*, Introducing Qualitative
   Methods, 2nd ed., Sage, 2009.

Wolf, Gary, review of *The Curse of Xanadu*, by Ted Nelson, *Wired*, June 1995.

Wolfe, Tom, *The Electric Kool-Aid Acid Test*, Black Swan, 1989.

— 'The "Me" Decade and the Third Great Awakening', *New York Magazine* (1976).

— 'What If He Is Right?', *The New York Herald Tribune* (1965).

Wong, Jamie, 'The Rise Of The Micro-Entrepreneurship Economy', *Fast Company* (29 May 2012).

Worstall, Tim, 'On the New York Times Stupidity Over Amazon's Mechanical Turk', *Forbes* (19 March 2013).

Wortham, Jenna, 'Success of Crowdfunding Puts Pressure on Entrepreneurs', *The New York Times*
   (17 September 2012).

Yee, Nick, 'The Labor of Fun', *Sage Journals* (2006).

Yu, Lixiu, and Jeffrey V. Nickerson, 'Cooks or Cobblers?: Crowd Creativity through Combination', in
   Proceedings of the SIGCHI Conference on Human Factors in Computing Systems, CHI '11, ACM (2011)
   1393–1402.

Zichermann, Gabe, *Gamification by Design: Implementing Game Mechanics in Web and Mobile Apps*, O'Reilly
   Media, 2011.

— 'The Purpose of Gamification', *O'Reilly Radar* (26 April 2011).

Zittrain, Jonathan, *The Future of the Internet and How to Stop It*, Yale University Press, 2008.

— *Ubiquitous Human Computing*, Social Science Research Network, 2008.

Zuboff, Shoshana, *In the Age of the Smart Machine: The Future of Work and Power*, Heinemann Professional,
   1989.

Project management: Lisa Schulze
Production: Katja Jaeger
Layout and typography: Sven Schrape
Design Concept BIRD: Christian Riis Ruggaber, Formal
Paper: 110 g/m² Multi Offset
Printing: BELTZ Grafische Betriebe, Bad Langensalza

Library of Congress Cataloging-in-Publication data
A CIP catalog record for this book has been applied for at the Library of Congress.

Bibliographic information published by the German National Library
The German National Library lists this publication in the Deutsche Nationalbibliografie;
detailed bibliographic data are available on the Internet at http://dnb.dnb.de.

This publication is also available as an e-book (ISBN PDF 978-3-0356-1067-3;
ISBN EPUB 978-3-0356-1051-2).

© 2017 Birkhäuser Verlag GmbH, Basel
P.O. Box 44, 4009 Basel, Switzerland
Part of Walter de Gruyter GmbH, Berlin/Boston

Printed on acid-free paper produced from chlorine-free pulp. TCF ∞

Printed in Germany

ISBN 978-3-0356-1198-4